The Post-Soviet States

The Post-Soviet States

Mapping the Politics of Transition

GRAHAM SMITH
University of Cambridge

A member of the Hodder Headline Group
LONDON • SYDNEY • AUCKLAND
Co-published in the United States of America by
Oxford University Press Inc., New York

First published in Great Britain in 1999 by
Arnold, a member of the Hodder Headline Group
338 Euston Road, London NW1 3BH

http://www.arnoldpublishers.com

Co-published in the United States of America by
Oxford University Press Inc.,
198 Madison Avenue, New York 10016

British Library Cataloguing in Publication Data
A catalogue entry for this book is available from the British Library

Library of Congress Cataloging-in-Publication Data
A catalog record for this book is available from the Library of Congress

ISBN 0 340 67791 0 (pb)
ISBN 0 340 67790 2 (hb)

1 2 3 4 5 6 7 8 9 10

Production Editor: Wendy Rooke
Production Controller: Sarah Kett
Cover designer: Terry Griffiths

Typeset in 10/12pt Sabon by Phoenix Photosetting, Chatham, Kent
Printed and bound in Great Britain by
MPG Books Ltd, Bodmin, Cornwall

What do you think about this book? Or any other Arnold title?
Please send your comments to feedback.arnold@hodder.co.uk

This book is dedicated to my brother

CALLUM SMITH

1957–98

Contents

Part II: Experimenting with democracy

Part III: Geopolitical economy, the market and privatisation

Conclusions

Appendix

Figures

Tables

Preface

Just before his death in November 1995, the political philosopher and east Europeanist, Ernest Gellner, wrote of the post-communist world: 'The problem of erecting a liberal, stable and prosperous society on the ruins of a totalitarian industrial ideocracy is historically absolutely new, no one knows what the answer or answers is or may be, or indeed whether there is one'.[1] Besides signalling the scale of political and geographical upheaval occurring in the post-Soviet states and in eastern-central Europe, Gellner was also cautioning in his inimitable way against those foolhardy enough to propose either ready solutions to difficult problems or to assume that history is somehow predetermined, as if liberal democracy and *laissez-faire* capitalism are the logical and only outcomes. Whatever else the prospects are for the post-Soviet transition, it cannot be assumed to be neatly determined. And nor is it developing uniformly throughout post-Soviet space.

The initial impetus for writing this book was a dissatisfaction with a specialist paper that I had started teaching in Cambridge following the inevitable transition from a previous course that I had taught on the Soviet Union. Timothy Colton has eloquently summed up the problem that post-Sovietologists faced in the first half of the 1990s:

> Getting a fix on post-Soviet politics ... is about as easy as judging a symphony by its opening bars. The ear picks out isolated notes and chords; melody and rhythm elude it. Worse, we risk being misled by false echoes of some half-remembered music.[2]

As the post-Soviet states move into the twenty-first century, the orchestra has not stopped playing but it is now easier with hindsight, I think, to judge the symphony. I leave to the reader whether I have understood it properly.

In writing this book, I have been fortunate enough in having the opportunity to discuss chapters with a number of friends and colleagues, although needless to say none should be held responsible for any textual errors or misjudgements. I am especially indebted to three of my colleagues on the

Post-Soviet States in Transition Programme at Sidney Sussex College, Annette Bohr, Penny Morvant and Andrew Wilson, for taking the time to read through and comment on parts of the manuscript. Penny's input, in particular, has been invaluable in providing research material which explicated greatly the writing of this book. I am also grateful to Alan Ingram and Alena Ledeneva for their comments on particular chapters. As with so many other projects, I am indebted to Ian Agnew for turning my thumbnail sketches into maps and diagrams. Alex Smith also needs to be thanked for assisting with photocopying. Special thanks are due to Laura McKelvie, at Arnold, who provided the necessary coaxing and good humour to get me to finish. Finally, it is a pleasure to acknowledge The Leverhulme Trust for its generous financial support which enabled me to undertake research in Russia, the Baltic states and in eastern Europe between 1995 and 1998.

Where a standard English form of proper names or place names already exists, I have retained that spelling; in other cases, and in all transliterations of books and articles from the Russian language, I have adopted the system used by the journal *Europe–Asia Studies* (formerly *Soviet Studies*).

GRAHAM SMITH
Sidney Sussex College, Cambridge
October 1998

1   E. Gellner, 'Return of a native', *The Political Quarterly*, 67(1), 1996, p. 12.
2   T. Colton, 'Politics', in T. Colton and R. Levgold (eds), *After the Soviet Union. From Empire to Nations* (New York and London, W.W. Norton and Co., 1992), p. 17.

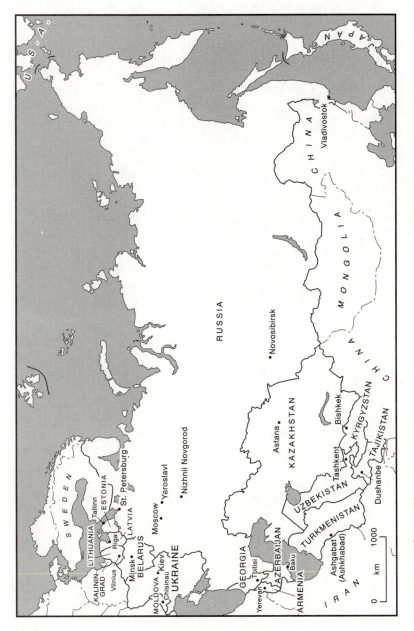

Figure 0.1 The post-Soviet states.

1

Trials of transition

The post-Soviet states are in the throes of what is undoubtedly one of the most momentous and critical political transformations of our times. Predicated upon the dismantling of state socialism and the simultaneous fragmentation of the Soviet Union into 15 sovereign states, the post-Soviet transition has entailed a scale and intensity of political, social and economic upheaval unparalleled in any other region of the world since World War II. The challenges that confront the post-Soviet states are formidable and include: states coming into existence at precisely the moment when the very sovereign powers of states have never been so much in question; new regional power blocs and alliances having to be forged out of a geopoliti-cally changing post-Cold-War world order; nation-builders aspiring to cre-ate new forms of citizen-polities but whose very projects inspire political tension rather than coexistence; and states committed to restructuring their economies on the Western neo-liberal model of market exchange, but having to manage the political ramifications of competing as late entrants on the margins of the global economy.

This book is about the post-Soviet states and the challenges they will face well into the twenty-first century. But it also takes up the intellectual challenge of finding new ways to understand the nature of the post-Soviet transition. From time to time, social scientists are forced into radically rethinking how to approach and analyse the polities, peoples and places they study. Nowhere is this more true than in the case of the post-Soviet world. The theories, models and methodologies of Sovietology – that branch of social science which focused on exploring the Soviet Union – are no longer applicable. New approaches are needed, offering the opportu-nity to intellectually retool, to open up new vistas for political and social enquiry and to locate post-Soviet studies more firmly within the social sci-ences. The aim of this book is therefore to examine ways of making sense of the post-Soviet transition by contributing both to the opening up of post-Soviet studies to more recent developments in political and social

theory while at the same time grounding such explorations in solid, empir-
ical enquiry.

Thinking through transition

In focusing on transition as a basis for framing a study of the post-Soviet
states, this book makes use of a convenient label for polities undergoing
changes of epochal proportions. The best way of viewing polities in transition is, of course, subject to considerable debate, and a wide range of theories and models have already been applied to the post-Soviet experience in
an attempt to shed light upon it. However, there is an overall consensus that
transition constitutes a process of change from beginning to end, a series of
multidimensional, fluctuating and interdependent stages, embodying the
remaking of institutions, social values and ways of doing things. If such an
approach is to have further usefulness, it is important to question some of
the assumptions that have already been made about transition in the post-
Soviet states. This section looks at the limitations of those assumptions.

First, the post-Soviet transition should not be regarded as preordained, as
if there is an inevitability about the future form the post-Soviet states will
take. The most familiar of such claims is the triumphalist one. According to
this theory, the end of the Cold War not only represented a victory for both
Western liberal democracy and capitalism over state socialism but also
implied that the only course now open to the post-Soviet states was to adopt
the political values and economic system of the West. For Fukuyama, what
occurred between the 1989 revolutions in eastern Europe and the subsequent collapse and fragmentation of the homeland of socialism itself, the
Soviet Union, constituted nothing less than 'the end of history'.[1] Fixed to the
view that Russia and the other post-Soviet states can only succeed by emulating the West, it is a thesis which is unquestioning in its teleological
assumptions about the post-Soviet trajectory. But this is not just an intellectual interpretation. It is also a thesis which underpins the prevailing attitude
of most Western states and global financial institutions: that successful market reform will lead to democracy. Yet as the post-Soviet transition unfolds,
it has become only too apparent that the unequivocal onward march
towards 'market democracy' that was envisaged has not materialised. Some
of the post-communist countries that have been most successful in democratic state-building, such as Lithuania, Hungary and Poland, have periodically re-elected socialist governments, and others, such as Uzbekistan,
Kazakhstan and Turkmenistan, have continued to experiment with market
reform while preserving authoritarian or semi-authoritarian forms of governance.

While triumphalists paint a rosy picture of the region's political and economic prospects, an alternative, more pessimistic school of thought regards
the cultural divisions and ethnic conflicts of the past as equally inevitable.[2]

Having secured emancipation from the Soviet Union, which froze the geopolitical map for several decades, nations, ethnic groups and religious communities, it is argued, are now competing in a tribal form of politics. For Huntington, what is taking place in the post-communist world is a clash of civilisations around what he sees as the enduring markers of history: Western Christendom, Slavic-Orthodoxy and Islam.[3] Accordingly, the future is predetermined, filled by nationalism, inter-communal violence and regional instability. That inter-communal tensions have undoubtedly played a significant part in shaping the post-Soviet transition cannot be doubted: the experiences of Chechnya, Georgia and Azerbaijan all illustrate the role that ethnic and religious divisions have played in shaping the politics of transition. Yet inter-communal violence has not had the all-pervasive impact on the post-Soviet transition that such essentialist thinking would suggest.[4] Framing discussion in this way therefore not only downplays the multidimensional character of transition but also overplays the significance of inter-ethnic violence as the central and overarching feature of the post-Soviet experience. It is therefore essential to acknowledge the possibility that differing and overlapping forms of identities are in the making, which refuse to follow the totalising contours of such essentialist theorising.

In a similar vein, it is also important to question those theories which hold that, as Russian history and culture are quintessentially different from Europe's, Russia will be unable to adjust to liberal and democratic values that are deemed exclusively a product of Europe and its greatest project, the eighteenth-century Enlightenment.[5] The peoples of the European post-Soviet states, such as the Estonians and Lithuanians, it is argued, are, after decades of rule by the East, on course to return to Europe and the political culture and values they have long since shared as members of the Common European Home as Europe's 'backward and semi-Asiatic Other'. In contrast, Russia is condemned to a path of authoritarianism, imperialism and anti-Westernism. In short, its future is already fixed and immutable.

Second, in theorising about transition, the post-Soviet states' past cannot be ignored, nor can the possibility that the break with the past may not be as sudden or as transformational as it appears. Simply labelling the post-Soviet states as in transition from an analytically predetermined and unreconstructed given, such as totalitarian rule, state capitalism or state socialism, without unpacking such designations, not only leaves too many stones unturned but also obfuscates the exact nature of the phenomenon under study. Thus, any examination of the post-Soviet transition should be preceded by a closer look at the Soviet Union – in particular, the extent to which it represented an alternative route to modernity to that pursued by the West, and the reasons for its ultimate failure to meet the expectations of its citizenry.

No transition, however radical, completely eradicates the past: memories, cultural values and even political institutions are not obliterated from the political landscape overnight. As one commentator aptly notes:

what is most instructive about historical experience is that it shows that transitions to new forms of economy, society and culture, usually take longer, are more complex, and are more conservative than the commentators of the time, who fix on the new, tend to realise.[6]

In particular, one should be sensitive to what is implied by regime breakdown and its relationship to transition. Major historical events, such as the 1789 French Revolution and the 1917 Russian Revolution, were truly revolutionary in that they resulted in a breakdown and destruction of the *ancien régime* and were followed by transitions that gradually brought about a new political and economic order. The breakdown of those regimes and the early stages of their transitions were accompanied by widespread violence and bloodshed. In contrast, the post-Soviet transition has not been marked by revolution.[7] At least in its early stages (1986–90), it was a transition initiated from above, by reform-minded political elites wishing to embark upon a belated attempt to reform communism – a drive that became known as *perestroika*, or restructuring. Ultimately the experiment failed, but it did not end due to a revolution of the sort that occurred in 1789 or 1917. Rather, the Soviet regime received its final blow from an unsuccessful *coup d'état* by Communist Party hard-liners in Moscow in August 1991, anxious to preserve the integrity of the Soviet system, and a remarkably ordered and peaceful assumption of power by Russia's newly elected leader, Boris Yeltsin. These political events quickly paved the way for the creation of a sovereign Russia and the establishment of 14 other independent states. The nature of the handover of political power has had a number of implications for the post-Soviet transition. Most notably, despite the creation of new polities and political institutions, and contested elections, there has been a remarkable continuity in political elites, particularly in Russia and the southern borderland states, many of whose leaders held positions of power in the mid-1980s or even earlier.

Finally, the post-Soviet transition cannot be adequately understood if analyses of 'domestic' and 'international' processes and events are separated. One of the major problems with Sovietology was that it tended to bifurcate the two, with often little consideration given to the impact of external processes on internal political events or of internal social and political changes on foreign policy. Given that the post-Soviet states have entered onto the world stage at a time when such globalising processes as the internationalisation of capital, the growth of regional trading blocs, and the spatial diffusion of a world-wide mass media are restructuring the world in which we live, it is even more vital to recognise the complex relationship which exists between global and local processes of change. Especially vital is the impact of globalisation on the sovereign power of the post-Soviet states. Transnational corporations and global financial institutions in particular limit the post-Soviet states' ability to shape their own transitions. Moreover, access to the global economy has also created new demands and opportunities for regenerating local political identities. As in Catalonia or Scotland, Russia's regions – in particular, Tatarstan, Chechnya and Sakha (Yakutia) – have seized upon the opportunities to bypass formal state structures and connect directly with other parts of the global market place. While such opportunities may be conducive to new patterns of economic co-operation, a more open and tolerant citizenry, and new forms of social interaction, they may also provoke resistance. Globalising processes can therefore also be destabilising and unsettling, producing in their wake new political and cultural tensions – such as anti-Westernism – which has already become a feature of the post-Soviet transition.

While arguing that the post-Soviet transition should be understood as a singular and particular type of transition, this book will also look at the transition from a comparative perspective. In so doing, its aim is to open up post-Soviet studies further to the sort of comparative theory-building that has already done much to shed light on the post-Soviet transition. Such research has included comparative studies of the collapse of multiethnic empires (e.g. Ottoman, French, British and Tsarist);[8] the transition from military-authoritarian rule to democracy (e.g. Latin America, southern Europe);[9] and the impact of differing experiments with market reform (e.g. China, Latin America, eastern Europe).[10] While traditional area-studies specialists maintain that the changes occurring in the post-communist world are unique and that comparative enquiry has tended to sacrifice the importance of place-specificity and the significance of local histories for quick generality, this should not imply that comparative work is of little value.[11] Above all, what is needed are comparative studies that recognise that the various elements that constitute the post-Soviet transition may be neither similar to nor different from other transitions.[12] In other words, both the specificity and similarity of transitions must be recognised. At the same time, while traditional area studies may have suffered from under-theorisation, one of its main strengths was its rich empiricism in adversity. It is this tradition, in particular, that it is important not to lose sight of when engaging in comparative theory-building.

Challenges of transition

Most observers regard the post-Soviet states as undergoing 'a dual' or 'double transition'. According to this viewpoint, what makes the transition in the post-Soviet states more complex and different from those experienced elsewhere, such as Latin America and eastern Europe in the 1990s, is that Russia and most of the other post-Soviet states are undergoing for the first time in their history the processes of democratisation and the introduction of a market economy simultaneously. We can take this argument further by suggesting that what the post-Soviet states are undergoing is a triple transition: from colonialism to post-colonialism (*decolonisation*); from totalitarianism to post-totalitarianism (*democratisation*); and from the command to a market economy (*economic liberalisation*). The way in which these processes of transition are unfolding also differs intra-regionally, for, as Burawoy notes, each of the post-Soviet states is following 'multiple trajectories'.[13] To understand the difference in impact of these processes of transition across the region requires an acknowledgement that, despite the common Soviet legacy, the post-Soviet states comprise very different cultures and traditions, contrasting pre-Soviet experiences of governance, and sharply and increasingly differing levels of development (ranging from the urban-industrial states of Russia, Ukraine and the Baltic republics to the rural-agrarian polities of the post-Soviet Central Asian states). Some of these intra-regional differences are shown in Table 1.1.

Decolonisation: from 'colonialism' to post-colonialism

The process of decolonisation entails the transition from a Soviet multi-ethnic empire to the establishment of post-colonial sovereign states. Most significantly, it is a process that has involved the post-Soviet states' attempting to fashion a national identity out of polities that consist of multiethnic communities. However, determining what sort of political community should be created has proved no easy task. As developments elsewhere in the twentieth century have shown, post-colonial regimes tend to give low priority to the establishment of political communities based on inclusion, political equality and universal citizenship, and, ultimately, to securing democratic governance. Rather, following independence, the state-building process invariably involves one section of the community, made up of members of the newly emergent titular national group, imposing some form of political and cultural hegemony on the rest. Not surprisingly, ethnic tension is frequently the result. If the desire of decolonised communities is for a coherent post-Soviet national identity, then that identity is being shaped as much by the politics of ethnic particularism and division as it is by universalism and coexistence.

How such a politics of decolonisation is being played out differs between the borderland states and Russia. For the new political leaders in the borderlands, the process of decolonisation is commonly, and usually unambiguously, interpreted as the transition from colonial rule. Thus, the nationalist struggles in the late 1980s are interpreted as having secured the liberation of national homelands from the Soviet Union, which granted the borderland Union republics only limited autonomy despite its claim to be a multiethnic federation made up of equal sovereign nationality-based Union republics. Thus, for many of the borderlands, imagining their nations as unimaginable without a political homeland is based on the claim that up

Table 1.1   Socio-economic differences between the post-Soviet states, 1997

	Population (millions, 1 Jan. 1997)	Urban population (%, 1 Jan. 1995)	Life expectancy at birth (years, 1996)	GDP per capita (1997, US$, purchasing power parities)	Industrial output growth (%, 1996)	Consumer price inflation (%, 1997, annual average)	Unemployment (%, end of year, 1996)	Average monthly wage (US$, 1996)
Russian Federation	147.5	73	65.9	4,280	–5.0	14.6	9.3	157 (Sept. 96)
Ukraine	50.89	39	69[a]	2,131	–5.1	15.9	1.5	83 (Sept. 96)
Belarus	10.28	69	68.6	4,131	3.2	63.8	3.9	88 (Sept. 96)
Moldova	4.32	47	66.7	1,637	–8.5	11.9	1.5[b]	43 (Oct. 96)
Estonia	1.47[c]	70	70[a]	5,633	1.1	11.1	5.6	246 (net, July–Sept. 96)
Latvia	2.4[c]	70	69[a]	3,847	0.7	8.4	7.2	199 (public sector, May 96)
Lithuania	3.71[c]	68	69[a]	4,164	2.8	8.9	6.2	163 (May 96)
Armenia	3.78	68[d]	70.9[a]	2,389	1.0	13.9	9.7	–
Azerbaijan	7.57	53	–	1,080	–6.7	19.8	1.1[e]	–
Georgia	5.42	56[d]	–	1,303	7.7	7.1	3.2	–
Kazakhstan	15.99	56	69[a]	2,734	0.3	17.4	4.1[f]	117 (Sept. 96)
Uzbekistan	23.44	68	70[a]	1,998	6.0	58.8	0.4	–
Kyrgyzstan	4.74[c]	35	66.6	1,529	10.8	26	4.5	–
Tajikistan	5.97[c]	28	67[a]	680	–19.8	90	2.4	–
Turkmenistan	4.4[c]	45	–	1,053	17.9	84 (est.)	–	–

Notes: 'Unemployment' refers to registered unemployment at the end of the period except for the Russian Federation (Goskomstat estimates based on the ILO definition) and Estonia (registered unemployed job seekers, which has a broader definition with regard to age and past employment record).
[a] Mid-1995.
[b] Excluding Trans-Dniestria.
[c] Mid-1997.
[d] 1 Jan. 1994.
[e] According to the UN, *Economic Survey of Europe* (see sources, below). *EIU Country Profile, Azerbaijan, 1997–98*, gives a figure of 2.6%.
[f] Unregistered unemployed in 1995 formed 10.8% of the labour force.

Sources: CIS Interstate Statistical Committee, *Sodruzhestvo Nezavisimykh Gosudarstv v 1997 godu* (Moscow, CIS Interstate Statistical Committee); CIS Interstate Statistical Committee, *Official Statistics of the Countries of the CIS, 1997–2* [CD-ROM] (Moscow, CIS Interstate Statistical Committee, 1998); International Monetary Fund, *International Financial Statistics*, August 1997; Economist Intelligence Unit, various country profiles and country reports for the post-Soviet states published in 1997 and 1998; World Bank, *World Development Report 1997* (New York, Oxford University Press, 1997); World Bank, *Statistical Handbook 1996. States of the former USSR, Studies of Economies in Transformation*, no. 21 (Washington DC, World Bank, 1996); Secretariat of the UN, *Economic Survey of Europe in 1996–1997* (New York and Geneva, UN, 1997); *Russian Economic Trends*, various 1997–99 issues; *Belarusian Economic Trends*, various 1997 issues; *Kazakstan Economic Trends*, various 1997 issues; *OMRI Economic Digest*, various 1996–97 issues; CIS Interstate Statistical Committee, *Demograficheskii yezhegodnik 1994* (Moscow, CIS Interstate Statistical Committee, 1995).

until 1991 their homelands existed as colonial appendages of a Russian-dominated Soviet empire.

Since 1991, competing visions of what form these political homelands should take have become a universal feature of politics in the post-Soviet borderlands. First, there are members of the titular nation who hold to the view that their polity is still somehow incomplete – not quite a nation-state – despite the obtention of sovereign statehood. To varying degrees, therefore, those political elites wish to complete the process of nation-building, aspiring to what Gellner calls the principle of national congruence: namely, making national and political space one and the same.[14] At minimum, this means a wish to see the titular nation – its language, culture and people – elevated to a key place within the state's political institutions and social life of the country. For others, it also entails a desire to see the creation of a larger, more spatially inclusive national homeland in which those co-nationals who still reside outside the polity can be reunited with their brethren. Such representations of homeland compete with and are fuelled by two other visions. Foremost are those of ethnic minorities uncomfortable with their place in the new polities who wish to see their own people and cultures provided with autonomous or even sovereign political homelands. Then there is the vision of those who do not wish to fit into such neat ethnic or religious divides, who identify with neither the homeland politics of the titular nor minority ethnic groups, but wish to see their homeland based on a politics of identity able to transcend such differences. It is a vision of homeland that plays down ethnic or religious differences and holds that all residents who live and work within the sovereign state should have an equal right to membership of the citizen-polity. Its supporters celebrate a vision of statehood in which the political homeland is for all and overlapping layers of identity are seen as the basis for reconstructing a more inclusionary and universal understanding of politics. Such new but still weakly developed forms of identity politics mobilise around issues such as multiculturalism, the environment, workers' rights and the women's movement. In the post-Soviet context, they constitute truly post-colonial forms of identity politics.

In Russia, the politics of decolonisation differs primarily because of the unique and special place that Russia and the Russians occupied within the Soviet Union. The Russians, more than any other nationality, were encouraged during the Soviet period to think of their homeland as synonymous with the spatial expanse of the Soviet Union. Because Russians have throughout recent history been used to identifying with such a larger homeland, either in the form of the tsarist empire or the Soviet Union, many have found it difficult to adjust to the loss of that homeland. Consequently, the geographical imagination of what and wherein lies Russia's homeland remains far less clear-cut. While for many Russians decolonisation is about focusing on the creation of a new sovereign and democratic Russia, for others the idea of re-establishing, in whole or in part, an empire abroad and recolonising the former Soviet borderlands is inextricably bound up with Russian national identity.

Besides its external sovereign borders, there also exist differing claims as to how the internal political community of Russia itself should be defined. Because Russia is made up of numerous ethnic groups, each with its own distinct set of identities and federated homeland administrations, Russia's state-builders are faced with the task of forming a political community out of differing and competing political identities. At one end of the spectrum, state-builders are faced with ethnic minorities, such as the Chechens, Tatars and Yakuts, who aspire to greater control over their homelands, and even the creation of their own nation-states (see Fig. 6.2). Such expectations, which for some observers have raised the spectre of Russia's Balkanisation, fuel and compete with the homeland vision of Russian nationalists, who wish to secure Russian political and cultural hegemony and have no sympathy for even the more modest homeland aspirations of minorities.

Democratisation: from totalitarianism to post-totalitarianism

At a minimum, the process of democratisation can be considered as the transition from a non-democratic to a democratic form of governance.[15] Although the post-Soviet states have undergone a transition from a territorially centralised totalitarian regime, which relied heavily on coercive state power to secure both socio-spatial transformation and political stability, it would be wrong to assume that they are all *en route* or have completed the journey to democracy. Their future paths are still uncertain. Indeed, while some of the post-Soviet states can be labelled proto-democracies in that they are developing or have developed those political institutions and features of socio-political life generally associated with democracies, others have slid with relative ease from totalitarian into authoritarian forms of governance.

Successful democratisation has certain preconditions. As Przeworski notes, 'if democracy is to be sustained, the state must guarantee territorial integrity and physical security; it must maintain the conditions necessary for an effective exercise of citizenship, it must mobilise public savings, co-ordinate resource allocation, and correct income distribution'.[16] If this interpretation of democracy is used, it is clear that the post-Soviet states still face many challenges, though some more than others. One of the major problems facing some of the states is the challenge posed by particular localities and communities to the state's monopoly over the rule of law. In some areas, for instance, armed insurgent movements challenge the authority of democratically elected governments. Organised crime syndicates have also taken advantage of the political and economic turmoil associated with transition to subvert the rule of law, assuming control over large sections of social and economic life in some neighbourhoods, cities, regions and even entire polities.

A widely recognised democratic building block is a civil society – generally understood to mean the presence of a network of social groups, modes of thinking and cultural traditions which operate autonomously from the state and its political institutions. The Soviet state, as a totalitarian entity, did not tolerate a civil society. Rather it attempted to absorb it by bringing all types of organisations – from trade unions to environmental groups – within the party-state apparatus and thus under its administrative control. Autonomous social movements did however begin to emerge in the Union republics, regions, coalfields and cities during the late 1980s and play a key part in challenging the legitimacy and moral authority of the Soviet state. But since then many have floundered, now offering a poor challenge to the political agendas set by the Soviet Union's successor regimes. Consequently, in most of the post-Soviet states, civil society remains weak. In most of the republics of Central Asia, where the highly centralised authoritarian state continues to extend its tentacles into the life of its communities, a pluralist politics capable of challenging the state or functioning autonomously from the state bureaucracy has yet to be realised. In contrast, in the Baltic states, a vibrant civil society is in the making. Here, voluntary associations, business organisations and pressure groups are contributing to the democratisation of political life at a variety of geographical levels, from national to local politics.

Finally, a functioning democracy requires an effective and accountable bureaucracy. All modern states need bureaucracies in order to administer the rule of law and to ensure that the rights of their citizens are guaranteed and protected. The Soviet state possessed a huge bureaucratic apparatus, but it was neither effective nor accountable to its citizens. Overly centralised and inflexibly hierarchical, it rigidly and mechanically administered Soviet space. For the post-Soviet states, the question of who controls the state bureaucracy and how it is used is therefore vital. But these states also require a bureaucracy that functions efficiently in the new political and economic climate. As Linz and Stepan note in relation to democratising states more generally, 'insufficient state taxing capacity or a weak normative and bureaucratic presence in much of the territory, such that citizens cannot effectively demand that their rights be respected or receive any basic entitlements, is a great problem . . .'.[17] In the post-Soviet states, tax collection has been especially problematic. The inability to collect taxes efficiently and fairly – be it from regions, cities, economic enterprises or individuals – has damaged citizens' welfare: wages are not paid, and vital local, regional and national public services receive inadequate funding and other resources. In short, state bureaucracy has found it hard to offer a modicum of social support for their citizens or to guarantee their safety.

Economic liberalisation: from the command to a market economy

Integral also to mapping out the politics of transformation is the region's transition from a command to a market economy. The process of liberalising the centrally administered Soviet economy has included privatising state property, ending state-regulated price controls (including prices of basic goods and services) and further opening up the region to international trade and investment. Such changes raise fundamental questions, not least concerning the degree of political autonomy the post-Soviet states enjoy in shaping their own economic futures, the ability of economic reform to proceed hand in hand with democratisation, and the implications of economic globalisation for redefining geopolitical alliances and creating opportunities for sub-national political communities to establish relations within the global economy.

While democratisation has opened up opportunities for the post-Soviet states to become integrated into the world economy, the success of their economic reforms is conditioned in part by those economic and political forces that play a major role in the global economic system, in which neo-liberal rules of capitalist competition predominate. As Kagarlitsky notes, the major problem facing the post-Soviet states is that they are entering into what he calls 'the semi-periphery of the new world order'.[18] In other words, the post-Soviet states are, to varying degrees, all faced with the task of finding markets for uncompetitive products while at the same time engaging in economic reform. Their specific circumstances do however differ considerably: some states, most notably the Baltic republics, are adjusting more quickly than for instance the less developed economies of Central Asia. Yet all recognise the importance of reform and of attracting external sources of investment and assistance, including the need to secure large loans from global financial institutions. Inevitably, such limits to economic sovereignty have led to accusations that the West is able to openly meddle in shaping post-Soviet agendas, by prescribing how their economies and societies should be structured.

Economic liberalisation can have a major impact on the prospects for both democratisation and geopolitical stability. However, the assumption, prevalent in the West, that economic liberalisation is integral to facilitating both democratisation and geopolitical stability remains doubtful. While democracy and economic liberalisation may accompany one another, as Leftwich notes, it does not necessarily follow that democracy is a major cause of the success of economic liberalisation.[19] Indeed, economic liberalisation may have the contrary effect to what is intended. Rapid economic reform can in the short-term lead to social hardships, thus throwing into doubt the prospects for political stability and democracy. Such considerations were one of the main reasons why in the early

1990s Russia and Ukraine abandoned their brief experiments with 'shock therapy' – or swift and comprehensive economic reform – for a policy of economic gradualism.[20] Indeed, successful economic reform, at least in its initial stages, may require a more rather than less *dirigiste* state. There is some evidence from the states of Central Asia, notably Kazakhstan, to suggest that authoritarian rule may facilitate economic reform.

Another factor that has emerged as crucial to shaping the politics of the economic transition is the need in a world economy that has become more regionalised in its patterns of trade to form new regional trading blocs. For the post-Soviet states, the exact nature of their regional project – the Commonwealth of Independent States (CIS) – has been shaped by a legacy of economic interdependency and limited trade with the rest of the world economy. While for some of the post-Soviet states, notably Russia, the CIS is also connected with geopolitical security interests, for others it represents little more than a short-term economic necessity, which, when they join alternative regional economic and geopolitical alliances, will largely disappear. For the moment at least, there is little evidence to suggest that the post-Soviet region is likely to emerge as a major trading bloc comparable with North America or the European Union.[21]

Finally, sub-national regions and cities are playing an increasingly important part in shaping the post-Soviet economic transition. Their rise to prominence has been fuelled largely by the crisis of the Soviet Union's economic fragmentation and subsequent state mismanagement of the economic transition. The difficulties that some of the post-Soviet states have had in managing their economies have produced dysfunctional local markets whose regions and cities have intervened to protect their own interests. In the process, the localities have gone further, seizing upon the opportunities that economic globalisation offers to trade and seek investment both across and beyond post-Soviet space. Consequently, the economic sovereignty of many of the post-Soviet states is being challenged not only from above but also from below as the regions and localities attempt to shape their own economies of transition.

Plan of the book

The rest of this book is concerned with exploring these three interconnected processes of transition. As signalled in this chapter, any consideration of the post-Soviet states must begin with examining the Soviet Union. Chapter 2 is devoted to this task. The main body of the rest of the book is divided into three main parts. Part I examines the process of decolonisation. Chapter 3 focuses on Russia and how Russian identities and political representations of homeland have been reformulated since 1991, and the implications such changes are having on Russia's envisaged geopolitical role within Eurasia. Chapter 4 considers how the politics of national identities is shaping the nation-building process in the borderland states, exploring in particular the relationship between the new titular-dominated regimes in power and the Russian diaspora, especially in the Baltic republics and Central Asia. Part II explores the relationship between the post-Soviet transition and democracy. Chapter 5 examines some of the limits to democracy in relation to the changing role that social movements are playing in the post-Soviet transition, the problems at a local level of establishing more democratic forms of urban governance, and the challenges that democracy faces from organised crime. Chapter 6 considers the relationship between democracy and multiculturalism, in which various strategies adopted by the post-Soviet states in relation to their national and ethnic groups are explored, and the consequences in particular that Russia's experiment with federation is having on securing a more democratic multicultural future. Part III examines the geopolitical economy of transition. Chapter 7 focuses on the region's economic power bloc, the CIS, and the role that it is playing in redefining economic and geopolitical relations amongst the post-Soviet states. Chapter 8 focuses on the role of Russia's regions in re-shaping its geopolitical economy and the differing strategies that the regions are pursuing in relation to the central state, local market reform and integration into the global economy. Finally, in the concluding section, Chapter 9 examines the usefulness of both comparative and geopolitical theories of transition in helping us to understand the nature of and prospects for the post-Soviet transition.

Notes to Chapter 1

1 F. Fukuyama, *The End of History and the Last Man* (London, Hamish Hamilton, 1992).
2 See, in particular, S. Avineri, 'The End of the Soviet Union and the Return to History', in M. Keren and G. Ofer (eds), *Trials of Transition. Economic Reform in the Former Communist Bloc* (Boulder, CO, Westview Press, 1992), pp. 11–18; S. Huntington, 'The clash of civilisations', *Foreign Affairs*, 72(3), 1993, pp. 22–49.
3 Huntington, 'The clash of civilisations', p. 31.
4 See, in particular, B. Rubin and J. Snyder (eds), *Post-Soviet Political Order. Conflict and State-Building* (London, Routledge, 1998).
5 See, for example, M. Kundera, 'The tragedy of Central Europe', *New Review of Books*, 26 April 1984, pp. 3–19; R. Kapuscinski, *Imperium* (London, Granta Books, 1996).
6 N. Thrift, 'New times and spaces? The perils of transition models', *Environment and Planning D. Society and Space*, 7, 1989, p. 127.
7 G. Szablowski and H.-D. Derlien, 'East European transitions, elites, bureaucracies, and the European Community', *Governance*, 6(3), 1993, pp. 304–24.
8 See, for example, D. Lieven, 'The Russian empire and the Soviet Union as imperial polities', *Journal of Contemporary History*, 30, 1995, pp. 605–36; A. Motyl, 'Competing Discourses and Inter-state Conflict in Post-imperial Eastern Europe', in Rubin and Snyder (eds), *Post-Soviet Political Order*, pp. 14–33.
9 G. Pridham and J. Vanhenen, *Democratisation in Eastern Europe. Domestic and International Perspectives* (London, Routledge, 1994); A. Przeworski,

Sustainable Democracy (Cambridge, Cambridge University Press, 1995); J. Linz and A. Stepan, *Problems of Democratic Transition and Consolidation. Southern Europe, South America, and Post-Communist Europe* (Baltimore, The Johns Hopkins University Press, 1996).

10 M. Burawoy, 'The state and economic involution: Russia through a China lens', *World Development*, 24(6), 1996, pp. 1105–17.

11 See, in particular, P. Schmitter and T. Karl, 'The conceptual travels of transitologists and consolidologists: How far to the East should they attempt to go?', *Slavic Review*, 53(1), 1994, pp. 173–85.

12 V. Bunce, 'Should transitologists be grounded?', *Slavic Review*, 54(1), 1995, p. 115.

13 M. Burawoy, 'From Sovietology to Comparative Political Economy', in D. Orlovsky (ed.), *Beyond Soviet Studies* (Washington DC, Woodrow Wilson Center Press, 1995), pp. 72–104.

14 E. Gellner, *Nationalism* (London, Weidenfeld and Nicholson, 1997).

15 G. Sorensen, *Democracy and Democratisation* (Boulder, CO, Westview Press, 1993).

16 Przeworski, *Sustainable Democracy*, p. 12.

17 Linz and Stepan, *Problems of Democratic Transition and Consolidation*, p. 11.

18 B. Kagarlitsky, *The Mirage of Modernization* (New York, Monthly Review Press, 1995), p. 218.

19 A. Leftwich (ed.), *Democracy and Development* (Oxford, Polity Press, 1996).

20 W. Adams and J. Brock, *Adam Smith Goes to Moscow. A Dialogue on Radical Reform* (Princeton, Princeton University Press, 1993).

21 A. Gamble and A. Payne (eds), *Regionalism and World Order* (London, Macmillan Press, 1996).

|2|

From transformation to fragmentation

At its height, the Soviet Union formed the core of a geopolitical system which, whether regarded as 'an empire', 'socialist world system' or 'military bloc', was global in its power and influence. In addition to Russia proper (the Russian Soviet Federative Socialist Republic or RSFSR), this system was made up of three main components: the borderland non-Russian Union republics, or 'inner empire'; the communist states of eastern Europe, or 'external empire', which owed their existence and survival very largely to Soviet force, whether applied or threatened; and Third World client states, including Cuba, Vietnam and a number of other countries in Africa and Asia, whose socialist revolutions had indigenous roots but where the Soviet Union provided the inspiration and model for development as well as a degree of material support. But what distinguishes the Soviet Union, which many commentators have labelled a totalitarian state, from other classic twentieth-century totalitarian regimes, such as Germany (1933–45) and Italy (1922–43), is not only that it proved more capable of global influence and lasted much longer, but also that it underwent more significant changes.[1] It was, in short, more dynamic and successful.

This chapter considers why the Soviet Union survived for most of the twentieth century. The first part examines how the Soviet system was able so effectively to transform the poor, backward and overwhelmingly rural-peasant society that its architects inherited following the 1917 Bolshevik Revolution into a global military–industrial superpower. This involves exploring how, in periods of both socio-spatial transformation and subsequent political stasis, the Soviet state was able to ensure regime maintenance and social stability. The first explanation examined here is the totalitarian thesis, but although it provides some important insights, it is argued that its ability to account for regime longevity in particular is limited. Other possible explanations are then examined on the supposition that the Soviet state and its relations with society were more complex and dynamic than totalitarian theories suggest. The second part of the chapter focuses on the reasons for the Soviet Union's eventual collapse. It examines the belated but unsuccessful attempt through *perestroika* or reform communism to return to socio-spatial transformation as a way of securing a stable and more prosperous socialist society, and the role that particular localities of resistance played in challenging that endeavour.

Totalitarianism revisited

The most commonly conceived and pervasive Western image of the Soviet Union is that, propounded by totalitarian theorists, of a territorially over-centralised, omnipresent and coercive state which sought to control all aspects of society. Linked to early 1950s US Cold War geopolitical thinking, this thesis identified two types of industrial states: liberal democracies and totalitarian regimes (both communist and fascist). Through the construction of such a binary distinction, totalitarian thinking came to form an integral part of a Western anti-Soviet discourse that survived in Atlanticist foreign policy circles throughout the Cold War. Friedrich, in what is probably the most frequently quoted definition of totalitarianism, describes it as 'a system of autocratic rule for realising totalist intentions under modern conditions'.[2] Its main features, as formulated by Friedrich and Brzezinski in their classic work,[3] are as follows:

1. A totalist ideology
2. A single mass party committed to this ideology (typically headed by one leader)
3. A system of terroristic police control over the population
4. State monopoly over mass communications [surveillance] and military force
5. Centralised control of the economy.

In keeping with this typology, the legitimacy of Soviet power rested upon a single ideology and guiding charter: Marxism–Leninism. Its purported goal was to create an alternative and superior form of social organisation to that of capitalism. The state's founding fathers drew upon a vision of history that equated social progress with the creation of a socialist, and ultimately classless, political order. In translating 'utopia into development', what was envisaged was a society that would no longer be characterised by town and country or inter-regional differences and would be one in which citizens, irrespective of their place in the social division of labour, would be equal. The responsibility for building this classless society lay with the Communist Party of the Soviet Union (CPSU), which enjoyed a territorial monopoly on state power through its control, management and spatial organisation of society. The party-state was omnipresent, existing at all geographical levels – from the factory, farm and neighbourhood, up through the cities, regions and Union republics to the centre – with each level of organisation responsible to the one above, and ultimately to the political leadership in the Kremlin. With its monopoly over the mass media and surveillance systems, the party-state had the power to mobilise its citizenry, monitor their actions and exert control in ways unimaginable in liberal democracies. Moreover, with its near monopoly over the means of production, the party-state was able centrally to plan, manage and control the economy – including industry, agriculture, transport, trade and technology – and oversee economic development throughout its territory. The state also determined social resource allocation, including education, status, income, wages and housing. It could allocate and redistribute social resources between basic socio-spatial groups in accordance with its own political preferences. As a consequence of this monopoly over the distribution of rewards and benefits, the party-state had at its disposal a powerful means to facilitate social change and maintain stability.

For totalitarian theorists, it was, however, the state's capacity and willingness to use coercion on a daily and systematic basis that was its central hallmark. Terror, it is argued, became the driving force of Soviet socialism, in part out of necessity because the 1917 revolution did not command mass social support. Backed primarily by a handful of the larger cities, the events and ideals of October 1917 did not capture the political imagination of the rural peasantry, who in the early 1920s constituted over four-fifths of the Soviet population. Consequently, one of the main aims of the Communist Party was to extend its control beyond the cities to the countryside. This the state embarked upon in 1928–29 with the launching of Stalin's industrialisation drive and the forced collectivisation of the countryside.

It was a programme of socio-spatial transformation undertaken for economic as well as political reasons. As Arnason put it,

> there is no doubt that those who launched the operation [of forced collectivisation] had both a political and economic rationale: Stalin's strategy of state-building and mobilisation could not be implemented without more effective control over the rural majority of the population, and the transfer of resources from the agricultural sector was seen as essential to rapid industrialisation.[4]

While rapid industrialisation was also achieved through the efforts of the existing urban-industrial labour force, the internal social and external geopolitical pressures the Soviet leadership faced prompted it to adopt a spatial strategy which entailed using the rural surplus of capital and labour in the industrialisation drive.[5] Industrialisation, Stalin's leadership believed, had to be achieved sooner rather than later in order to ensure that the Soviet Union was militarily and industrially strong enough to withstand the threat of capitalist encirclement.

In a feat unsurpassed by any state either before or since, the industrialisation and collectivisation drive transformed the country's economy in a remarkably short period. By 1937, 93 per cent of peasant households had been collectivised. This compares with a figure of only 1.7 per cent in 1928.[6] By the mid-1930s, the vast majority of the 25 million individual peasant households that existed in 1928 had been combined into some 250,000 collective farms (*kolkhozy*). Totalitarian theorists argue that this transformation was made possible only by utilising and expanding the coercive and administrative apparatus of the party-state and by the use of terror. Stalin, they argue, resolved the issue of peasant voluntarism through a ruthless policy of state coercion. Thus, socialist industrialisation was achieved through 'an act of political will exercised through revolutionary coercion, in short by quasi-military means'.[7] In the towns as well as the countryside, it is claimed, society had no choice but to acquiesce. Moreover, it was the arbitrariness of state terror that was crucial to socio-spatial transformation. Irrespective of whether the individual was an urban worker or rural peasant, a party or non-party member, nobody was safe. This use of state power reached its height in the 1930s when millions of so-called 'enemies of the state', ordinary workers, peasants and those drawn from the professional classes, were liquidated or imprisoned in the work camps of the Gulag Archipelago. As Brzezinksi put it, 'failure to adjust to the Stalinist system can mean extinction of life. But success in adjusting ... does not guarantee liberty or safety'.[8] For totalitarianists, it was the centrality and pervasiveness of terror that were pivotal to accounting for both the scale and speed of the transformation.

The administrative powers and territorial reach of the party-state expanded in the 1930s as a result of the incorporation of the countryside into the centrally planned economy. The party-state determined what the countryside should produce and in what quantity. By establishing a near monopoly over the purchase of agricultural goods, it was also able to fix the price paid for its produce. Industrialisation also made it easier for the Communist Party to extend its territorial control. This was not only because the population had become more urbanised as a consequence of the 1930s industrialisation drive, but also because of the way in which the large cities functioned as 'command outposts of the territorial organisation of society'. Small towns and the countryside became directly accountable to such centres as part of the hierarchical, super-centralised systems of party-state power.[9] The party-state was therefore able to use its surveillance techniques more effectively and over a wider area.

The Stalinist State established a form of urban-industrial economy geared primarily towards heavy industry and the military–industrial complex. In Lange's term, it was a war economy, which sacrificed balanced sectoral development for military-industrialism.[10] 'In reality', writes one totalitarian theorist, '. . . the Soviet Union in its prime was never more than a great military–industrial complex and a Party-state superpower'. What was built in the 1930s, it is argued, 'was a crude, but serviceable imitation of a Pittsburgh–Detroit or Ruhr–Lorraine economy'.[11] Indeed, war provided the formative experience and a major underpinning for the Soviet economy throughout its existence. However, the centrality of the military–industrial complex was also to become the Soviet Union's Achilles' heel, for it lowered the priority of investment in social consumption and other sectors of the economy vital for more balanced development.

Another consequence of the specific character of Soviet industrialisation and urbanisation was the lack of housing relative to the demand for and supply of industrial labour in the largest cities. The massive influx of rural migrants to the cities in the wake of break-neck industrialisation, combined with limited state spending on house-building, resulted in an acute housing shortage, especially in large cities such as Moscow and Leningrad. In 1932–33, in order to manage this crisis, the state introduced an internal passport and residence permit (*propiska*) system to monitor and restrict migration into large cities (Fig. 2.1). The majority of rural residents were not issued internal passports, and it was difficult to obtain the *propiska* needed to live in cities such as Moscow, Leningrad and other major cities. Although this did not halt the mass movement of rural labour into restricted cities during the Stalin years, the system became an important means of regulating not only migration but also access to privileges as large cities came to offer better public services, amenities and social opportunities than did smaller towns and the countryside.[12]

For totalitarian theorists, the Soviet model, shaped during the extensive industrialisation drive of the 1930s, represented a deviant form of modernity based upon state power through terror. As Koltakowski puts it, the Soviet model symbolised 'the greatest fantasy of our century' because, despite 'utopia in power', the ideals of 1917 were never translated into practice.[13] Thus, the Soviet Union was based on the myth not only that the ideals of socialism had been achieved following the country's socio-spatial transformation but also that socialism was possible in the first place. Rather than creating utopia, it established 'a Stalinist mausoleum'.[14] Attempts at subsequent political or economic reform, as undertaken by Nikita Khrushchev in the latter half of the 1950s and Mikhail Gorbachev three decades later, were doomed to fail precisely because the political and economic system created by the Stalinist state was unreformable. Although commentators like Friedrich note that the totalitarian techniques used by the state were characterised by 'notable ups and downs', these did not alter the essential nature of the regime. Yet such accounts mask at least one important ingredient in Soviet social stability. While state terror was integral to socialist industrialisation, social consent also played a part, especially amongst the urban industrial working class, the backbone of support for the revolution. Many citizens could identify with and did support the socialist ideals that Stalinism espoused. By combining a socialist symbolism (of building a better society) with nationalist rhetoric, which drew heavily upon the Soviet Union's geopolitical vulnerability to capitalist encirclement, the Stalinist State created a vision of homeland that was able to mobilise society. The

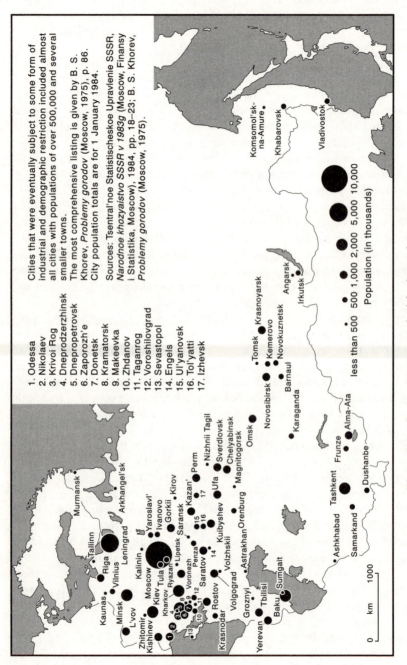

Figure 2.1 Soviet cities earmarked for limited in-migration.

symbolic power of *Sovetskaya rodina* (Soviet homeland) was further cemented by the sacrifices of some 27 million Soviet citizens who gave their lives during the 'Great Patriotic War' (1941–45) in defence of the socialist motherland. Later, during the Cold War era, this sense of identity also played a part in mobilising support against what was constructed as the Soviet state's 'imperial Other', the United States of America.

Revisionist interpretations

The organised consensus

While coercion was a central feature of the Soviet system, the totalitarian model is less applicable to the post-Stalin era. Revisionist accounts emphasise that the state changed in two vital senses after Stalin's death in 1953 and that those changes imbued it with a new vitality. First, while state power remained highly centralised, political power within the party-state apparatus became more fragmented, with vested institutional interests such as the economic ministries and military–industrial complex vying for influence over political decisions. Thus, after Stalin, the Soviet Union resembled more a political oligarchy than a Leviathan State. Second, although the party-state continued to use coercion to maintain social stability, it also recognised the need to forge a greater degree of consensus by fulfilling more of the social and economic aspirations of its citizenry. This change was most clearly expressed in Khrushchev's late 1950s speech which emphasised the need to mobilise the support of society in the building of communism. As a result, what emerged was, as Zaslavsky calls it, 'an organised consensus',[15] or, in Cook's words, 'a social contract'.[16] As Zaslavsky explains, 'basic social groups accepted the existing highly centralised nature of power and their lack of access to the decision-making process, in exchange for a number of rewards'.[17] These social concessions included guarantees of job security, some workers' rights (including a maximum number of hours in the working day), upward social mobility (based increasingly on educational merit), a slow but steady rise in material living standards (better diet, house-building programmes, rise in incomes, improved medical and childcare) and the guaranteed continuation of state-subsidised prices for basic commodities such as foods and housing. In return, society continued to be denied any meaningful say in the political decisions that affected people's everyday lives, including the continued imposition of strict limits on civil and political rights.

Three aspects of the organised consensus are particularly important. First, certain social groups, especially those pivotal to ensuring regime stability, benefited more from the material and social rewards of the organised consensus than others. One way in which the state continued to manipulate access to benefits was through the passport–*propiska* system. With its increased application, the state ensured the reproduction of privilege because the children of those who resided in large cities had automatic access by birth to a *propiska* and thus all the benefits of city living. The opposite was true for those who lived in the smaller towns or the country-side, where the material benefits of socialism were usually far less apparent. Non-*propiska* holders also included millions of urban commuters who resided in the suburbs but travelled daily into the large cities, where demand for unskilled labour continued to grow. Thus, the population of large cities, where the share of professionals and skilled workers had always been greater, became increasingly stratified and hereditary in composition. As Zaslavsky writes, 'the interaction between class stratification and geograph-ical stratification seems to be of primary importance for understanding the internal development of Soviet society'.[18]

Second, the organised consensus under Brezhnev in the 1970s and early 1980s reflected a deliberate strategy in which social stability was prioritised over engagement in economic or political reform. Under such conditions the organised consensus could not prevail. By the late 1970s, living standards were no longer able to keep up with the rising consumer expectations of this more urbanised and educated society. Differentials in living standards, espe-cially between town and country, were becoming greater. Moreover, the vested material interests in social stability of those social groups who had benefited from the organised consensus were becoming an economic burden to the state. For instance, one of the consequences of the over-production and over-concentration of the professional classes in large cities was a chronic shortage of specialist skills in the smaller towns, the countryside and Siberia. The need to create employment for specialists in the cities where they chose to live was therefore a considerable economic cost for the regime.

Finally, the continued existence and expansion of the second or shadow economy became even more important to regime stability. Coexisting in an uneasy and tense relationship with the state socialist or 'first economy', the second economy covered a vast and varied set of socio-economic activities, ranging from the outright illegal (the so-called black market), involving the pilfering of state property from the workplace, through activities such as providing dental, hairdressing or teaching services 'on the side' in the so-called grey market, which were technically legal but outside the structure of the formal economy, to 'the white market' whose activities were tolerated, such as peasants selling fruit and vegetables produced on their private household plots on the open market. In short, the second economy fulfilled consumer demand for a range of vital goods and services that the state socialist sector could not effectively provide. In all, it contributed a stagger-ing 30 to 40 per cent of personal income and involved an estimated 20 mil-lion citizens. By providing a modicum of material well-being for the ordinary Soviet citizen, the second economy was an important ingredient in social stability. Yet the growth of the second economy questioned the very legitimacy of the socialist sector because of the shortages that socialist central planning generated as a result of loopholes in the economic system.[19]

Socio-spatial change: the urban transformation thesis

Both the totalitarian model and the social contract or organised consensus thesis are state-centric theories of stability. Both emphasise the central role of the state and its political institutions in controlling and manipulating society. While not questioning the central role of state power in shaping transformation and stability, an alternative interpretation argues that social transformation, linked to Soviet urbanisation, is also important to understanding both the changing nature of relations between state and society and why a particular urban social stratum emerged, able and willing from the mid-1980s onwards to engage in economic and political reform.

The most compelling account is provided by Lewin.[20] He argues that the social transformation of the Soviet Union involved two essential stages: first 'the ruralisation of the cities' in the 1930s, and second, 'the urbanisation of society' from the 1960s onwards. By the ruralisation of the cities he means the way in which, during Stalinist rapid industrialisation, the cities not only demographically but also in terms of their socio-cultural values became predominantly peasant. Especially important was the way in which Stalinist industrialisation put together a hurriedly formed state bureaucracy 'peopled' by a large proportion of individuals drawn from peasant backgrounds. This new *nomenklatura* therefore brought a particular set of cultural values which fulfilled one of the central requirements of Stalinism, the need for a loyal and deferential social stratum. The political and economic system that was created in the 1930s included a culture wholly commensurate with the functioning of a totalitarian order, i.e. loyal lieutenants willing to carry out orders and commands. Individual upward mobility or what Fitzpatrick calls the *vydvizhenchestvo* of the 1930s – the promotion of peasants and workers to non-manual positions – was secured not so much on the basis of merit but through displaying loyalty and deference to the party.[21] Social change, in effect, played a more proactive role in structuring the nature and value system of the despotic state than other theories suggest.

By the 1960s a predominantly urban society had emerged, with the majority of Soviet citizens now living in cities. By the mid-1980s the proportion of urban dwellers in the total Soviet population had grown to over two-thirds (Fig. 2.2). Soviet society was therefore undergoing a vital urban transformation at precisely the moment when the Brezhnev administration was shying away from any engagement with economic or political reform. It was, in particular, the emergence of a new urban social grouping of highly educated and qualified specialists which Lewin singles out as being crucial to this transformation, a stratum which in the 1960–86 period had grown fourfold. It was a disparate stratum made up of managerial–administrative, educational, scientific and political elites who increasingly came to occupy prominent positions within the party-state apparatus, as well as becoming a more influential social force more generally. The proportion of party members with higher education grew rapidly throughout this period: whereas in

(a) Total and urban population growth, 1917–89

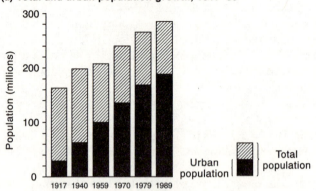

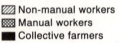

(b) Occupational class background, 1940–87

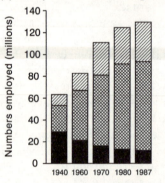

(c) Higher education of party members, 1957–89

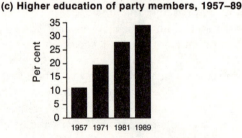

Figure 2.2 Urban transformation and social change, 1917–89. Sources: (a) from *Pravda*, 29 April 1989; (b) and (c) from data compiled by D. Lane, *Soviet Society under Perestroika* (London, Unwin Hyman, 1990).

1957 only 10 per cent of party members had had a higher education, by 1971 this had doubled to 20 per cent, increasing by 1989 to over 30 per cent.[22] It was this well-educated and more urban stratum who came to challenge the position and authority of those party functionaries (or *praktiki*) who owed their position and status to loyalty to the party, and who had a vested interest in maintaining the social and political status quo. This new stratum was hindered by a political, economic and social system whose institutions and ways of doing things were largely a product of the system created under Stalin: a technical intelligentsia, made up of engineers, scientists and factory managers whose professionalism was straightjacketed by a production system that was still stuck in an earlier technological age and inhibited economic growth; and a cultural intelligentsia, composed of teachers, journalists and artists who were restricted in their ability to write, paint, teach or compose what they wished. In short, this new urban world, complete with a new and increasingly challenging social formation, sat uneasily with a communist system which stifled economic and political change. It was this new stratum, Lewin argues, that by the mid-1980s had secured significant positions of power within the party-state apparatus. The generation of *perestroika* and of reform communism had come of age.

While such a set of arguments tends to down play the manipulative role of the state and over-play the role of diploma holders as a natural and automatically progressive force, it is nonetheless a powerful thesis and one which provides insight into why a new political leadership committed to economic liberalisation and later political reform was able to secure political power in the mid-1980s.

Bringing in global perspectives

One of the main problems with the above accounts is that explanations of transformation and stability are framed within an endogenous context. Yet any account of the Soviet phenomenon must also locate it within a global framework. By taking as its starting point the global economy and interpreting the state and its external relations as bound up with the political organisation of a changing world economy, world systems theory offers one such interpretative mapping. It seeks to explain the particular path and limits to Soviet modernity within the context of its place and role within a functioning capitalist world economy. For Wallerstein, the modern world embraces one mode of production, founded on market exchange, which determines the nature of inter-state relations based on a state's location within the world economy. Soviet socialism therefore did not constitute a separate mode of production.[23] On the eve of the Bolshevik Revolution, Russia, as the least developed of the European powers, occupied a semi-peripheral position within the world economy, with all the internal contradictions and tensions that such a position generated. Although the empire's trading capacity lay primarily as an exporter of raw materials and grain, it had already established an urban-industrialising base, a large proportion of which was foreign-owned and also, to a lesser extent, foreign managed.[24] Indeed, socialism, as an anti-systemic movement that came to power with the 1917 Bolshevik Revolution, was largely a product of an urban industrial proletariat impoverished by the inequalities generated by Russia's location within the world system. Thus, 1917 brought to state power a social movement which attempted to challenge capitalism and redress the Soviet Union's more peripheral position within the world economy, primarily through pursuing what became known as the Stalinist strategy of 'socialism in one country'. This strategy, while representing a successful autarkic attempt to industrialise, gradually gave way after 1945 to the Soviet Union's functioning as a fuller member of the world economy. So although having secured after World War II its own geographic bloc of trading countries, the Soviet Union also functioned as an integral part of a capitalist world order. As Wallerstein puts it, the Soviet state pursued 'in Marxist clothing a mercantilist strategy of "catching up" and "surpassing" rival states'.[25]

The Soviet Union traded as part of the world economy in order to gain a core status that eluded it. Because it lacked the economic, technological or ideological clout necessary to make it a truly global power, it remained what Dibb has called 'the incomplete superpower'.[26] As a functioning part of the world economy, it was more closely bound up and susceptible to changes and fluctuations in global markets than either official Soviet versions or the scale of East–West geopolitical rivalry might suggest. There is therefore little evidence to support Syzmanski's thesis that 'a socialist world system' functioned separately from the capitalist world economy.[27] While most of Soviet trade occurred between Soviet bloc countries, the Soviet Union became increasingly dependent on the wider global economy. In seeking to protect its own industries from intense global competition by maintaining a state monopoly over foreign trade, the Soviet Union actively sought and secured trading links with the capitalist core countries, notably with the United States of America, western Europe and Japan. The Soviet Union supplied these core states with raw materials and fossil fuels in return for importing high technology (in an attempt to reduce the East–West technology gap) and overseas grain (to compensate for the failings of Soviet collectivisation). In all, by the early 1980s, just under a fifth of all Soviet foreign trade was with the capitalist West.[28] As Shmelev and Popov put it, 'imports were looked at as ways of "plugging the holes" in an economy that was unbalanced in all its indicators, and exports were seen as the unpleasant but unavoidable cost of imports.'[29] In the absence of economic reforms at home, the Soviet Union therefore needed the capitalist world economy. As world systems theorists argue, it was the nature of the economic system created during the Stalinist period and the inability of the economic system to reform itself which meant that in the longer term the Soviet Union was unable to take on board, or compete with, the new technological changes that were the driving force of the more dynamic and innovating core capitalist world economies of the 1970s and 1980s.

Despite the importance that world systems theorists place on locating the Soviet Union within the global economic context, they downplay the geopolitical dimension to global relations or what Deutscher called 'The Great Contest'.[30] Ultimately, this West–East geopolitical rivalry played an important part in determining the fate of the Soviet Union. In this regard, Kennedy's thesis is particularly insightful.[31] Throughout recent history, Kennedy argues, 'great powers' have a habit of overstretching themselves in terms of their global geopolitical and economic commitments, which can lead to their decline if such global commitments are not matched by economic and technological innovation at home. In the Soviet case, the absence of economic reform affected not only national economic growth but also the capacity of the Soviet Union to finance both its large empire abroad and the increasingly expensive military technology, armaments and armies necessary to compete with the USA in the Cold War. During the 1970s and 1980s, finding the resources to maintain its external empire was becoming increasingly difficult. As Bunce notes, whereas in certain respects (primarily in terms of geopolitical security), Soviet–east European relations can be considered in the first 15 years of post-Stalinism as 'Soviet assets', in the last 15 years they were being transformed into 'Soviet liabilities'. This was the result of: first, the economic and political dependence of eastern Europe on the Soviet Union; second, the costs to the Soviet Union of maintaining its east European monopoly of political and, to a lesser extent, economic power; and third, the costs which accompanied the bloc's limited re-integration with global capitalism in a period of economic downswing.[32] Whereas increases in costs of energy from 1973 onwards in the world economy strengthened Soviet hegemony over eastern Europe, falling oil prices on the world market in the mid-1980s had the opposite effect. Unable to provide the resources necessary to stimulate economic growth in eastern Europe or to permit reform, the east European countries had increasingly to finance their own modernisation by looking westwards, a process which included borrowing heavily from Western states and global economic institutions.

The Soviet Union's inability to redress economic stagnation (*zastoi*) at home or to guarantee improved living standards within its geopolitical sphere of influence was highlighted by the comparative geopolitical context – in particular, by comparisons that ordinary Soviet citizens began to make between the record of Soviet-style communism and that of Western-style capitalism. This carried profound implications for the legitimacy of the Soviet state. The contrast between an ideology that viewed the decline of capitalism as inevitable, and Soviet-style communism as invincible, and the record of the Soviet Union, which had manifestly failed to catch up with, let alone overtake, capitalism, discredited the entire state-projected image of Soviet socialism. Moreover, the dynamics of capitalism contained a new dimension vital to its global impact: the increasing role of new information technology, from which the Soviet Union and its client states in eastern Europe could not insulate themselves, despite attempts to maintain a cordon sanitaire. Advances in media technology gave the people of the Baltic republics, for example, access to Finnish television and hence an electronic window through which they could compare the reality of life under Soviet rule with the projected image of Western-style capitalism.

Reform communism

While such conditions were eventually to ensure the beginning of the end of Soviet-style communism, what separated the revolutions in 1989 in eastern Europe from the homeland of the Bolshevik Revolution itself was that communism in the latter was considered as reformable. Moreover, while the above accounts of social change and regime stasis further our understanding of why by the mid-1980s Soviet socialism was in decline, they do not explain why a reform-minded leadership under Mikhail Gorbachev failed ultimately to breathe new life into the system or why this failure led to both the end of Soviet-style communism and the Soviet Union's geopolitical disintegration.

Reform communism or *perestroika* (restructuring) was initiated in February 1986, just under a year after Mikhail Gorbachev took over as CPSU general secretary. It began as an attempt to modernise a stagnating socialist economy but became increasingly radical and far-reaching as the 1980s drew to a close. Economic restructuring contained three main elements. The first was economic modernisation through *uskorenie* (or economic acceleration).

As the state could no longer rely on endless sources of indigenous capital and surplus rural labour, its leaders decided that the only way to modernise the economy was through technological innovation and gains in labour efficiency. Many of the large smoke-stack industries in the industrial regions of the Urals, the Donbas and the Leningrad area, for example, which had been built during Stalin's time, were in desperate need of modernisation. Later the idea of *uskorenie* was linked to a further opening up of the Soviet economy to outside trade, with a view to gaining greater access both to Western technology and to Western investment. In encouraging a new climate of East–West *détente* as part of its strategy for economic modernisation, the new reform-minded leadership was also signalling its realisation of the need to switch part of the huge, economically crippling public expenditure on the military-defence sector to investment in factory technology and diversifying production in order to meet popular demand for consumer goods. In Gorbachev's economic modernisation plans, labour was to be encouraged to be more innovative and productive. This included improving discipline in the workplace, increasing worker motivation, strengthening managerial initiative and authority, and rationalising the labour force. This was also the motivation behind the anti-alcohol campaign launched in 1985. What in effect *perestroika* was attacking were those labour practices summed up in the often quoted saying: 'we pretend to work and they pretend to pay us'. In emphasising 'work, sobriety, order and honesty', the Gorbachev administration was attempting to address a number of problems, including excessive labour absenteeism, overmanning (it has been estimated that by the mid-1980s factory enterprises were engaged in a scale of 'labour hoarding' that involved retaining around a fifth more labour than was necessary to fulfil production schedules), and high labour turnover (labour tended to vote with its feet by moving to and from those sectors and localities where wages and conditions were better).

Second, economic modernisation sought to give the regions, factories and farms more say in the running of their localities and enterprises. This included plans to decentralise, giving enterprises and localities greater responsibility over their own budgets (*khozrashchet*). The argument was based on the premise that greater local financial accountability would not only lead to greater economic efficiency but would also take power away from a cumbersome and overcentralised party-state bureaucracy which was often insensitive to local needs and economic conditions.

Finally, *perestroika* introduced a limited market sector. Here the idea was not only to roll back part of the centralised command economy but also to provide the economic space for the establishment of new market-type enterprises, especially in the underdeveloped sphere of urban consumer services. In acknowledging for the first time that the centrally planned economy could not meet the needs of its consumers, the regime envisaged the establishment of small, flexible, non-state enterprises that could react much more quickly to local fluctuations in demand than the more centralised and larger state enterprises. Thus, enterprise and co-operative laws of 1987–88 made it possible for groups of individuals within certain service activities, such as shops and restaurants, waste processing and agricultural co-operatives, to form their own companies and to fix their own prices.[33] These, however, had to be strictly co-operative ventures, involving a minimum of three persons but no hired labour. Moreover, given also that co-operatives were to be subject to heavy rates of taxation, the reformist state was signalling that it had no intention of opening the door to a petty-bourgeoisie or runaway capitalism.

Gorbachev's chief economic adviser, Abel Aganbegyan, linked the introduction of co-operatives to what he called 'the democratisation of economic life'. For him, 'the development of co-operatives and self-employment is not a departure from socialist principles of economic management. In Soviet conditions, a co-operative is a socialist form of economic management'. He went on to justify their introduction by reference to Lenin:

As is well known, Lenin's last articles were dictated by him. He was extremely ill and sensed his imminent death; these articles are rightly

seen as his last will. It is symbolic that among the various questions to
which Lenin wished to draw society's attention, was the question of co-
operatives as an important form of socialist economic development.[34]

Thus, the introduction of one of the central economic planks of *perestroika*
was given legitimacy by claiming continuity with the Soviet Union's limited
experiment with a mixed economy – the so-called New Economic Policy
(NEP) – in the 1921–28 period. What had occurred in the interim, Stalinist
industrialisation and the neo-Stalinist policies pursued by successive Soviet
leaders, was regarded as a deviation from socialism's true path.

The co-operative experiment immediately ran into a number of problems
not envisaged by the reformers, particularly in obtaining supplies. State sector
enterprises, faced with their own production and distribution problems, neither could nor wanted to meet the supply needs of co-operatives. Thus, to
obtain supplies, many co-operatives were forced to turn elsewhere, to the black
market, which made them easy targets for arbitrary prosecution. As the short-
age-economy fuelled high prices in the co-operative sector, public resentment
also developed, particularly as the living standards of the average Soviet citizen were continuing to deteriorate. Many ordinary Soviet citizens appeared to
feel that co-operatives had spawned a *nouveau riche*, a development that was
not in their interests and had no place in a socialist society. There were even
sporadic demonstrations and arson attacks against co-operatives. A major reason for the riots in Turkmenistan's capital, Ashkhabad, in May 1989, were the
high prices charged by local co-operatives for their produce.

Communism's reformers also began to acknowledge that economic modernisation required greater openness (*glasnost'*) and democratisation.
Beginning as a stratagem to expose inefficient and corrupt practices
amongst intransigent elements within the central and local party-state
bureaucracies and in central economic management, *glasnost'* quickly
evolved into public debates, encouraged by the leadership, over the failings
of Soviet socialism and the appropriate way forward, contributing to an
increasingly open society. The long held tenet that socialism was superior to
capitalism and that Soviet-style socialism had resolved problems such as
social inequality, urban decay and corruption, supposedly endemic only to
capitalism, was debunked and those problems were publicly acknowledged.
Glasnost set out to involve society in reforming communism, but in the
process the carefully orchestrated calls for 'reform from above' were over-
taken by demands for reform from below, as *glasnost'* enabled a fledgling
civil society to engage in social and political change for the first time in
Soviet history. These new opportunities spawned a wide range of social
movements: citizens began to participate in various forms of collective
action mobilised around issues such as environmental degradation, better
wages for workers, women's rights and more autonomy for the nationality-
based Union republics. A new oppositional identity politics emerged, a
process further strengthened by political reform, particularly from 1989

onwards, following the elections to the first USSR Congress of People's Deputies in March.

Not surprisingly, the backbone of support for reform communism was the urban intelligentsia. *Perestroika* was not only 'a revolution of the educated classes' but also, as Walker put it, a reform programme with which this social stratum could most readily identify:

> the folk doing well out of Gorbachev's *perestroika* are the chattering classes, never very popular with the lads on the shop floor. All this *glasnost'* is exciting for the intellectuals, the media, the film-makers and novelists and playwrights and rock musicians

but, as he continues, all this contrasts sharply with 'the worried Soviet worker facing a three hour queue to buy a bottle of vodka, with a hole in his pay-packet, an empty larder, and the prospect of being re-deployed to another and possibly worse job'.[35]

Instead of achieving increased prosperity, the Soviet economy deteriorated throughout the late 1980s. Thus, a widening gap arose between the aspirations raised by the rhetoric of reform and the reality of food queues and empty shelves, thus creating a growing constituency of opposition to reform communism. This opposition took an increasingly political form of resistance, leading to strikes and demonstrations. Protests in two localities, the coalfields and the Union republics, were particularly important. In both, resistance identities were fuelled by two underlying grievances: first, a sense of alienation from reform communism, and second, resentment against exclusion, whether political, economic or social in form.

Localities of resistance I: the coalfields

Protests in the coalfields, culminating in a series of economically crippling strikes from 1989 to 1991, not only damaged the national economy and thus the prospects for economic recovery, but also carried immense symbolic importance. This was because the state was being openly challenged by the very stratum upon which its legitimacy rested, the urban industrial working class, the supposed support base of state socialism. Moreover, the miners had long enjoyed a special relationship with the Soviet state. Compared with most other workers, the 2.2 million coalfield workers enjoyed higher wages and other perks and privileges, reflecting the vital role played in the Soviet economy by the coal industry, which met over a fifth of the state's energy needs.[36]

Frustration at the failure of *perestroika* to fulfil the aspirations it had generated in the coalfields was an important factor leading coalfield workers to take strike action. Three very different coalfields were at the heart of the protest movement: the Kuzbass (western Siberia), Donbas (eastern Ukraine) and Vorkuta (Russian Arctic) coalfields (Fig. 2.3). Of these, the Donbas was

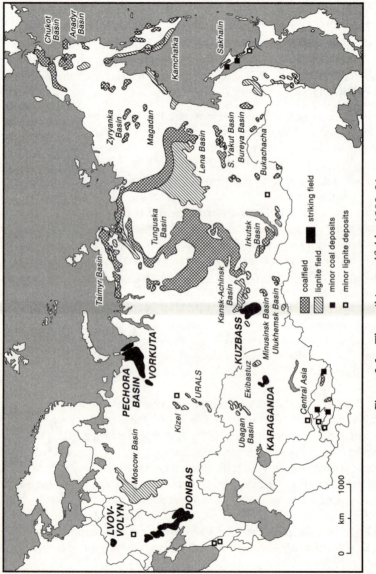

Figure 2.3   The striking coalfields, 1989–91.

by far the largest, employing some 300,000 miners in a region which produced a quarter of all Soviet coal. As a traditional mining area, many of its
mines were nearing exhaustion. Indeed, over the previous two decades, it
had been receiving less and less state investment. In contrast, the second-
largest coalfield, the Kuzbass, was a mining area established only in the
1930s. Its rich and relatively accessible deposits resulted in high production
levels, and its workers qualified for regional wage bonuses by virtue of the
coalfield's remote location. By far the smallest of the three, the Vorkuta
coalfield had originally been established as part of the Gulag labour-camp
system. In more recent times, in an attempt to attract workers to Vorkuta,
wages were purposely inflated, but this policy did not compensate for either
the extremely harsh working environment or the higher cost of living.
Consequently, labour turnover there was especially high.

The strikes began in July 1989 in the Kuzbass and quickly spread to other
coalfields. The miners' demands were initially fairly modest – for basic supplies, notably soap, and better food – but quickly expanded to include calls
for higher wages to cope with the higher prices and for better housing and
an improvement in the appalling working conditions. For the first time in
Soviet history, the strikers also began to make political demands, such as
greater workers' participation in management. Highly organised through
strike committees at both the pit and regional level, the coalminers quickly
marginalised the local trade unions, which had long been regarded as part
of the apparatus of the central party-state and as being largely unsympa-
thetic to workers' demands. Part of the effectiveness of the strike committees was their ability to draw upon a strong sense of local community-based
solidarity and identity. In an unprecedented move, Moscow showed that it
was willing to deal directly with the local strike committees, quickly settling
with each coalfield individually. In responding so speedily, the Gorbachev
administration was acknowledging the seriousness of the problem and the
potential harm that a prolonged strike could do both to economic recovery
and to the legitimacy of the reform programme. In short, 'the government's
priority ... was to contain the strike, to neutralise or co-opt its leadership,
and to demobilise the workers. In this it was remarkably successful'.[37]

It soon became apparent, however, that the state's promises were not
being kept. In the spring of 1991 there was another wave of strikes, beginning this time in the Donbas but spreading to the Kuzbass and Vorkuta.
This time the government took a harder line, declaring much of the strike
action illegal, but the strikes rolled on for about 2 months, and a wide range
of broad political as well as economic demands were made. Although local
workers' committees again took the lead, this time a co-ordinating Inter-
Regional Council of Strike Committees was established, which provided the
basis for a more nationally co-ordinated response to negotiations with the
state. While this made the strikes more effective, it quickly became evident
that varying attitudes towards reform communism had emerged within the
coalfields, reflecting differing local economic and political circumstances.

On the one hand, the Kuzbass miners adopted a more radical posture, calling for the implementation of further market reforms, Gorbachev's ouster and the establishment of a sovereign and independent Russia. In contrast, in the less productive and competitive Donbas coalfield, where mining was more dependent on state subsidies and where the miners were more suspicious of market reform and its possible implications for employment, a more defensive posture prevailed.[38]

By openly supporting the Kuzbass miners against the Gorbachev administration, Yeltsin, who had been elected chairman of the Russian Supreme Soviet in 1990, secured a crucial ally. In April and May of 1991, control over the coalfield, as over mines in the far northern Komi republic (which included Vorkuta) and the southern Rostov region, was transferred from all-Union jurisdiction to that of the Russian republic, and the strikes were called off almost immediately. The events in the coalfields were a good illustration of the inability of reform communism to satisfactorily respond to the demands of ordinary urban industrial workers, the increasing radicalisation and politicisation of the work force and, in the case of Russia, the workers' growing identification with the republican leadership against the centre.

Localities of resistance II: the borderland Union republics

The other and ultimately more destructive focus of resistance to reform communism was the nationality based Union republics. Based on a 'historic compromise' between the Russian-dominated Communist Party and its urban-based non-Russian allies in the borderlands, the Soviet Federation had provided the Union republics with a degree of cultural and administrative autonomy, and in return they gave up their homeland sovereignty and became constituent units of a highly centralised federation.[39] Until the late 1980s, the Soviet Federation served in effect as a means of managing a multiethnic empire, but it was not a form of rule analogous to 'internal colonialism' or, as officially claimed, 'a federation of equal sovereign states'. Rather, relations between Moscow and the borderland Union republics resembled what I have called elsewhere a form of federal colonialism, containing three main features.[40]

1. The people of the Union republics were denied the right to national self-determination, but from the 1960s onwards their political leaders were granted some leeway in running their own republics' affairs. During most of the Brezhnev years, in particular, relations between Moscow and Union-republican leaders were amicable. In part, this was because Moscow demanded from the republican leaderships only a moderate overall commitment to economic growth targets, though it required absolute political loyalty. Moreover, Moscow's policy of placing greater

trust in local and native party functionaries made life in the Union republics less volatile and more comfortable for the local political elites. They, in return, could be relied upon to ensure the preservation of local stability whenever events threatened to undermine the status quo. In short, Union-republican leaders closely identified themselves with the centre and its conservative leadership and were rewarded accordingly.

2. The federal system included affirmative action policies (or *korenizatsiya*) designed to ensure that the Union-republican nationalities were fairly represented within the top echelons of local political and public life. These included granting members of the indigenous population preferential access to higher education and membership of the local Communist Party, which in turn ensured that the titular nation was well represented within the Union-republican party-state leadership. *Korenizatsiya* also facilitated native upward social mobility more generally and the subsequent growth or consolidation of a native urban intelligentsia. Affirmative action policies were complemented by the central leadership's policy of creating employment opportunities for the republics' native populations even if there was an overabundance or overconcentration of particular skills or types of specialist labour.

3. As a result of their federal status, the Union republics' titular nationalities were provided with a range of local institutional and cultural supports, including, most notably, a native language-based education system, which helped to ensure the reproduction of national cultures and languages, as well as the continuation of an identifiable association with a particular administrative homeland. Such institutional supports also furnished the republics' nationalities with a basis to resist centralising pressure to assimilate linguistically and culturally with the Union's dominant nationality, the Russians. As Table 2.1 shows, while a knowledge of the Russian language was widespread among all the Union-republican people, particularly the more urban-industrialised strata, native languages showed no signs of disappearing and continued to remain pivotal to political and social life within the republics. This was despite the fact that knowledge of the Russian language was a prerequisite for upward mobility. Federal supports also enabled the native language to remain a vital badge of national difference and identity.

Already statelets in embryonic form, the Union republics possessed many of the institutional and symbolic supports of governance, including their own national symbols, native language educational systems, their own Party organisations, and even the (theoretical) right to secede as embodied in the federal constitution. Moreover, by the mid-1980s, the relationship with the centre was becoming increasingly tense. Opportunities for upward social mobility for non-Russians continued to be confined largely to the horizons of the Union republic; the Moscow-dominated, overly centralised production system inhibited local economic and professional initiative; centrally

Table 2.1 Population and language knowledge in the Union republics, 1989

	Total population	Nationality breakdown (%)			Native language (%)		Fluency in second language of the Soviet Union	
		Titular nationality	Russians	Other	Titular nationality not claiming titular language as native language	Titular nationality claiming Russian as native language	Titular nationality claiming Russian	Russians claiming titular language
RSFSR	147,021,869	81.53	–	18.47	0.05	–	–	–
Ukraine	51,452,034	72.73	22.07	5.2	12.28	12.24	59.49	32.77
Belarus	10,151,806	77.86	13.22	8.92	19.78	19.73	60.42	24.49
Moldavia (Moldova)	4,335,360	64.46	12.96	22.58	4.58	4.31	53.27	11.22
Estonia	1,565,662	61.53	30.33	8.14	1.06	1.05	33.57	13.69
Latvia	2,666,567	52.04	33.96	14	2.63	2.57	65.72	21.12
Lithuania	3,674,802	79.58	9.37	11.05	0.41	0.26	37.36	33.45
Armenia	3,304,776	93.31	1.56	5.13	0.35	0.31	44.27	32.2
Azerbaijan	7,021,178	82.68	5.59	11.73	0.87	0.42	31.69	14.3
Georgia	5,400,841	70.13	6.32	23.55	0.27	0.23	31.78	22.54
Kazakhstan	16,464,464	39.69	37.82	22.49	1.43	1.36	62.84	0.86
Uzbekistan	19,810,077	71.39	8.35	20.26	1.32	0.45	22.23	4.53
Kyrgyzia (Kyrgyzstan)	4,257,755	52.37	21.53	26.1	0.46	0.33	36.93	1.21
Tajikistan	5,092,603	62.3	7.63	30.07	0.75	0.51	30.03	3.5
Turkmenistan	3,522,717	72.01	9.48	18.51	0.76	0.71	27.55	2.51

Source: 1989 Soviet census.

imposed migration policy continued to bring Russian migrants into the borderland republics, increasing competition for local employment and housing; the culturally standardising centre remained insensitive to local linguistic and cultural interests; and centrally managed economic ministerial interests continued to ride roughshod over local environmental concerns. In particular, there were clear signs that the unwillingness of the centre to engage in economic reform meant that the standards of living enjoyed throughout the borderland Union republics in the 1960s and 1970s were no longer being sustained.[41]

With the accession of the Gorbachev leadership, relations between Moscow and the borderland Union republics began to change. By disabling many central control mechanisms through the introduction of the twin policies of *glasnost'* and democratisation, the centre was in effect inviting the Union republics and regions to contribute to *perestroika*, a policy that was to have far-reaching unintended consequences. At the same time, however, the Gorbachev leadership continued in the crucial first 3 years of its existence to treat the 'nationalities question' as tangential to the reform programme. Instead, Gorbachev chose to reiterate Brezhnev's faith in the idea that a new historic community of the Soviet people (*Sovetskii narod*) now existed, transcending identities based on ethnic or Union republic differences.[42] This insensitivity to the fact that the Soviet Union was a multiethnic society and that the borderland Union republican nationalities in particular had to varying degrees amassed grievances against the centre, began to have serious disruptive consequences for the centrally initiated reform agenda. In December 1986, as part of a campaign to stamp out local corruption, the first secretary of Kazakhstan's Communist Party organisation, a Kazakh, was replaced by a Russian from outside the republic, in a departure from what had become accepted practice throughout the Union republics of appointing natives to the top party post. Riots followed, the first of the Gorbachev era. In 1987 and 1988, a series of ethnic demonstrations erupted elsewhere as the Union republics tested the limits of Moscow's reform programme. In an attempt to contain such developments, Moscow dealt with each crisis as it arose on a case-by-case basis rather than incorporating the nationalities question into the reform agenda. One example was the handling of the Nagorno-Karabakh issue. In response to the demands of the Armenians of Nagorno-Karabakh in 1988 to transfer their enclave from Azerbaijan to their native republic of Armenia, Moscow took the view that the problem could be resolved by an economic development package for the region. When this failed to halt the escalation of local ethnic conflict, the enclave was transferred to direct control from Moscow in January 1989, only to be handed back to Azerbaijan 10 months later, further fuelling conflict over the disputed territory. The idea that federal boundaries might be renegotiated was not on the centre's agenda.

Glasnost' inadvertently created space for ethnoregional movements to emerge in the Union republics. Many locally organised social movements, which the centre initially encouraged to facilitate the reform process, quickly took on a nationalist hue, beginning to call for greater autonomy and eventually independent statehood. The evolution of these ethnoregional movements (or popular fronts) tended to follow a three-stage pattern. First, with the advent of *glasnost*, national consciousness was able to express itself openly within the public political arena. This enabled the Union republics' nationalities to rediscover and debate their history, to bring out into the open long-held national beliefs and prejudices rooted in the collective imagination and to re-examine publicly past and current ethnic inequalities. At this stage, grassroots activities took a variety of forms, espousing issue-specific cultural, linguistic, environmental and other concerns. The second stage, beginning in the Baltic republics in mid-1988 but quickly spreading to Transcaucasia and Moldavia (Moldova), and eventually to the other republics as well, saw the mobilisation of issue-oriented groups behind republican-based popular front movements. Led mainly by urban intellectuals, these movements began to reflect a particular type of identity politics geared towards securing greater self-determination for the Union republics. Finally, a third stage followed in some Union republics in which the local Communist Party became increasingly weak and marginalised, and the popular fronts emerged as the focus of political power in the 1989 and 1990 elections. In some republics, this process entailed the fragmentation of the Communist Party, with its more radical wing throwing in its lot with the popular fronts. But even where the Communist Party held on to power, the popular fronts were able to exert considerable pressure upon conservative political leaders, who realised that in order to continue in office they had to accommodate some of the aspirations engendered by nationalism. Setting the pace were the Baltic republics, with Lithuania becoming the first nationalist elected government to declare its republic's political independence from Moscow in March 1990. By the end of that year, all the Union republics, including Russia, had publicly demanded some form of national sovereignty, although only Lithuania had gone so far as to declare outright independent statehood (Table 2.2).

Despite recognising the need to rethink the nationalities question, Moscow remained consistent in its opposition to any proposals emanating from the Union republics that could challenge the state's territorial integrity. Rather, for the reform communists, rethinking the nationalities question followed a similar logic to many other aspects of Gorbachev-initiated reform. The political system established under Stalin and his successors provided the framework for a critique of past failings, and a return to Leninist principles as the basis for renewal. Thus, it was not the original conception of the Leninist federation as embodied in the constitution ratified in 1924 that was deemed to be faulty, but rather the political and economic system that followed. Accordingly, as Lenin's notion of national self-determination and social justice for the Union republic nationalities had never been effectively implemented, it was argued, responsibility for the nationalities

Table 2.2 Sovereignty declarations and ethnoregional movements in the Union republics, 1989–91

Union republic	Sovereignty declaration	Ethnoregional movement (date of foundation)
Russian Republic	June 1990	The Democratic Russian Movement (1991)
Estonia	March 1990 (declared a transitional period to independence)	Estonian Popular Front (April 1988)
Latvia	May 1990 (declared a transitional period to independence)	Latvian Popular Front (July 1988)
Lithuania	March 1990 (declaration of independent statehood)	*Sajudis* (June 1988)
Ukraine	July 1990	Popular Front of Ukraine for Perestroika (*Rukh*) (November 1988)
Belorussia (Belarus)	July 1990	Renewal (*Adradzhen'ne*) (June 1989)
Moldavia (Moldova)	June 1990	Moldovan Popular Front (*Al Moldovei*) (January 1989)
Armenia	August 1990	Karabakh Committee (February 1988); also the Armenian Pan-National Movement (Spring 1990)
Azerbaijan	September 1989	Azeri Popular Front (July 1988)
Georgia	November 1990	Committee for National Salvation (October 1989), but in May 1990 split into two organisations, 'The Round Table' and 'The Co-ordinating Committee'
Kazakhstan	October 1990	Coalition of groups, the most prominent of which was the Nevada Semipalatinsk Movement (February 1989)
Uzbekistan	June 1990	Unity (*Birlik*) (November 1988), but fell apart by 1990
Turkmenistan	August 1990	Unity (*Agzybirlik*) (January 1990)
Kyrgyzia (Kyrgyzstan)	October 1990	Openness (*Ashar*) (July 1989)
Tajikistan	July 1990	Openness (*Ashkara*) (June 1989); also Rebirth (*Rastokhez*)

Source: G. Smith, 'The State, Nationalism and the Nationalities Question in the Soviet Republics', in C. Merridale and C. Ward (eds), *Perestroika. The Historical Perspective* (London, Edward Arnold, 1991), p. 211.

problem lay in the way in which the successor regimes had deviated from the path of preserving the right of nations to self-determination. As Gorbachev noted in July 1989, the factors underlying current ethnic tensions emanated from a variety of distortions and past acts of lawlessness, the result of which was a nationalities policy that displayed

> indifference towards ethnic interests, the failure to resolve many of the socio-economic problems of the republics and autonomous territories, deformations in the development of the languages and cultures of the country's people, the deterioration in the demographic situation, and many other negative consequences.[43]

In response in particular to events in Lithuania, there was now an urgent need, as Gorbachev saw it in a March 1990 speech, 'to draft a new federal treaty that is in keeping with present day realities and with the demands of the development of our federation and of each of its peoples'.[44]

The new Federal Treaty, which although in its earlier drafts was dictated by the centre and imposed strict limits on the permissible, in its final formulation involved the participation of those Union republics willing to enter into a *voluntary* federal arrangement and offered considerable scope for Union republic autonomy.[45] It envisaged a federation in which the Union republics would be able to choose freely what powers to delegate to the centre and what republican laws would have priority over federal laws, and vice versa. Membership could only be entered into voluntarily: this in effect recognised what had been constitutionally enshrined in Lenin's original, centrally imposed federal treaty but had never amounted to more than a theoretical notion. Thus, in striking a new compromise between the centre and nine pro-Union republics (all except the Baltic states, Georgia, Moldavia and Armenia), Gorbachev had in effect rejected imposing a federal arrangement by force. The final draft of the new Union Treaty, published in Moscow in mid-August and scheduled to be signed on 20 August 1991, not only signalled Gorbachev's recognition of the republics' sovereignty but also the right of those, such as the Baltic republics and Georgia, to opt out of the Soviet Union. The attempted coup launched by hard-liners in Moscow on 19 August sought to pre-empt the signing of the treaty and prepare the way for the reinstatement of a centralised system. Its collapse, however, dealt a fatal blow to the idea of the decentralised federation envisaged by the treaty and signed the Soviet Union's final death warrant. Nationalism had triumphed over reform communism.

Ultimately the Soviet federation, albeit even in the form of its more decentralised variant, could no longer be justified for a number of reasons. First, the official ideology that underpinned Gorbachev's conception of federation was bankrupt. As Gellner puts it, 'The . . . secular ideology was strong enough to suppress . . . nationalism, as long as it retained faith in itself and the determination to use all means to retain control'.[46] Having renounced repression, in part to retain Western goodwill, Gorbachev generally resisted using coercion to keep the federation together. This helped to make the end of the Soviet Union a far less violent affair than the disintegration of Yugoslavia in 1990–91. Second, a federation often serves as a means of uniting people against a common enemy, a strategy Lenin pursued skilfully in the early 1920s. With the end of the Cold War, however, any justification for a federation on the grounds of common geopolitical security had disappeared, while new geographical fault lines were opening up, exploding the myth of a federal society based on a united Soviet people. Finally, the idea that a federation was crucial to the economic well-being of citizens also floundered. Gorbachev had made great play out of the Union republics' being united by an interdependent 'common economic space', in which fragmentation would spell economic disaster even for the richer republics. But this argument had only limited appeal in the republics, not least because of the failure of the federation's reformers to revitalise the national economy and to reverse falling living standards. Also, in the world of the 1990s, economic sovereignty was no longer conceived by most of the republics as a precondition for nation-statehood. Indeed, the more secessionist-minded emphasised the idea that their future well-being lay in going simultaneously national and global, through attaining political sovereignty while securing material prosperity by joining new international markets and supra-regional trading blocs. For the least developed and less separatist-minded Central Asian republics, however, with their higher degree of economy dependency on the Union, the argument against secession had greater appeal. Indeed, this is also one reason why some of the Central Asian republics have been keen to preserve greater economic links with Russia and some of the other post-Soviet states since 1991.

Notes to Chapter 2

1 See, in particular, J. Arnason, *The Future that Failed. Origins and Destinies of the Soviet Model* (London, Routledge, 1993).
2 C. Friedrich *et al.*, *Totalitarianism in Perspective. Three Views* (New York, Praeger, 1969), p. 126.
3 C. Friedrich and Z. Brzezinski, *Totalitarian Dictatorship and Autonomy* (New York, Praeger, 1961).
4 Arnason, *The Future that Failed*, p. 97.
5 See, in particular, R. Davies, M. Harrison and S. Wheatcroft (eds), *The Economic Transformation of the Soviet Union, 1913–1945* (Cambridge, Cambridge University Press, 1994); J. Millar and A. Nove, 'A debate on Soviet collectivisation. Was Stalin really necessary?', *Problems of Communism*, July/August, 1967, pp. 49–62; G. Smith, *Planned Development in the Socialist World* (Cambridge, Cambridge University Press, 1989).
6 Tsentral'noe statisticheskoe upravlenie pri Sovete Ministrov SSSR, *Narodnoe khozyaistvo SSSR v 1958g* (Moscow, 1959), p. 346.
7 Arnason, *The Future that Failed*, p. 114.
8 Z. Brzezinski, *The Permanent Purge. Politics in Soviet Totalitarianism* (Cambridge, MA, Harvard University Press, 1956), p. 1.

9 V. Zaslavsky, *The Neo-Stalinist State. Class, Ethnicity and Consensus in Soviet Society*, 2nd edition (London, M.E. Sharpe, 1992), p. 139.
10 O. Lange (ed.), *Problems of the Political Economy of Socialism* (New Delhi, 1962).
11 Z (pseudonym for M. Malia), 'To the Stalin Mausoleum', in W. Brinton and A. Rinzler (eds), *Without Force or Lies. Voices from the Revolution of Central Europe in 1989–90* (San Francisco, Mercury House Books, 1991), p. 399.
12 G. Smith, 'Privilege and Place in Soviet Society', in D. Gregory and R. Walford (eds), *New Horizons in Human Geography* (London, The Macmillan Press, 1989), pp. 320–40.
13 L. Koltakowski, *Main Currents of Marxism*, vol. 3 (Oxford, Clarendon Press, 1978), p. 523.
14 Z, 'To the Stalin Mausoleum', p. 399.
15 Zaslavsky, *The Neo-Stalinist State*.
16 L.J. Cook, *The Soviet Social Contract and Why it Failed. Welfare Policy and Workers' Politics from Brezhnev to Yeltsin* (Cambridge, MA, Harvard University Press, 1993).
17 Zaslavsky, *The Neo-Stalinist State*, p. viii.
18 Zaslavsky, *The Neo-Stalinist State*, p. 76.
19 L. Holmes, *The End of Communist Power. Anti-Corruption Campaigns and Legitimation Crisis* (Oxford, Polity Press, 1993).
20 M. Lewin, *The Gorbachev Phenomenon. A Historical Interpretation* (Berkeley, University of California Press, 1991).
21 S. Fitzpatrick, *Education and Social Mobility in the Soviet Union, 1921–34* (Cambridge, Cambridge University Press, 1979).
22 From Soviet sources compiled by D. Lane, *Soviet Society under Perestroika* (London, Unwin Hyman, 1990).
23 I. Wallerstein, *The Politics of the World Economy. The States, the Movements and the Civilisations* (Cambridge, Cambridge University Press, 1984).
24 Davies, Harrison and Wheatcroft (eds), *The Economic Transformation of the Soviet Union*.
25 Wallerstein, *The Politics of the World Economy*, p. 89.
26 M. Dibb, *The Soviet Union. The Incomplete Superpower*, 2nd edition (London, Macmillan, 1988), p. 280.
27 A. Syzmanski, 'The Socialist World System', in C. Chase-Dunn (ed.), *Socialist States in the World System* (London, Sage, 1982), pp. 57–84.
28 These data refer to OECD countries. The exact percentages of imports to and exports from OECD countries was 18.2 and 17.6 per cent, respectively. This compares with 8.5 and 8.8 per cent in the early 1970s. Data from *Vneshnyaya torgovlya SSSR* (Moscow, 1982).
29 N. Shmelev and V. Popov, *The Turning Point. Revitalising the Soviet Economy* (London, I.B. Tauris, 1990).
30 I. Deutscher, *The Great Contest. Russia and the West* (Oxford, Oxford University Press, 1960).
31 P. Kennedy, *The Rise and Fall of the Great Powers* (London, Fontana, 1989).
32 V. Bunce, 'The empire strikes back. The evolution of the eastern bloc from a Soviet asset to a Soviet liability', *International Organisation*, 39(1), 1985, pp. 1–46.
33 K. Plokker, 'The development of individual and cooperative labour activity in the Soviet Union', *Soviet Studies*, 42(7), 1990, pp. 403–28.
34 A. Aganbegyan, *The Challenge. Economics of Perestroika* (London, Hutchinson, 1988), p. 30.
35 M. Walker, *The Waking Giant* (London, Abakas, 1987).
36 This section draws on the following accounts: B. Kagarlitsky, *Farewell*

Perestroika (London, Verso, 1990); P. Rutland, 'Labour unrest and movement in 1989 and 1990', *Soviet Economy,* 6(4), 1990, pp. 345–84; S. Clarke *et al., What about the Workers? Workers and the Transition to Capitalism in Russia* (London, Verso, 1993).

37 Clarke *et al., What about the Workers?,* p. 132.
38 Rutland, 'Labour Unrest and Movement in 1989 and 1990', 354–84.
39 For a fuller discussion, see G. Smith (ed.), *The Nationalities Question in the Post-Soviet States,* 2nd edition (London, Longman, 1996).
40 G. Smith, 'The Soviet Federation. From Corporatist to Crisis Politics', in M. Chisholm and D. Smith (eds), *Shared Space: Divided Space* (London, Unwin Hyman, 1990), pp. 84–105.
41 G. Smith, 'The Soviet Federation. From Corporatist to Crisis Politics'.
42 M. Gorbachev, *Politicheskii doklad tsentral'nogo komiteta KPSS XXVII S″ezdu Kommunisticheskoi Partii Sovetskogo Soyuza* (Moscow, 1986).
43 *Pravda,* 6 July 1989.
44 *Izvestiya,* 16 March 1990.
45 *Izvestiya,* 24 April 1991.
46 E. Gellner, 'Nationalism and politics in Eastern Europe', *New Left Review,* 189, 1991, p. 132.

PART

I

Postcolonialism and the
politics of national identities

|3|

Russia: identity, geopolitics and homeland

Russia differs from the other post-Soviet states in the nature and scale of the task that it faces in coming to terms with its redefined status as a sovereign homeland. As experiences of the end of other twentieth-century empires have shown, adjusting to post-colonial status is especially difficult for the people of the former metropolitan homeland. For Russia and the Russians, this is particularly true for a number of reasons.

For Russians, the territory that constituted the Soviet Union – unlike the classical empires of Britain, Portugal or even France – had long been considered an integral and largely undifferentiated part of Russia. As far back as medieval Muscovy, Russia had been colonising contiguous territories which, following their incorporation, were regarded by empire-builders as an integral part of the homeland. The fact that expansion resulted in the creation of an overland empire – unlike the maritime empires of Britain or Portugal – also favoured the blurring of boundaries between metropole and colonies. Moreover, in contrast with the experiences of most other empires, where the formation of the national identity of the metropole preceded empire-building, the formation of the modern Russian nation coincided with colonial expansion. In short, as Beissinger notes, Russia as an overland empire 'had a difficult time defining who was a citizen and who was a subject, faced extraordinary difficulties in any effort to segregate the two and could not delineate what were the physical boundaries of Russia and what were occupied territories'.[1] The image that most Russians had of their homeland (*rodina*) was based on the conception of Russia as a multiethnic (*rossiiskii*) rather than a specifically Russian (*russkii*) empire. As such, the Russians' view of their homeland was more inclusive and their relationship with their colonies more ambiguous than the association between the British or Portuguese and their overseas empires.

This relationship between the Russian national identity and the homeland-empire was further reinforced during the Soviet period by the peculiar position that the Russian Soviet Federative Socialist Republic (RSFSR) – the official administrative homeland of the Russians – occupied within the USSR. More than any other Soviet nationality, the Russians were encouraged to identify the Soviet Union as their homeland (*Sovetskaya rodina*). The Soviet state placed considerable emphasis on promoting a symbolic and institutional association in the Russian mind-set between Russian nation-building and the Soviet Union. In contrast with the borderland Union republics, the Russian republic did not provide the titular nation with its own Communist Party, KGB or Academy of Sciences. Instead, Russians were encouraged to look upon all-Union institutions as the social basis and identific framework of support for their nation. One consequence of this was that, irrespective of where Russians lived in the Soviet Union, the state provided them with schools and mass media in their own language. Moreover, because Russian was the state lingua franca, Russians faced few obstacles to social mobility, regardless of their place of residence. The presence of such institutional supports at the all-Union level helped furnish Russians with a sense of identity that was inseparable from that of the Soviet homeland. Russian identification with *Sovetskaya rodina* was further strengthened by the mass migration of Russians into the borderland republics, a process of settlement that Moscow actively encouraged in the name of promoting proletarian internationalism. As a consequence, on the eve of the collapse of the Soviet Union, one in seven Russians – some 25 million – resided in the borderland republics.

In contrast with the experience of the British and the Portuguese when their empires disintegrated, the Russians also had to adjust to the creation, for the first time in their history, of their own sovereign homeland. Moreover, this was a Russia that its peoples had neither expected nor fought for. The unplanned end to the Soviet empire meant that virtually overnight Russians had to adjust from being members of a global superpower to being citizens of a polity forced by circumstance to occupy a more peripheral position within the world arena. As Gellner has noted, while Russian faith in the idea of *Sovetskaya rodina* as a socialist project and what had been achieved in its name was largely bankrupt by the late 1980s, nonetheless the Soviet Union had provided its largest nationality with a sense of pride in its status as a global superpower.[2] Loss of that status stripped Russians of their national dignity. For Russians, adjusting to their new homeland status has therefore been disorientating and painful. They have had to come to terms not only with the fall of the once powerful Russian-dominated USSR, but also with post-colonial dependency on their former Cold War adversary for economic aid and investment, and the reality of a US-dominated unipolar world in which Russia has little choice but to play a more marginal role.

Yet not all Russians have felt ill at ease with the loss of the homeland-empire. As Lieven and McGarry note,

> whereas the English nationalist identifies wholeheartedly with the Union Jack and glorified in the British empire, the Russian was always

more equivocal in his [*sic*] support for the Tsarist and Soviet empire. In part this is for the simple reason that life under the imperial state, Tsarist and Soviet, has been thoroughly unpleasant for most Russians, who, unlike the English, had never either chosen or controlled the state's rulers. Moreover, unlike the English, the majority of Russians had good reason to believe that they were, in economic terms, losers rather than gainers from empire.[3]

In the last few months of Soviet rule, many Russians rejoiced in the prospect that Russia would no longer subsidise the poorer borderland republics and that Russian soldiers would not have to sacrifice themselves in local ethnic and tribal wars in Afghanistan or Azerbaijan. For many Russians, the collapse of the Soviet Union signalled a welcome end not only to communism and totalitarianism but also to the burdens of empire, and offered the hope that Russians would be able to channel their resources into building a more prosperous homeland-nation.

Finally, the end of empire carries far greater implications for Russia's own territorial integrity than it did for Britain or France following the collapse of their imperial systems. As a multiethnic homeland, in which one in five inhabitants are not Russian, post-Soviet Russia has had to face up to the prospect of its own internal fragmentation – a scenario that many in some of Russia's own ethnorepublics (most notably Chechnya, Tatarstan and Bashkortostan) view as the next logical stage of imperial disintegration. While the majority of Russians have adjusted to the loss of the former Soviet borderlands, the idea of losing part of Russia is regarded by most as wholly unacceptable. However, the costs of preventing Russia's own Balkanisation have already proven high, particularly with regard to the small but geostrategically important republic of Chechnya. When in December 1994 Moscow launched an all-out military offensive to bring the breakaway republic back into the federal fold, it was confident of achieving a rapid victory. Instead, federal forces became bogged down in a bloody 21-month conflict that not only severely dented Russian national pride but also failed to guarantee Russia's future control over what most Russians viewed as an integral part of their homeland. The fear in the minds of many Moscow politicians is that the still unresolved question of Chechnya's status leaves the door open to further secessionist demands, especially in the other geopolitically volatile North Caucasian republics of Ingushetia, North Ossetia and Dagestan.

Consequently, Russia is faced with an identity crisis: it must define what it means to be Russian without empire, where the boundaries of Russia should lie, and what role the country should play within the post-Cold-War world order. Above all, this search for place and meaning for Russians represents a crisis of homeland, of finding and negotiating a new role, borders and identity for a country and its people in the post-colonial world. After all, as Billig reminds us, 'a nation is more than an imagined community of people, for a place – a homeland – also has to be imagined'.[4] The way in which such a homeland identity is being reformulated by Russia's political and cultural elites may be considered in terms of endogenous power struggles, as different political factions and groups struggle to translate their understanding of what Russia should be into political reality. This chapter examines this search by the country's political and cultural elites for a new role, borders and identity for Russia and the Russians.

Eurasian dilemmas: Russia's place in Eurasia

Although Russians have never been so preoccupied with their place in the world as they are at present, such considerations are far from new. From the nineteenth century onwards, the Eurasian question – of exactly what Russia's place is and should be within Eurasian civilisations – has exercised Russian political and intellectual elites. Three schools of thought can be identified: those who regard Russia as part of Europe and the West, those who see Russia as distinctively different from both Europe and Asia, and those who envisage Russia as a bridge between the two.

The first – placing Russia within Europe – has its roots in the vision of Russia of Peter the Great (1672–1725) and the desire of the Petrine State to transform Russia in the image of the West. It embraces what Kristof has coined 'the St. Petersburg image of Russia',[5] as exemplified by the construction in 1703 of a quintessentially European, outward-looking capital city. As Russia's 'window to the West', built in the style of French and Italian grand planning, St. Petersburg evoked an image of Russia emerging from socioeconomic and cultural isolation and backwardness by connecting up with the grand eighteenth-century European projects of the Enlightenment and, later, with capitalist industrialisation, of Russia viewing its destiny not outside Europe but as an integral and equal member of it. Reinvented in the nineteenth century as the project of Russia's 'Westernisers' (*zapadniki*), the idea of Russia following a European route to modernity remained influential in the development of the empire in the late nineteenth century. While united in their aversion to the empire's centralised-autocratic style of rule, differences did exist amongst Westernisers, especially between liberals and socialists. For liberals, Russia was merely 'Europe's backward stepchild',[6] which, if it imitated Europe's political and social institutions, could be transformed from a predominantly peasant society into a modern European nation. Europe was also an important reference point for Russian Marxists. As the proclaimed heirs of the European Enlightenment, they were preoccupied with what Russia could learn from the European experience, notably how to secure modernity without the dire social consequences of capitalist-led urban industrialisation. However, with the 1917 Bolshevik Revolution and the subsequent formation of the Soviet state, they seized the initiative by proclaiming that Russia had secured the high ground of European modernity. Rather than following Europe, successive leaders from Lenin to Brezhnev proclaimed the moral superiority of the Russian experiment over the capitalist West, holding up the socialist Soviet Union, based on social equality and political justice, as the future vision for Europe.

In post-Soviet Russia, the 'Russia as Europe' school is espoused by those who see their homeland as once again 'returning to civilisation'. In the absence of any other specific identity, Russia is again to become 'an apprentice of Europe'.[7] Thus, the solution to Russia's current socio-economic problems rests in adopting Western models of capitalist development, in emulating the political institutions and power structures of Western-liberal democracies and in Russia reclaiming its place as an equal and willing partner of the West. Indeed, one of the leading pro-Western political parties in the new Russia, Russia's Choice (later renamed Russia's Democratic Choice) took as its symbol 'the bronze horseman' of Peter the Great, which still stands on the bank of the Neva in the city that he founded. The Western neo-classical economists, Hayek and Friedman, replace Marx and Lenin as the icons of the new order. Cosmopolitanism and Western integration are favoured over Russian national particularism. As it was put by Andrei Kozyrev, the Yeltsin administration's first minister of foreign affairs, this 'return to civilisation is about a pragmatic politics, of helping meet the internal needs of Russia'.[8] For Westernisers, returning to the common European home is therefore about securing the economic and social prosperity that eluded Russia throughout the twentieth century.

In contrast with the Westernisers, proponents of the second school of thought are highly suspicious of the West. They take their inspiration from those who see Russia as a world apart from Europe, as culturally and geopolitically distinct. Russia, it is claimed, is destined to follow its own particular and unique path of development. Viewing Russia's future as lying within Eurasia, advocates of the second school are heavily influenced by nineteenth-century Slavophilism, a movement which, as Bassin notes, was 'stirred by a growing uneasiness over the Russians' unquestioning assumption regarding their country's European identity and its unity of purpose with the west'.[9] For the Slavophiles, the Russians had created their own unique culture that was destined to provide the building block for the country's spiritual salvation. It was and is above all a pre-Petrine image of Russia, which identifies the country's spiritual and geopolitical heartland with medieval Muscovy and its successful battle to survive intrusion from both 'the advanced West' and 'the barbaric East'. It is an image of Russianness symbolised by the Russian patriot, and it borrows heavily from nineteenth-century folk nationalism, which locates the spiritual purity of Russia in a pre-industrial countryside uncontaminated by external cultural influences. It is within the peasant commune, the *mir*, where the Russian sense of community is deemed to be at its spiritual purest, representing a superior form of social and cultural organisation to Western individualism and identity. It also envisages the Russian Orthodox Church as the cornerstone of Russian values and way of life, and cannot imagine Russia without a 'Eurasian empire'. For the nineteenth-century Slavophiles, it was Russia's educated urban classes, seduced and corrupted by Western cultural and material values, who had betrayed the social and spiritual backbone of Russia, the rural peasantry.

As Greenfeld notes, this process of looking inward towards Russian cultural values was inextricably bound up with a view of the West as the anti-model: 'It was *ressentiment* [of Europe], not social concerns, that fueled Russian national consciousness, and it was *ressentiment*, not sympathy for the peasantry, that made the peasant a symbol of the Russian nation'.[10] It was only by pursuing its own distinctive course that Russia would avoid being infected by the runaway urbanisation and industrial decay of the capitalist West. It should reject the West, its neo-liberal economic model and form of democracy, and embark instead upon a programme of cultural and economic renewal distinctively and uniquely Russian.

In the 1920s, this particular conception of Eurasianism was reconstituted by an influential circle of Russian *émigrés* living in the West. Opposed to the establishment of Bolshevism in Russia and calling themselves Eurasianists (*yevraziisty*), they argued that Europe and civilisation were not synonymous and that the specific Romano-German culture which had dominated Europe and represented 'a formula of chauvinistic cosmopolitanism', as exemplified in Marxism, was the worst possible outcome of Western culture for Russia. The task of Russians at that particular moment should have been, as one of Eurasianism's leading theorists, Trubeskoi, put it, to convince their own Europeanised intelligentsias that Russia should seek allies in Asia against Europe. The geographer Peter Savitsky took this Eurasian conception of Russia further by arguing that it was Russia's ribbon-like natural environmental zones of steppe and taiga crosscutting the Urals – which he suggested were wrongly labelled as the geographical divide between Europe and Asia – that provided Russia with a sense of natural coherence and social unity, and distinguished both Siberia and western Russia from the rest of Europe.[11]

By rejecting both European and Asian experiments with state-building, those who today see Russia in such exceptionalist terms argue that a prosperous future can only be secured by promoting 'a third way'. As Borodaj, a spokesperson for neo-Slavophile ideology, proclaims,

> we have to seek our direction between the East and West as it corresponds to our spiritual and geopolitical position in the world. Not western individualism with imposed sociality . . . Nor on the other hand, the Asiatic cults with monolithic sociality, where the individual is nothing . . . We have to create the Orthodox confession and the corresponding communitarian life and economy. This is our third path.[12]

One recent manifestation of this sentiment was the welcome many Russians gave to a law passed in September 1997 making life more difficult for religions not traditionally found in Russia. Moreover, by tightening registration requirements for so-called 'imported religions', such as Scientology and Mormonism, the opportunity has been created for the Russian Orthodox Church to play an even greater role in public affairs. In its more extreme form, Eurasianism also gives the Russians and their Slavic cousins the task of reasserting a place for Russia within post-Soviet Eurasian space by playing a leading cultural as well as geopolitical role.

The third school of thought imagines Russia functioning as a cultural and geopolitical bridge between the continents of Europe and Asia.[13] Like Slavophilism, this school was a product of the nineteenth century, of 'a redirected Russian nationalism that had been rebuffed by Europe, and a growing consciousness of Russia's presence and opportunity in Asia'.[14] It was a vision of Russia forged by the country's colonisation of Asia, by its southern and eastward expansion during the nineteenth century into the Caucasus and Central Asia and its consolidation of its hold over Siberia. While many nineteenth-century Russian imperialists embraced a vision of Russia's frontiers extending to Constantinople and even India, Russia's relationship with Asia was an ambivalent one. Hauner notes 'the almost unlimited capacity among Russians to identify themselves with Asia while showing their contempt for the Asian peoples and civilisations as utterly barbaric'.[15] Above all, Asia was a geopolitical project for imperial Russia rather than the basis of an imagined community grounded in Russians identifying themselves as both European and Asian.

Within the Soviet Union this idea of Eurasianism was refashioned to accommodate a different project, that of socialism. The socialist homeland was represented not only as embracing Europe and Asia but also as reflecting a regime committed to ensuring the economic and social prosperity of both. The Soviet Union was held up as symbolising a multicultural and internationalist brotherhood of people committed to and living in harmony with both its European and Asian halves. The most conspicuous symbol of this supposedly harmonious Soviet Union united in its commitment to fraternal socialist internationalism was embodied in the idea of the Soviet Federation, representing more than a hundred different nationalities from the Tajiks of Central Asia to the Estonians to the west, which comprised a unique and superior experiment of state 'unity in diversity' (*yedinstvo v mnogoobrazii*). Under Gorbachev's *perestroika*, the Eurasian idea was extended to become a tool for promoting East–West coexistence as part of the so-called 'new thinking' in late 1980s Soviet foreign policy. Eager to play up his country's willingness to find a new and lasting rapprochement with the West and to de-emphasise the competitive bipolarity that had become the centrepiece of the Cold War, Gorbachev made it clear that the Soviet Union's interests were truly Eurasian in their geopolitical scope: 'The Soviet Union', he declared, 'is an Asian as well as European country'.[16] Gorbachev emphasised this particular theme of Eurasianism in a number of other geopolitical settings. Thus, in a 1986 speech in Prague he reminded his European audience of the Soviet Union's commitment to 'a common European home', while in Vladivostok he later talked about the USSR as 'a Eurasian state ... to serve as a hopeful bridge bringing together two great continents'.[17] And in a speech in Murmansk, directed at Scandinavians and Canadians, he referred to Russia as part of our 'common Arctic house'.

In post-Soviet Russia, this Eurasian vision defines 'Eurasia' as both Slavic and Turkic, Christian and Muslim, Western and Eastern.[18] As Russia occupies a special place within northern Eurasia, it is held that the goal of multicultural Russia should be to ensure 'the cultural self-preservation and further development of national traditions and co-operation among Slavic, Turkic, Caucasian, Finno-Ugric, Mongolian and other peoples of Russia within the framework of Eurasian national-cultural space'.[19] Here the centuries-long intermingling of European and Asian cultures is seen as a beneficial and enriching force, providing the potential for coexistence between the peoples of Eurasia on the basis of mutual recognition of the equal value of all national cultures.

Discourses of homeland

While the above interpretations of Russia's *place* within Eurasian civilisation inform present-day visions of what sort of polity and society Russia should be, they provide only a partial insight into the complexity of Russian geopolitics. Some commentaries have focused on what is considered to be the binary nature of Russia's geopolitical aspirations – the so-called 'empire-rebuilders', who wish to recreate a Russia which again includes part or even all of northern Eurasia, on the one hand, and the 'nation-statists', who accept Russia's present post-1991 boundaries as the basis for its people's political and economic future, on the other.[20] However, during the 1990s a variety of competing political ideologies, geopolitical programmes and visions of Russia's place within the new world order have unfolded. These constitute differing visions of homeland – sets of policies or stances based on a particular normative understanding of what the homeland and its geopolitical boundaries should be and the particular role that is ascribed to Russia within the new world geopolitical order.[21] Four such homeland stances can be identified: liberal-Westernist, neo-nationalist, neo-Soviet and democratic statist (Table 3.1). Integral to these discourses of homeland is the way in which each is scripted in relation to the other.

Liberal: return to the West

The liberal-Westernist conception of Russia, which formed the official political discourse from 1990 until 1992 and remained influential thereafter, accepts the sovereign boundaries of Russia's new political home-

Table 3.1 A typology of Russia's images of Eurasia

	Liberal-Westernist (European/Western)	Neo-nationalist (Russia is a Eurasian, non-Western country)	Neo-Soviet (Russia is a Eurasian, non-Western country in which capitalism is foreign to Russian culture and way of life)	Democratic statist (Russia is a Eurasian, non-Western country but one which accepts that it has something to learn from both West and East)
Perceived role in Eurasia				
Geopolitical borders	Fixed	Slavic lands or Russian empire	USSR	Fixed
Cultural identity	Pluralist	Russian (*Russkii*)	Pluralist but Russia as 'first among equals'	Slavic-Turkic
Type of state	Federation	Empire	Confederation of Soviet states	Confederation
Attitude towards Russians in the 'near abroad'	Encourage them to become citizens of country of residence	Incorporate the lands settled by ethnic Russians into Russia	Incorporate the lands settled by ethnic Russians into Russia	Dual citizenship
Geopolitical relations				
Attitude towards the post-Soviet states	Non-threatening	Threatening until they are reintegrated into a larger Russia	Threatening because they are increasingly influenced by capitalist geopolitical powers	Some are threatening to Russia because of internal military and ethnic conflicts
Attitude towards the West	Friendly, in favour of co-operation	Openly hostile towards USA but less so towards Europe because it may become an ally in Russian–USA geopolitical struggle	Openly hostile: the West is a foreign culture	Neutral or implicitly hostile: can co-operate on some issues
Attitude towards East Asia	Generally friendly but cool: Russia's interests are in the West	Generally hostile	Generally suspicious and hostile, especially towards China	Neutral: Russia has special interests in developing better relations with east Asia

Source: developed from Shenfield (1994) and Tsygankov (1997).

land. It is based on the idea of promoting a civic nation, of creating a citizenship united by an identity and commitment to Russia as a political community. On the one hand, it is an inclusive and pluralist conception of the citizen-homeland in that it envisages membership of the polity as being open to all its inhabitants, irrespective of ethnicity, language or religion. But it is also exclusive in viewing all those living outside the present-day boundaries of Russia, including Russians residing in the post-Soviet borderlands, as citizens of the polities in which they live and work. Imperialising practices, interpreted as both tsarist and Soviet, are, for liberals, to become closed chapters in Russia's geopolitical history. Instead, Russia must accept that, with the collapse of empire, northern Eurasia has now been irrevocably transformed into 15 nation-states whose sovereign spaces and right to political self-determination must form the basis of the continent's new geopolitical order. It is therefore only by acknowledging this geopolitical reality that a prosperous and stable future for the region will be ensured.

Liberal-Westernists do have reference points in Russia's own history to draw upon, including the aborted attempt by the Mensheviks in February to October 1917 to establish a liberal democracy. Yet given the limited impact of liberalism on state-building in Russia, liberals recognise that the more formative and inspirational reference point is the post-Cold-War West. Having abandoned the European path of capitalism and liberal democracy in 1917 for an alternative route to modernity, Russia, liberals believe, must now seize the opportunity to rectify its deviant path by 'returning to Europe'. In order to fulfil this ideal and to resolve Russia's acute economic and political problems, Russia must follow the successful Western model of modernity. Moreover, rather than trying to regain its superpower status, Russia should focus its energies on putting its own house in order. Thus, 'the greatest patriotism is not to boast so much about large territory and resources but to learn how to make the most sensible use of them'.[22] To this end, liberals acknowledge that the mammoth task of economic and political restructuring requires Western financial support, technologies and markets. Russia's geopolitical future is therefore envisaged as best served by adopting an avowedly Western strategy of partnership and coexistence and participating fully in Western-dominated institutions of transnational governance.

Neo-nationalist: return to empire

In contrast with the liberals, the neo-nationalist discourse seeks a 'return to empire'. Although Russian neo-nationalism of the Far Right takes a variety of forms, its advocates share a conception of Russia which looks back to the pre-1917 empire as the building block for the future. Neo-nationalists appropriate and valorise an imperial, pre-communist golden age to frame and legitimise their programme for the post-colonial present. It is a discourse which is resolute in its rejection of Soviet rule and of what one of its intellectual historians, Pozdnyakov, calls 'the barbary of communism'.[23] Interpreted as a historical aberration in Russia's history, the 1917 Bolshevik Revolution is understood as an inherently non-Russian even 'foreign' event, forced from 'outside' and/or 'from above' upon a reluctant Russian people. But besides rejecting communism, it is also a discourse that renounces Western capitalism as an inappropriate way forward. The neo-nationalist right not only treat the West and Russia's urban cosmopolitans with suspicion and contempt but also reject Western coexistence and integration. For neo-nationalists, Russia instead must pursue its own distinctive path. Theirs is thus a discourse that accords to Russia a special place within Eurasian civilisation.

While advocating a return to the larger homeland, neo-nationalists differ in their views on where the geopolitical boundaries of Russia should lie. At one end of the spectrum is a conception of Russia's boundaries that is informed by Slavophilism. One of its main proponents is the former Russian *émigré* and Nobel prize winner Alexander Solzhenitsyn. On his return to his native Russia in the early 1990s, Solzhenitsyn sought to spur Russians into thinking about the implications of the USSR's collapse for their sense of national identity: 'What exactly is Russia ... who, today considers himself part of the future Russia? And where do Russians envisage the boundaries of Russia?'.[24] For Solzhenitsyn, Russia's future did not lie in what he considered 'a return to empire'. For post-imperial metropoles, he noted, shedding colonies could be economically and politically beneficial. He cited the case of post-World-War-II Japan as an example of decolonisation providing a sound basis for economic recovery and long-term prosperity. But rather than becoming part of a Western culture epitomised by material consumerism, Russia's future was seen by Solzhenitsyn in 'the spiritual and bodily salvation of the Russian people' and their Slavic brethren, the Ukrainians and Belarusians. In geopolitical terms, this meant Russia should be reunited with the other Slav-populated lands of eastern Ukraine, Belarus and northern Kazakhstan in a voluntary confederation or pan-Russian Union (*Rossiiskii soyuz*).

Other neo-nationalists, informed in particular by the ideas and writings of classical Western geopolitics, take a less ambiguous and more forthright view of the virtues of a 'return to empire'. For Aleksandr Dugin, a political geographer and former member of the extreme nationalist movement *Pamyat'*, Russia's geopolitical interests reflect its location at 'the geographical pivot of history', a concept borrowed from the early twentieth-century British geographer Mackinder. For Dugin, Russia is a continental power engaged in a struggle for *Grossraum* in Eurasia, which is held to be its natural sphere of influence.[25] It is therefore Russia's destiny to re-secure its influence and control over northern Eurasia, for it is only by doing so that Russia will again become a global superpower (Fig. 3.1). Just as Mackinder

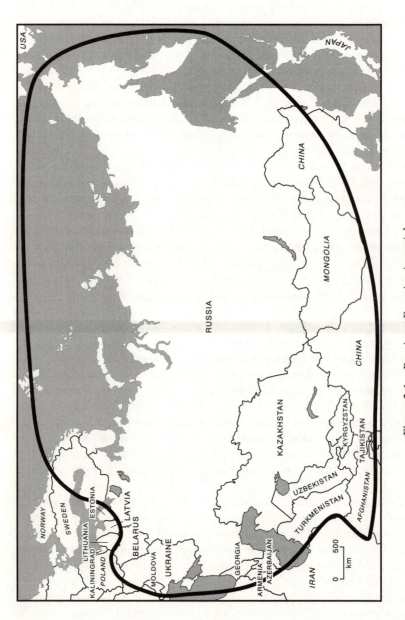

Figure 3.1 Russia as Eurasian imperial power.

Source: redrawn from A. Dugin, *Osnovy geopolitiki. Geopoliticheskoe budushchee Rossii* (Moscow, Arktoreya, 1997).

had presented the struggle for global supremacy between continental and maritime worlds, so Dugin argues that it is only through striking an alliance with western Europe's major continental power, Germany, against the maritime powers of the USA and Britain that Russia will be able to weaken the geopolitical and economic influence that the USA currently possesses over part of northern Eurasia. Russia should therefore forge alliances with continental Europe against the USA.

For the notorious *bête noire* of Russian politics and self-styled geopolitician Zhirinovsky, restoring empire is also seen as the only basis for ensuring Russia's renewed prosperity. In his book entitled *Last Thrust to the South*, Zhirinovsky advocates a return to Russia's borders as they were in 1913, when the empire had reached its apogee;[26] his vision of Russia's boundaries is set out in Fig. 3.2. Besides retaking the Soviet borderlands, including the Baltic states (minus Tallinn and Kaunas, which would become city states), the empire would reincorporate parts of Poland (the western part going to Germany). Slovakia too might become part of Russia, thereby extending Moscow's influence into Central Europe. Finland, which was part of the tsarist empire until its collapse, is excluded from this map, although elsewhere it is included in his vision. Zhirinovsky also envisages Russia's geopolitical influence stretching southwards to warm-water outlets on the Indian Ocean and Persian Gulf, a goal he describes as a strategic priority in Russia's imperial history. For him, this represents 'the last thrust to the south. I dream of Russian soldiers washing their boots in the warm waters of the Indian Ocean, and changing permanently into their summer uniforms'.[27]

Although the fact is not acknowledged, Zhirinovsky borrows heavily from the ideas and concepts developed by *geopolitik*, a school of thought in inter-war Germany which developed a particular concept of superpower domination. Its leading practitioner, Karl Haushofer, envisaged a world dominated by north–south-constituted pan regions, and his ideas are clearly evident in Zhirinovsky's writings. In his version of a Monroe doctrine for Russia, for example, Zhirinovsky talks about the world being divided into natural spheres of influence: 'Regional co-operation is better,' he writes, 'division into spheres of influence is better, and by the principle of north–south . . . we must come to an agreement that we divide the whole planet, with spheres of economic influence, and operate on a north–south axis'.[28] In Zhirinovsky's world, four pan regions are therefore proposed, identical to those envisaged by Haushofer: a Russian sphere of influence, including Afghanistan, Iraq and Turkey; western Europe (with its former African colonies); the USA (including the Americas); and Japan (dominating eastern Asia and Australia). Like Dugin, Zhirinovsky is also keen to ensure the neat division of Central Europe between Russia and what he regards as western Europe's major geopolitical actor, Germany.

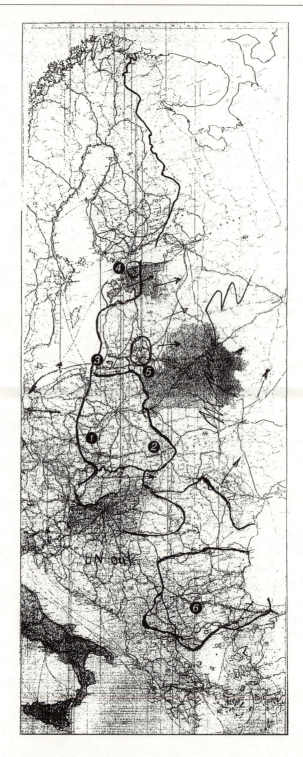

The neo-Soviet: Russia as socialist motherland

In contrast to the neo-nationalist right, those who subscribe to a neo-Soviet vision of Russia take as their reference point – even golden age – the idea and values of a Russia embodied within the Soviet homeland. This nostalgic representation of Russia's future looks back to the Soviet years as a positive period in Russia's history, which provided Russians with job security, an extensive welfare system, strong leadership, international respect, and pride in their country's superpower status. This vision of the Soviet past is juxtaposed with Russia's experiences since the fall of communism. Besides directing animosity towards liberal intellectuals and Russia's *nouveaux riches*, the neo-Soviet view holds the West in contempt, blaming Russia's economic, moral and global decline on Western capitalism and the USA in particular. Indeed, much of the rage generated by the collapse of 'the socialist motherland' is directed against what the more ardent conspiracy theorists interpreted as the grand American plan, supported by Russian liberals, to break up the Soviet Union. It is only by returning to a communist path that US global hegemony will end and Russia will stop being treated as the West's 'junior partner'.[29] The main organisational force behind neo-Sovietism is the Communist Party of the Russian Federation (CPRF), which emerged out of the Russian Communist Party, a hard-line group founded by opponents of Gorbachev in 1990, banned after the August 1991 putsch and legalized again by a Constitutional Court ruling in late 1992. The CPRF has found a ready constituency amongst those who have benefited least and suffered most from economic liberalisation, notably urban pensioners, the unemployed, and residents of the conservative provinces of the Russian *glubinka* ('the deep countryside').

In its homeland discourse, neo-Sovietism combines unreconstructed class politics and nationalist rhetoric. Indeed, 'the real success of the CPRF's rejuvenation has undoubtedly been grounded in its encapsulation

---

Figure 3.2 A neo-nationalist vision of Russia's western borders.
Note: The map was drawn by Vladimir Zhirinovsky for the former Swedish ambassador Rolf Gauffin. It shows the boundaries of Europe as conceived by Zhirinovsky. The key to the map is as follows: (1) Poland is to be partitioned between Russia and Germany; (2) in compensation, Poland is to acquire the district of Lvov from Ukraine; (3) Kaliningrad (Königsberg) is to be returned to Germany; (4) with the exception of Tallinn, which would become 'a city state', the three Baltic republics are to be returned to Russia; (5) Kaunas, which was the capital of Lithuania between the two world wars, is to become part of Russia; (?) Slovakia might also become part of Russia; (6) a Greater Bulgaria would absorb Macedonia, Thrace and Bucharest.
Source: *Le Monde*, 29 January 1994, p. 7.

and embodiment of the nationalist cause in Russia'.[30] For Gennadii Zyuganov, who has led the Communist Party since 1993, Russia differs from the rest of European civilisation in that capitalism remains alien to its culture, which is based on centuries of communal social values and sociability.[31] Bourgeois values, it is argued, are both foreign and unsuited to the Russian mentality, not least because until the 1990s Russians were innocent of 'the sin of ownership'. The distinctiveness of the Russian nation therefore rests on its being quintessentially socialist in orientation. Its struggle is to resist capitalist globalisation, which can only be reversed through Russia's again becoming economically and militarily strong enough to resist economic and cultural colonisation by the West. So while it is important for Russia to focus its energies on state-directed modernisation through the renationalisation of the economy and a return to socialist welfarism, any such programme of economic growth should not come at the expense of Russia's military-security needs.

Geopolitically, neo-Sovietism envisages Russia once again as part of a socialist Eurasian homeland. What exists at present, the Russian republic, is neither 'historical' nor 'ethnic Russia'. Its boundaries are 'unnatural'. The 'weak' and 'subservient' Russia of today is destined to 'disappear'.[32] In its place Zyuganov wants 'to provide conditions for the gradual restoration of a Union-state on a voluntary basis'.[33] Indeed, in 1996, the Communists in the lower house of the Russian Parliament, the State Duma, voted to renounce the Belavezha accords of 7–8 December 1991 that recognised the formal dissolution of the Soviet homeland and its replacement by 15 post-Soviet states.

Neo-Sovietism has a number of internal contradictions. Although it extols the virtues of incorporation, embracing universalistic aspirations of an 'international brotherhood' based on the idea of equality between nations within a common Eurasian homeland, it also regards socialism as a singularly Russian idea and aim. As the motherland of socialism, Russia is deemed to be the socialist archetype and the Russian nation 'the agent for remaking history'. The 1917 Bolshevik Revolution is interpreted as a Russian Revolution, reflecting the innate, superior socialist values of the Russian people.[34] Among the post-Soviet nations, Russia, it is argued, will again lead the way in re-establishing Soviet socialism. Thus, coexisting uneasily with the theme of international brotherhood is that of Russia's national greatness. Although the core aim is to rebuild a socialist Eurasia, this project is dependent upon strengthening Russian statehood because 'the Russian people should bind together all nations and people by their common historical destiny'. The appeal of this largely unreconstructed form of Communism therefore relies on re-establishing Russian hegemony. So, just like the Soviet Union, the restorationist political order would be a specifically Russian achievement, with the reconstituted socialist homeland constructed on the basis of Russia as 'first among equals'.

Democratic statist: the new orthodoxy

Finally, there is the vision of Russia of the democratic statists (*gosu-darstvenniki*), so labelled because its proponents call for a strong Russia yet are committed to democracy. More than any other reading of Russia and its future, it constitutes a hybrid or compromise drawing upon a combination of Western liberalism and neo-nationalism to produce a syncretic discourse of homeland. On the one hand, democratic statists see Russia as a distinctive civilisation differing from the West both in terms of its cultural values and its geopolitical interests. While accepting Russia's new geopolitical boundaries, they see Russia as a great Eurasian power whose role is to organise and stabilise Eurasia's heartland, so operating as a buffer or bridge between Europe and Asia. Thus, 'our state emerged and grew strong as a peculiar historical and cultural mixture of Slavic and Turkic, and of Orthodox and Muslim components'.[35] Russia is regarded as different from the West not only culturally but also geopolitically, having different needs and security interests. The new world order did not automatically imply the convergence of Russian interests with those of the West. Russia therefore must play a more active, even interventionist, role within Eurasia, not only to secure its own geopolitical concerns but also to ensure regional stability.

On the other hand, statists also remain committed to the project of capitalism and wish to see Russia playing a full and active part within the world capitalist economy. Although statism is suspicious of Atlanticism as a geopolitical project, it is pragmatic enough to recognise that Russia must work with the West, and that it is in the interests of Russia to co-operate with the world's major economic and geopolitical powers in such Western-dominated global institutions as the G8, the Organisation for Security and Co-operation in Europe (OSCE), the Council of Europe and NATO.

Statism is now the most influential geopolitical discourse in Russia, not least because 'it provides the most scope for pragmatic manoeuvre'.[36] Its post-1992 ascendancy reflects important shifts in official geopolitical discourse within the post-Cold-War world order. As Neumann notes, these changes in effect signal 'a contraction of the scope of discourse around the ideas of Russia as a great power, with an ambiguous status as a Eurasian state'.[37] The revival of this revisionist and more assertive stance within Russian foreign policy making was largely a product of two sets of developments. The first was the disquiet with which political elites and the electorate more generally viewed Russia's Western-liberal experiment. The economic reform package of the early 1990s Gaidar administration was generally interpreted by Russians as what could happen in emulating too quickly the Western-liberal model, leading as it did to hyperinflation, unemployment, dramatic falls in living standards, and rising crime. In short, there was a feeling that Russia was no longer in control of its own political actions and that it must find alternative, more appropriate solutions to the country's problems. Second, it was also felt that Russia had conceded too much to the West.

Not only had Russia ceased to be a great power, it seemed merely to follow the West's plans for restructuring the post-Cold-War political order. This disquiet with both the state of the Russian economy and Russia's weakness within the world community was reflected in the success of Zhirinovsky's Liberal Democratic Party of Russia (LDPR) in the December 1993 parliamentary elections (it gained 11.4 per cent of the party-list vote). In the 1995 Duma and 1996 presidential elections, communist candidates were also major contenders. The Yeltsin administration could not afford to ignore the politics espoused by the opposition. It therefore sought to outbid nationalists on both the right and left by playing the nationalist card more assertively, a strategy that appeared to have a wide appeal.

Geopolitical shifts in Eurasianism

As Malcolm and Pravda note, 'from an early liberal westernist position, associated with a policy of unqualified support for the West, Yeltsin and his government moved in late 1992 and early 1993 to adopt a more pragmatic nationalism stance'.[38] This switch in emphasis was also embodied in a change in foreign policy to what Tsygankov labels *defensive realism*.[39] By this he means that 'realists [in Russia] emphasise the importance of power in relation to control, domination and conflict, while de-emphasising the elements of co-operation and regeneration. The goal is to maintain the existing balance of power and geopolitical stability'. This is to be achieved peacefully and not through the use of force. This shift in thinking in Russian foreign policy reflects a tendency once again to view the world in terms of the balance of power, in which one country's gain is considered to be another one's loss. This differs from the early 1990s liberal-Westernist position when Moscow was concerned above all with the *geopolitics of international security*. At that time Moscow sought to safeguard Russia's security through co-operation with the West and with its neighbours, and by giving a high priority to active participation in international economic and political organisations.

These changes in how Russia percieves its role and interests in the geopolitical arena have four main components: first, that Russia's security interests necessitate taking a more active role in the affairs of the post-Soviet borderlands; second, that Russia should protect the interests of all Russians within the post-Soviet space; third, that Atlanticism is no longer the most appropriate cornerstone for Russia's foreign policy; and finally, that it is also in Russia's interests to play a more active and accommodating role in east Asia.

Geopolitical security

The first important change was Russia's eagerness to take a more active role in the affairs of the post-Soviet borderland states. Until 1993, Russia had largely ignored what it dubbed the countries of the 'near abroad' (*blizhnee zarubezhe*), preferring instead to focus on its own domestic reforms.[40] Wary of again falling into the trap of over-extending itself militarily and economically, Moscow had, since the late Soviet period, pursued in effect a policy of non-intervention, even of benign neglect, towards the borderlands. Under Gorbachev, Moscow withdrew its military presence from Afghanistan in 1988–89, and later, in 1994, it began the process of withdrawing troops from the newly independent Baltic states. Moreover, in the face of Chechnya's 1991 declaration that it did not wish to become part of the new Russia, Moscow decided not to intervene militarily to suppress the secessionist republic, preferring instead to concentrate on more pressing domestic problems while hoping that Chechnya would sort itself out.[41]

The shift in thinking in Russian foreign policy circles, in relation to the countries of the 'near abroad', reflected a growing unease over events in some of the borderland states and the consequent perception that Russia should play a more active role in the affairs of the borderlands. As Andrannik Migranyan, one of Yeltsin's advisors on foreign policy, put it:

> As a result of miscalculations in assessing the role and place of Russia and the deep-seated nature of relations between Russia and the countries of the near abroad, officials of the Russian Foreign Ministry and other political leaders in the country drew the strategically erroneous conclusion that Russia should return inward . . . thereby openly and publicly renouncing any special rights and interests in the post-Soviet space outside the Russian Federation . . . However, the events that occurred in Russia and in the republics during 1992 made some serious adjustments in the understanding of Russia's role and place in the post-Soviet space . . . A significant proportion of the political establishment . . . began to realise more and more clearly that a special role in the post-Soviet space belonged to Russia.[42]

Two issues in particular were of growing concern to many in Moscow: the fact that Russia had abrogated its responsibilities as Eurasia's regional policeman, thereby negating its role as a leading world power, and the political flash points within the borderlands that posed a potential threat to Russia's own internal security. Above all, it was felt that Russia should intervene to ensure the de-escalation of conflicts that could imperil Russian interests or spill over into Russia proper.[43] This included concern over the escalation of disputes in civil-war-torn Georgia, in particular secessionist struggles in South Ossetia. In keeping with this line, Moscow began to talk about the need to deploy Russian troops in the 'near abroad' for the purposes of peacekeeping.

In re-scripting security concerns, statists began to borrow the language and metaphors of geopolitics from neo-nationalists.[44] Moscow now talked about 'a geopolitical vacuum' and fears of 'geopolitical isolation' within 'post-Soviet space' and about the need to reassert Russia's 'natural' and 'regional sphere of influence' over the 'near abroad'. After all, it was argued, given Russia's long-standing historical ties with its neighbours, it was wholly legitimate for Russia to pursue its geopolitical interests in the borderlands.

In redefining the 'near abroad' as pivotal to Russia's geopolitical security, Moscow was signalling the emergence of a new Russian Monroe doctrine, or what might be more usefully labelled the 'Yeltsin doctrine'. Migranyan argued that, as a result of its low-key international stance between the late 1980s and 1992, Moscow had lost all its influence in global geopolitics, had failed to build up new geopolitical alliances and had been totally isolated by the West. Russia should, he argued, drop close co-operation with the West and pursue a more meaningful reintegration 'on former Soviet territory'. Migranyan argued that Russia could emerge as a superpower only by forging closer relationships with the countries of the near abroad. In contrast with neo-nationalists, however, the statists expressed the view that the borderlands should be reintegrated into Russia's regional sphere of influence without the use of force.[45]

The near abroad is therefore seen to be linked both to Russia's regional security concerns and to its prosperity, in that closer relations between Russia and the borderlands would offer greater economic opportunities. Russia is especially concerned about the growing influence of some 'far abroad' countries and regional alliances in the 'near abroad'. As regards the security of its western borders, Russia is preoccupied with NATO expansion, but it is also worried about the growing influence of the Islamic world on the region's southern rim. Russia has been prepared to intervene in the affairs of the near abroad, as in the civil war in Tajikistan, when fundamentalism is judged a potential threat to Russia's geopolitical interests. It is also concerned about the potential impact of militant Islam on Russia's own internal security, especially on stability in the republics of Chechnya, Dagestan and Tatarstan, where there is a large Muslim population. The rise of the Taliban in Afghanistan has intensified such concerns. In May 1998, such fears prompted Russia to sign an agreement with the Central Asian states of Uzbekistan and Tajikistan. As Russian presidential spokesman Sergei Yastrzhembsky put it, the 'troika' is dedicated 'above all to political co-operation . . . in the struggle with [Islamic] fundamentalism'.[46]

Russians in the near abroad

Security concerns were not the only reason for Moscow to take a more active stance in relation to the post-Soviet borderlands. Since 1992, the fate of the 25 million Russians living in the borderland states has emerged as a major focus of disquiet. Having recognised the sovereignty of the borderland republics, Russia had initially 'conceded *de facto* to rendering Russians living in these areas as "foreigners" '.[47] But it subsequently began to express concern that 'in the territory of the former USSR we are, in effect, seeing a restoration of the principle of ethnocracy and the formation of ethnocratic states', a tendency that 'is asserting itself throughout post-Soviet space . . . from the Europeanised Baltic regions to the clan societies of Central Asia'.[48] Within some of the borderland states, notably Moldova, the Baltic states and Ukraine, Russians were calling for Moscow to play a more active role in supporting those 'who have essentially been abandoned to the vagaries of fate'.[49] In the initial years of Russian statehood, the plight of Russians in the near abroad had been championed by the neo-nationalist right, but Moscow foreign policy makers now also began increasingly to think about their ethnic brethren outside Russia and the way in which they were being castigated as 'colonisers' and 'occupiers'. Indeed, 'concern for ethnic Russians [in the near abroad] is [now] one of the fundamental factors in Russia's foreign policy'.[50] The Russian state intervened militarily in the breakaway Russian-speaking enclave of Trans-Dniestria, which in 1991 had declared its secession from Moldova. The introduction of exclusionary citizenship legislation in Estonia (1992) and Latvia (1994) prompted Moscow to level highly charged accusations that these countries were pursuing policies of 'social apartheid' and 'ethnic cleansing'. It also threatened to impose trade embargoes and other economic sanctions, and signalled its unwillingness to withdraw Russian troops from the Baltic states until their governments respected what Russia coded as 'the end of human rights abuses'.[51] The Yeltsin administration was now in no doubt that 'the twenty-five million of our compatriots in these countries must not be forgotten'.[52]

In referring to Russians outside Russia as 'compatriots abroad', Russian statists were signalling an important change in Moscow's thinking on citizenship. Although the Russian state was still to offer citizenship to any former Soviet citizens, what now clearly concerned Russia above all were the near abroad Russians. Such a policy shift highlighted Russia's perceived role as the historic homeland of the Russians. For the *vykhodtsy* (literally, those who have left), Russia was their 'natural' homeland (*otechestvo*). The upshot is that the Russians in the near abroad have become a central concept in defining Russian national identity, with Russia being the 'historic homeland' of all Russians, and Moscow making it clear that it has responsibilities and obligations to protect their well-being. Moscow has therefore made periodic calls for action against recalcitrant borderland regimes, most recently in 1998 against Latvia, to protest against what Moscow views as that country's increasingly inflexible attitude towards its large Russian minority. Support for the 'near abroad' Russians is also reflected in Moscow's policy of earmarking funds for what it prefers to call 'humanitarian aid'.[53]

The idea of Russia as the homeland of the Russians has therefore been reinvented. By offering citizenship to all those who have a connection – ethnic or historic – with the Russian homeland, Russia has sought to redefine the boundaries of the Russian nation while at the same time acknowledging the inviolability of the borderland states' sovereign spaces. This differs from the stance adopted by the neo-nationalists, who do not accept that Russians in the borderlands should be politically separated from Russia, arguing that instead they should be reunited with their brethren within a common political homeland. Moscow's renewed willingness to protect Russians in the near abroad does not, however, mean that Moscow wishes to encourage 'return migration'. In the current economic climate, it is recognised that the large-scale migration of Russians to Russia would have disastrous consequences for the country's economic well-being and social stability.[54] Rather, statists have attempted to protect those who are deemed to be part of the Russian nation without either encouraging a grand gathering-in of Russians or calling for the establishment of a homeland-empire.

Attitudes towards the West: the retreat from Atlanticism

In the early 1990s, foreign policy was dominated by liberals who saw Russia's future as best served as part of a re-configured Atlantic Alliance in which Russia would work in partnership with the West, becoming an integral part of its dominant security and economic systems. From the mid-1990s onwards, however, important changes in attitudes towards the West began to emerge. As Neumann argues, this sea change was largely a reaction to 'the construction of a new wall in Europe along the wall between the CIS and those states bent on applying for EU and NATO membership'.[55] What in particular concerned Moscow were Western proposals to expand NATO's frontiers eastwards, initially to include three new members – Poland, Hungary and the Czech Republic – but with the further prospect of membership for the Baltic states as well. This meant not only that what once constituted Russia's vital sphere of influence was now being usurped by its traditional military adversary, the USA, but that such a military alliance was expanding to the very borders of Russia, threatening its own security. NATO's proposals shattered what Russia had envisaged as a common political and security system stretching from 'Vancouver to Vladivostock'. In a 1994 speech in Budapest, Yeltsin indicated his disquiet over NATO's proposed expansion by asserting that 'Europe has not yet freed itself from the heritage of the Cold War and is now in danger of lunging into a Cold War peace'.[56] For Moscow, NATO's 'new open-door policy' not only represented a breach of the old Iron Curtain but also signalled Western encroachment into what Moscow had for most of the twentieth century regarded as its natural sphere of influence. This growing mistrust of the West's geopolitical intentions not only showed Moscow that its geopolitical interests were no longer the same as those of the Atlantic Alliance but that Russia now needed to play a more assertive role in its relations with the West and the USA in particular.

Although statists recognise that Russia's geopolitical interests differ from those of the West's, Moscow continues to operate pragmatically. It acknowledges that Russia no longer possesses the superpower status of the Soviet Union nor has the capacity to recreate the bipolar world of yesteryear, and that it must adjust to being part of a multipolar world made up of competing but coexisting global power blocs. Statists also see the need to take into account the stark reality of the country's economic fortunes' being dependent on the goodwill of the West. For its part, the West has not been insensitive to Russia's geopolitical importance and new assertiveness within the international arena. In May 1998, Russia managed to upgrade its status from a participant in the G7 group of industrial countries to a full member of the G8. And in return for accepting US plans for NATO expansion, Moscow secured the establishment in 1997 of the NATO–Russia Permanent Joint Council under the NATO–Russia Founding Act, which was intended to provide a new security framework for the whole of Europe, thereby going at least some way towards reconciling Moscow's fears of the West as a threat to its national security.[57]

One consequence of US-led NATO expansionism has been to raise in Moscow once again the spectre of Russia's adopting different policies towards the USA and Europe. Many statists have increasingly embraced the rhetoric of the neo-nationalists by representing the USA as 'the reborn Cold War Other'. Europe, in contrast, is redefined as 'the good West' because of its perceived sensitivity towards Russia's geopolitical concerns. Yet, for many Russians, this is tantamount to a policy of divide and perish. As the deputy chairman of the lower house of the Russian Parliament put it,

> Objectively, most European countries share the American concept whereby the world is a single centre, a power house, uniting the Europeans in a major military bloc and other trans-Atlantic structures under America's aegis, a centre which brings order and peace into this chaotic world. With perceptions like this, why should Europeans open their arms to Russia and stand up to the United States? For us, too, it would be an unforgivable mistake to seek rapprochement with Europe with a view to harming the United States.[58]

Russia resents the current reality of the USA as the world's geopolitical hegemon and no longer wants to model its international relations on Western lines. This important change was succinctly put by Russian Foreign Minister Yevgenii Primakov:

> Initially, Russia's policy was one of 'strategic partnership' with the United States . . . a structure in which one country (the US) led the others was gradually created. . . . This is not what Russia wants. We want

equitable co-operation even though we realise that we are now weaker than the United States. I think we have secured such an objective . . . The world is becoming accustomed to the fact that *we have our distinct identity*. This is very important.[59] [*my emphasis*]

While no longer viewing the West as its enemy, Russia has neither lost its anti-Western instincts nor its desire to find a new identity for itself distinct from Atlanticism.

Attitudes towards the East: guarded rapprochement

Largely as a result of the independence of the six European post-Soviet western-borderland states, there is a general perception within Moscow foreign policy circles that Russia's centre of balance has moved eastwards, towards Asia.[60] Indeed, with the loss of the Slavic countries of Ukraine and Belarus, as well as the Baltic states, 'Russia stepped back to the European frontiers it had in the middle of the seventeenth century'.[61] While Moscow has long seen its presence in Asia as synonymous with its status as a world power, a growing rapprochement with its immediate Pacific neighbours – notably Japan and China – is also seen as crucial to developing the natural-resource- and energy-rich economy of Asiatic Russia (or Siberia). Moscow recognises that this vast region has the potential to give Russia the status of an economic superpower.

Moscow has not been slow to realise that if Siberia is to play a key part in the country's economic recovery, Russia must also provide the necessary conditions for its Pacific neighbours to participate in opening up the region's economic opportunities. Given that Moscow does not have sufficient capital of its own to invest in Siberia's development, this has meant recognising that Russia must strike a balance between its broader geopolitical interests and concerns in eastern Asia and the need to attract outside capital. In this regard, Japan is recognised as offering the greater potential. Since 1997 in particular, Russo-Japanese relations have shown signs of improvement. The major obstacle to closer ties has been the territorial dispute over the Kurile Islands, which the Soviet Union annexed from Japan after World War II. Yet while neo-nationalists in Russia view the islands as an inviolable part of Russia, the Yeltsin administration has adopted a more flexible stance, offering the prospect that some arrangement might be forthcoming over the ownership and administration of the islands. In return, Tokyo has looked increasingly favourably on the expansion of economic co-operation programmes with Russia, especially investment in Siberian gas and oil exploration.[62]

There has also been a similar rapprochement with China. Because of Russia's initial orientation towards the capitalist West, Beijing treated the new Russia with suspicion, viewing it as the gravedigger of communism.

Since the mid-1990s, however, Sino-Russian relations have improved considerably and are now better than at any time since the 1950s. In part, this is linked to a new confidence amongst China's political elites. For the first time in the twentieth century, China has not only surpassed Russia in economic development, but its northern neighbour no longer represents the geopolitical threat that it did during Soviet times. Both countries have also come to recognise the mutual benefits from cross-border trade and labour flows. In an attempt to facilitate movement across the Sino-Russian border, major defence agreements were signed in 1997 in which the two countries agreed not only to respect their common border but also to ensure its demilitarisation. Southern Siberia, in particular, has been a major economic beneficiary, because Chinese traders have seized upon the economic opportunities that this region offers. Such developments, however, have not been without their critics, having rekindled Russian fears of Siberia's vast underpopulated expanses providing *Lebensraum* for Chinese economic and geopolitical ambitions.[63] Yet the influx of Chinese settlers into Siberia's southern rim has not been enough of an issue to hamper progress towards a new Sino-Russian *détente*. As much as anything else, it is increasing mistrust of the USA and resentment at what is seen as its high-handed behaviour in Asia that have helped to facilitate what many in Moscow and Beijing hope will become 'a new strategic partnership' forming an 'alternative pole' to Atlanticism in global geopolitics.[64]

Notes to Chapter 3

1 M. Beissinger, 'Persistent ambiguities of empire', *Post-Soviet Affairs,* 11(2), 1995, p. 160.
2 E. Gellner, 'Return of a native', *The Political Quarterly,* 67(1), 1996, pp. 4–13.
3 D. Lieven and J. McGarry, 'Ethnic Conflict in the Soviet Union and its Successor States', in J. McGarry and B. O'Leary (eds), *The Politics of Ethnic Conflict Regulation* (London, Routledge, 1993), pp. 79–80.
4 M. Billig, *Banal Nationalism* (London, Sage, 1995), p. 74.
5 L. Kristof, 'The Russian Image of Russia. An Applied Study in Geopolitical Methodology', in C. Fisher (ed.), *Essays in Political Geography* (London, Methuen, 1969), pp. 345–87.
6 D. Lieven, 'The Russian empire and the Soviet Union as imperial polities', *Journal of Contemporary History,* 30, 1995, p. 617.
7 A. Kozyrev, *Preobrazhenie* (Moscow, Mezhdunarodnye Otnosheniya, 1994).
8 *Izvestiya,* 2 January 1992.
9 M. Bassin, 'Russia between Europe and Asia. The ideological construction of geographical space', *Slavic Review,* 50(1), 1991, p. 9.
10 L. Greenfeld, *Nationalism. Five Roads to Modernity* (Cambridge, MA, Harvard University Press, 1992), p. 258.
11 D. Mirsky, 'The Eurasian movement', *Slavonic and East European Review,* 6, 1927, pp. 311–20.
12 R. Borodaj and A. Nikiforov, 'Between east and west. Russian renewal and the future', *Studies in Eastern European Thought,* 47(1 and 2), 1993, p. 110.
13 I. Neumann, *Russia and the Idea of Europe* (London, Routledge, 1996).
14 Kristof, 'The Russian Image of Russia', p. 369.

15 M. Hauner, *What is Asia to Us? Russia's Asian Heartland Yesterday and Today* (London, Routledge, 1992).
16 M. Gorbachev, *Perestroika. New Thinking for our Country and the World* (London, Collins, 1987), p. 181.
17 Hauner, *What is Asia to Us?*, p. 249.
18 R. Szporluk, 'The National Question', in T. Colton and R. Levgold (eds), *After the Soviet Union. From Empire to Nations* (New York, W.W. Norton and Co., 1992), pp. 84–112.
19 *Rossiiskaya gazeta,* 10 July 1996, p. 5.
20 R. Szporluk, 'The National Question', pp. 84–112.
21 S. Shenfield, 'Post-Soviet Russia in Search of Identity', in D. Blum (ed.), *Russia's Future. Consolidation or Fragmentation?* (Boulder, CO, Westview Press, 1994), pp. 5–16; A. Tsygankov, 'From international institutionalism to revolutionary expansionism. The foreign policy discourse of contemporary Russia', *Mershon International Studies Review*, 41, 1997, pp. 247–68.
22 Y. Afanas'ev, *God posle avgusta, gorech i vybor* (Moscow, Literatura i politika, 1992).
23 *Nezavisimaya gazeta,* 5 March 1992.
24 A. Solzhenitsyn, *Rebuilding Russia. Reflections and Tentative Proposals* (London, Harvill Press, 1991).
25 A. Dugin, *Misterii Yevrazii* (Moscow, Arktoreya, 1996); A. Dugin, *Osnovy geopolitiki. Geopoliticheskoe budushchee Rossii* (Moscow, Arktoreya, 1997); also A. Solzhenitsyn, *Rossiya v obvale* (Moscow, Russkii put', 1998).
26 V. Zhirinovsky, *Poslednii brosok na yug* (Moscow, TOO Pisatel, 1993).
27 Zhirinovsky, *Poslednii brosok na yug*, p. 66.
28 As quoted in E. Klepikova and V. Solovyov, *Zhirinovsky. The paradoxes of Russian Fascism* (London, Viking, 1995), p. 157.
29 See, in particular, G. Zyuganov (ed.), *Sovremennaya russkaya ideya i gosudarstvo* (Moscow, RAN, 1995); G. Zyuganov, *Rossiya i sovremennyi mir* (Moscow, Obozrevatel', 1995).
30 Y. Vinokurov, 'Overdosing on nationalism. Gennadi Zyuganov and the Communist Party of the Russian Federation', *New Left Review*, 212, 1996, p. 36.
31 Zyuganov, *Rossiya i sovremennyi mir*.
32 Zyuganov, *Sovremennaya russkaya ideya i gosudarstvo*.
33 Zyuganov, *Sovremennaya russkaya ideya i gosudarstvo*.
34 *Pravda,* 25 June 1994.
35 *Nezavisimaya gazeta,* 28 March 1992.
36 Shenfield, 'Post-Soviet Russia in Search of Identity', p. 9.
37 I. Neumann, 'The Geopolitics of Delineating "Russia" and "Europe". The Creation of the "Other" in European and Russian Tradition', in O. Tunador *et al.* (eds), *Geopolitics in Post-Wall Europe. Security, Territory and Identity* (London, Sage, 1997), p. 149.
38 N. Malcolm and A. Pravda, 'Democratisation and Russian foreign policy', *International Affairs*, 72(3), 1996, p. 541.
39 Tsygankov, 'From international institutionalism to revolutionary expansionism', pp. 248–68.
40 K. Dawisha, 'Russian foreign policy in the near abroad and beyond', *Current History*, 95(603), 1996, pp. 330–4.
41 C. Gall and T. De Waal, *Chechnya. A Small Victorious War* (London, Pan, 1997), p. 111.
42 *Nezavisimaya gazeta,* 12 January 1994, p. 4.
43 Dawisha, 'Russian foreign policy in the near abroad and beyond', pp. 330–4.
44 P. Baev, 'Russia's Departure from Empire. Self-assertiveness and a New Retreat', in Tunador *et al.* (eds), *Geopolitics in Post-Wall Europe*, pp. 174–95.

45 *Nezavisimaya gazeta,* 12 January 1994, p. 4.
46 *Rossiiskaya gazeta,* 7 May 1998.
47 J. Dunlop, 'Russia: in Search of an Identity?', in I. Bremmer and R. Taras (eds), *New States. New Politics. Building the Post-Soviet Nations* (Cambridge, Cambridge University Press, 1997), p. 37.
48 A. Andreev, 'Etnicheskaya revolyutsiya i rekonstruktsiya postsovetskogo pros-transtva', *Obshchestvennye nauki i sovremennost',* 1, 1996, p. 105.
49 A. Andreev, 'Etnicheskaya revolyutsiya i rekonstruktsiya postsovetskogo pros-transtva', p. 112.
50 *Segodnya,* 12 July 1994.
51 G. Smith, 'The ethnic democracy thesis and the citizenship question in Estonia and Latvia', *Nationalities Papers,* 24(2), 1996, pp. 199–216.
52 *Nezavisimaya gazeta,* 1 January 1994.
53 *Rossiiskaya gazeta,* 10 July 1996, p. 5
54 I. Zevelev, 'Russia and the Russian diaspora', *Post-Soviet Affairs,* 12(3), 1996, pp. 265–84.
55 Neumann, *Russia and the Idea of Europe.*
56 *Rossiiskaya gazeta,* 7 December 1994.
57 For a discussion leading up to these events, see R. Walter, 'Rußland und die NATO-Osterweiterung', *Osteuropa,* 46(8), 1996, pp. 741–57.
58 *Nezavisimaya gazeta,* 31 December 1997.
59 *Izvestiya,* 23 December 1997.
60 D. Kerr, 'The New Eurasianism. The rise of geopolitics in Russia's foreign policy', *Europe–Asia Studies,* 47(6), 1995, pp. 977–88.
61 Y. Borko, 'Possible Scenarios for Geopolitical Shifts in Russian–European Relations', in Tunador, *et al.* (eds), *Geopolitics in Post-Wall Europe,* p. 202.
62 *Jamestown Foundation Monitor,* 14 July 1998.
63 V. Tsepkalo, 'The remaking of Eurasia', *Foreign Affairs,* 77(2), 1998, p. 117.
64 P. Ferdinand, 'China and Russia. A strategic partnership', *China Review,* Autumn/Winter, 1998.

4

The borderland states: nations, citizens and diasporas

Throughout the post-Soviet borderland states, there has been a tendency amongst the titular political and cultural elites to place heavy emphasis on nation-building in reshaping the political and cultural life of their newly emergent polities. For Brubaker, this reflects what he refers to as a nationalising tendency amongst the new regimes in power. Based upon the claim that the titular nation is the only legitimate homeland nation within the political space that it shares with other ethnic groups, such nations aspire to becoming the 'state of and for a particular ethnocultural "core nation" whose language, culture, demographic position, economic welfare and political hegemony must be protected and promoted by the state'.[1] In the most extreme cases, nation-building has come to reflect a vision of the political homeland in which nation and state should ideally become spatially congruent. However, by labelling the borderland states as nationalising regimes, it should not be inferred that they are all engaged in nationalising projects with the same degree of intensity or that they all pursue similar policies. With regard to language policy, for instance, there are very different sets of nationalising practices taking place in Latvia, where all residents are expected to speak Latvian as a condition of citizenship and where the Russian language now has no official status, and in Belarus, where both Belarusian and Russian are acknowledged as state languages. Nonetheless, exclusive claims to a special relationship between the titular nation and political homeland exist to varying degrees, with consequences for those minorities who are not considered members of the homeland nation and do not share its cultural attributes.

In securing a more privileged position for the titular nation, nationalising regimes have implications for the ethnic minorities of the borderlands. For no minority is this more significant than the 25 million Russians who are scattered throughout the borderland states (Fig. 4.1). Now the largest minority in northern Eurasia, they constitute an especially large and significant presence in Ukraine (11.4 million), Kazakhstan (5.1 million),

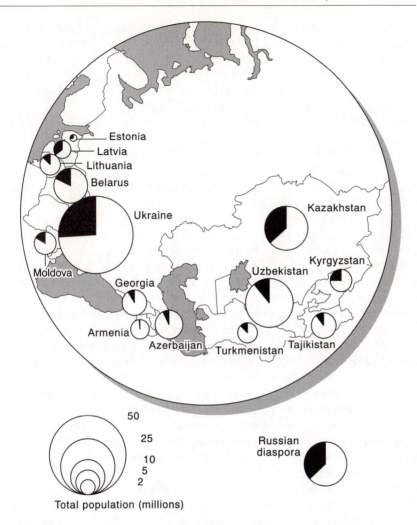

Figure 4.1 The Russian diaspora in the post-Soviet borderland states.
Sources: *Natsional'nyi sostav naseleniya SSSR* (Moscow, 1991); Yu. V. Arutynian
et al. Russkie. Etnosotsiologicheskie ocherki (Moscow, Nauka, 1992), p. 52.

Uzbekistan (1.5 million) and the Baltic states (1.6 million). Literally
overnight and without any sense of having emigrated, these borderland
Russians found themselves transformed into minorities in political homelands reconfigured and ostensibly claimed by and for others. Stripped of
their previous privileged status within the Soviet Union, it is the Russian
minorities, equated in the mind-set of many in the borderlands with the erstwhile colonial 'other', who have often the most to fear from such national-

ising tendencies. This chapter examines the relationship between these nationalising states and their Russian minorities. It explores how ethnic Russians are portrayed by the nationalising political and cultural elites within discourses of homeland politics and how these minorities are responding to their changed political status in two very different borderland regions: the Baltic states and Central Asia.

The borderland states as nationalising regimes

There are three notable nationalising projects that nation-builders in the post-Soviet borderlands have embarked upon. First, there is de-Sovietisation. This refers to the process by which nationalising political elites have removed the homeland symbols, political institutions and representatives of Soviet power from the social and political landscape, and replaced them with new national symbols and political institutions in order to safeguard what is deemed to be the national interest. In many of the borderland states, notably the Baltic states, Georgia and some of the Central Asian republics, the Communist Party, the main institution and symbol of Soviet power, has been removed from the political landscape. Bound up also with the self-interests of the new nationalising political elites and their desire to distance themselves, as well as the political homeland, from the Soviet era, its removal is legitimised on the basis of the wholesale rejection of the previous regime and is deemed to be commensurate with the homeland's geopolitical security and social well-being. Such a process is, however, also linked to mistrust of 'the former colonisers', the Russians, and unease about their perceived relationship with what is still seen as a neo-imperialist Russia. Thus, within some nationalist circles, de-Sovietisation is presented as synonymous with both decolonisation and de-Russification. Some political activists, notably in the Baltic states and Ukraine, even go so far as to suggest that the de-Sovietisation of their national homelands will only be complete when the Russians, still widely regarded as synonymous with communism and imperialism, return to Russia.

Second, nationalising political and cultural elites are also engaged in reinventing and recodifying the social boundaries that distinguish the homeland nation from other minorities.[2] Marking out distinctions between 'us' and 'them', i.e. differentiating between the titular nation and ethnic Russians, has become crucial to the way in which identities are represented in the mind-sets and politics of nationalising elites. This process includes a tendency to *essentialise* national identities, to single out one trait or characteristic in codifying a national or ethnic grouping. Here it is assumed that there is some intrinsic and essential context to any identity which is defined in terms of oppositions by either a common origin (our homeland, language community) or a common structure of experience (colonised/colonisers; immigrants/indigenous), or both. This representation of difference takes the form of offering one fully constituted, separate and distinct identity of 'us' which is different from 'them' (e.g. the titular nation as 'the chosen people' and Russian settlers as 'fifth columnists'). There is also a tendency to *historicise* identities. This has entailed reinventing and repackaging a supposed pre-colonial 'golden age' of yesteryear for the homeland-nation, which can inspire or forge unity amongst those who identify with that vision of nationhood. For Latvians, such a selective history is configured by an overly romanticised interpretation of the independent inter-war Latvian state (1918–40), which is juxtaposed with the more recent and negative period of Soviet rule. The pre-colonial past is therefore repackaged as a latent present in the reality of the nation's post-colonial status, one that can again be realised if political leaders only re-secure the elevation of the Latvian language and culture to the position they occupied during the inter-war years. Finally, there is a tendency to *totalise* difference between the titular nation and ethnic Russians, to turn relative differences between the two groups into absolute ones. Individuals are therefore squeezed into particular ethnicised categories in which one is either, for instance, an Uzbek or a Russian. There are no common concerns that transcend ethnic difference. Hence, nation-builders often seek to manufacture distance between the titular nation and ethnic Russians even though members of both nationalities may suffer equally from economic dislocation as a result of market reforms, speak a common language or even through marriage belong to the same family.

The third nationalising tendency is associated with a desire to standardise culturally the social, economic and political life of the polity, based upon the premise that a more homogenous polity dominated by one national culture is essential to the post-colonial state's political and economic modernisation. A rational, modern and efficient nation-state, it is argued, requires a uniform and standardised national culture. Thus, political elites contend that linguistic, cultural and educational homogenisation is necessary to run a more efficient national economy and state bureaucracy, as well as to produce a more loyal and harmonious citizenry. Of special importance is the goal of promoting a common national language. The institutionalisation and elevation of the titular language – in the state bureaucracy, government and education – are seen as a precondition for the running of a modern nation-state. This goal is also bound up with a desire to reverse the former 'colonial other's' policy of asymmetric bilingualism in which the titular nations learnt Russian while those Russian migrants who moved into the borderland Union republics during Soviet rule were given no incentive to learn the native language. If ethnic Russians want to become part of the new post-colonial order, they must, it is held, comply with this vision of nation-statism and learn the newly appointed language of position, status and social mobility.

Diasporic politics and the borderland Russians

The borderland ethnic Russians continue to occupy a pivotal place in defining relations between the post-Soviet borderland states and Russia. As Motyl argues, the collapse of empires can produce 'nationalising peripheries and imperialising cores, both of which define themselves in terms of the other and in terms of their abandoned brethren'.[3] The nature and extent of the regimes' nationalising projects can therefore only be fully understood in relation to the way in which Russia is represented in the mind-sets of the borderland states. Equally, Russia's interests and actions with regard to the near abroad will be shaped by Moscow's portrayal of the borderland regimes and, in particular, of the place it ascribes to Russians living in the near abroad as part of its own sense of nationhood.

For ethnic Russians, how they view their relationship with both their erstwhile homeland, Russia, and the polity in which they now reside will have a crucial bearing on what sort of community they imagine themselves to be. Most accounts contend that they constitute a diaspora because their imagined sense of community transcends the political boundaries of the polity in which they reside and where, in particular, there remains a strong sense of identity with their former homeland.[4] Yet in other respects, the borderland Russians do not easily conform to those features commonly ascribed to archetypal global diasporas like the Jews, Armenians or Palestinians. There are a number of reasons which lend themselves to such a conclusion:

1. The borderland Russians display a weak sense of communal identity or willingness to engage in a politics of collective action. This might seem especially surprising in the case of Russians in some of the borderland states, notably in Estonia and Latvia, whose regimes formally excluded large numbers of Russians, who moved into these republics during Soviet rule, from qualifying as members of the citizen-polity. If diasporic politics is about the politics of political mobilisation, then the Russians in the borderland states do not fit comfortably into being categorised as a diaspora.

2. In contrast with other global diasporas, a sense of solidarity with co-ethnic members of other countries is conspicuously weak or non-existent. The Russians, unlike many of the world's other diasporas, display little sense of a transnational solidarity linking their diasporic communities either symbolically or through established social networks. In other words, there is little sense of identity or social interaction between ethnic Russians living in, say, Estonia, Ukraine and Uzbekistan. In part, this lack of solidarity may be a product of Soviet rule, because Moscow discouraged any direct social or political interaction between the borderland republics, preferring to see all forms of social interaction flow from and to the centre. Consequently, in the post-Soviet era, inter-borderland

links among the diaspora remain either non-existent or at most weakly developed. Moreover, despite the opportunities opened up by cyber-space, it does not appear that the Russians are joining up with one another across time–space boundaries or that their identities are being symbolically reinvented through a shared imagination of community. At most, the identities of the borderland Russians are therefore highly localised and/or centred on the external homeland of Russia.

3. The borderland Russians were separated as a result of boundary changes from their external homeland rather than through forced or voluntary migration as in the case of archetypal diasporas. It was there-fore the collapse of the Soviet Union in 1991 that resulted in their changed status and position, and not the trauma of having to physically leave a homeland for a new life in a foreign country. In this sense, the ethnic Russians do not constitute a diaspora such as the Jews or Armenians who fled Europe for the USA in the late nineteenth and in the twentieth centuries.

It is the absence of such features of diasporaship which leads Cohen to prefer to label the borderland Russians as a 'stranded minority'.[5] Yet we should also be cautious concerning claims that the borderland Russians display no features commonly attributed to diasporas or that they are unlikely to become a diaspora in the future. Many ethnic Russians in the borderland states still subscribe to what can broadly be interpreted as a neo-imperial vision of Russia, celebrating the spiritual greatness and achievement of a Russian past, and even aspiring to be part of Russia's geopolitical renewal. Such views are found in a number of the border-lands' ethnic Russian enclaves, notably in northern Kazakhstan, north-east Estonia and Trans-Dniestria, where there is some support for a return to the Soviet homeland or to a geographically expanded Russia, though this is far less evident now than it was in the early 1990s. This does not mean, however, that the borderland Russians no longer display some form of affection or cultural affinity with the ancestral homeland. Even for Russians whose bonds with their former homeland are confined primarily to the cultural sphere, what happens in Russia is still of special interest. This is especially the case when ethnic Russians feel that they are being treated unfairly by the polity in which they reside and fear that they are becoming or have become 'victims' or 'second-class citizens'. If only for insurance purposes, ethnic Russians are likely to take more than a fleeting interest in the rhetoric of Russia's politicians and the policies that their former homeland may pursue *vis-à-vis* the near abroad.[6]

In sum, although the borderlands' ethnic Russians do not fulfil all the cri-teria generally associated with diasporas, they do display some diasporic features. Much, however, depends on the local context in which each bor-derland community finds itself.

Estonia and Latvia: the ethnic politics of exclusion

What distinguishes the two Baltic states of Estonia and Latvia from the other post-Soviet borderland states is that through their citizenship legislation they have introduced a particular variant of the nationalising state, what I have referred to elsewhere as characteristic of an ethnic democracy.[7] By this I mean that, on the one hand, the titular nation has secured an institutionally superior position and status for itself – in the political legislature, education, the law courts and in public administration – in part by successfully depriving the Russian settler communities of particular political rights and through state language policies. This includes denial of the right to form political parties and to stand as candidates for or vote in national elections, although in Estonia Soviet-era migrants do have a right to vote in municipal elections. Through language laws, the state has also insisted that a precondition to citizenship is a test of proficiency in the state language. As there was little pressure on Russians residing in the borderlands to learn the local languages under Soviet rule, some 60 per cent of Russians in Estonia and 40 per cent in Latvia have no knowledge of the post-1991 state language.[8] On the other hand, within ethnic democracies, certain universal principles of human rights are adhered to with regard to minorities, most notably within the sphere of civil and collective rights.

In order to legitimise the marginalisation of Soviet-era citizens, exclusionists in both polities were able to represent and to codify the Russians as a 'colonial other' in three particular ways, thus successfully outmanoeuvring inclusionists with their alternative vision of what the citizen-homeland should be.

First, Soviet-era settlers were successfully labelled as *illegal migrants*. As Estonia and Latvia had been illegally incorporated into the Soviet Union in 1940, it was claimed that their homeland-nations should have a right to reclaim their lost sovereignty. Thus, from the outset, the nationalist struggle to reclaim their political homeland was represented as 'a lawful struggle' against 'occupation' by 'a foreign power'.[9] However, the implications for citizen formation that flowed from this notion of connecting up with the interwar sovereign homeland were the subject of intense debate. On the one hand, inclusionists emphasised the idea of establishing a multicultural homeland in which all residents should have a stake in the citizen-polity irrespective of their ethnicity. The 'other', the common enemy, was not equated with a people (the Russians) or a homeland (Soviet Union/Russia) but with a particular ideology and socio-political system, those of Stalinism. In contrast, the exclusionists were able to draw upon a powerful set of legal and political arguments. As incorporation into the Soviet Union had been involuntary, it followed that those who had settled in Estonia and Latvia during the years of occupation were illegal migrants. Furthermore, by framing the citizenship debates within the context of homeland-descent rather than ethnic-descent – i.e. those citizens of the previous political homeland and their descendants should have the right to automatic citizenship – their argument was made more palatable to those who had initially supported a more inclusive stance. Moreover, labelling the diaspora 'illegal migrants' was also part of a political strategy to ensure that state power would be firmly in the hands of the homeland-nation and 'that Latvians would again be masters of their own land'. To do otherwise would 'legalise the occupation and incorporation of Latvia into the USSR'.[10] Exclusionists therefore deliberately blurred the difference between the historical and contemporary homeland, while the difference between the homeland-nation and the diaspora was accentuated.

The eventual codification of Soviet-era immigrants as illegal migrants cannot, however, be divorced from interest politics. If homeland-nation citizens can secure over-representation in the state's major institutions by excluding others, considerable benefits flow for those who are members of this new political class.[11] Besides minimising Russian representation in their respective parliaments (following the 1995 national elections in both countries, there are respectively six and seven Russians in their 101-strong national legislatures), other material benefits have accrued to members of the titular nation, from limiting the rights of Soviet-era settlers to profit from economic reform, most notably from property ownership. The implementation of policies designed to restore property to citizens of the inter-war homeland and their descendants, whose homes, farms and companies were expropriated during Soviet rule, has spawned a new class of property owners, drawn more or less exclusively from the titular nation.[12]

Second, the exclusionary discourse holds not only that Soviet-era settlers should be denied the automatic right to citizenship but also that they cannot be trusted to carry out those obligations and duties expected of homeland-citizens. This equation in the exclusionist mind-set between 'Russians' and 'the Soviet or Russian empire' is reflected in the claim that the citizen-homeland will only be fully secure if it is purged of the political institutions (notably the Communist Party), organisations and individuals that were responsible for the nation's repression in the first place. It was this successful representation of Russians as 'fifth columnists' that formed an important backdrop to the redrafting of Estonia's June 1993 Law on Aliens. Concerned that in being redesignated as 'aliens' they would not have the right to travel freely back and forth to Russia and that, with the threat of growing unemployment, as recodified aliens they would be more vulnerable either to being expelled or losing their livelihood, many ordinary Russian workers in north-east Estonia supported their local municipal leaders in calling for a local referendum on the region's future. Tallinn and certain elements of the Estonian media interpreted these moves as a threat to the nation's territorial sovereignty. As one deputy in Estonia's Parliament put it, 'if citizens of other countries, or people with no citizenship at all, meddle in Estonia's internal affairs, we will deport them. There will be no compromises'.[13] While more than four-fifths of those in the north-east who voted in the referendum favoured some form of regional autonomy, turnout was very low. In all, the referendum seemed less an attempt to secede from Estonia than a means of exerting pressure on the central government to modify its citizenship policies.

Finally, Russian settlers are also represented as a threat to the *cultural self-preservation* of the homeland-nation. Estonians and Latvians claim that, after 5 decades of facing near cultural genocide as a result of Soviet rule, they have the right to protect what they regard as the special relationship between the nation and their historic homeland. This was evident in discussions leading up to the formulation of Latvia's 1994 Citizenship Law. The centre-right governing coalition were able to link considerations of citizenship rights to cultural self-preservation. For the centre-right, crucial to preserving the Latvian language and culture is the idea of a 'one nation political community', in which it is proposed that the language and culture of the Latvians should be congruent with membership of the citizen-polity. To achieve this goal, admission into the citizen-polity must be carefully regulated through a quota system in which the numbers of non-citizens to be naturalised each year should be limited by means of the system of so-called naturalisation windows. Thus, in June 1994, the Latvian Parliament decreed that a proportion equivalent to only 0.1 per cent of Latvian citizens (or around 2,000 persons) could be naturalised annually.[14] Others wanted to go much further. The extreme but influential nationalist political party, Fatherland and Freedom, even advocated the diaspora's decolonisation.[15] Faced with increasing pressure from both within and outside Latvia at the slow rate at which naturalisation was occurring, in June 1998 the Latvian Parliament proposed that the system of 'naturalisation windows' be abolished.[16] In a national referendum 4 months later, Latvians voted in support of what their Parliament had earlier advocated.[17]

A crucial role in moderating citizenship legislation has been played by Western transnational political organizations, especially the Organisation for Security and Co-operation in Europe (OSCE), the Council of Europe and, more recently, the European Union. As Keohane has noted, Western-dominated European political institutions have at their disposal considerable geopolitical leverage to ensure that eastern Europe complies with the West's political agenda on human rights and questions of geopolitical security. The West can

> use the economic and technological dependence of East European societies on Western Europe as a source of leverage ... some combination of European Community as magnet and CSCE [now the OSCE] as encompassing framework of rules would seem to be the proper institutional antidote to the danger of hyper nationalism in Eastern Europe.[18]

For their part, the Baltic states, with their commitment to 'returning to Europe', have been keen to demonstrate their European credentials in order to attain the security, markets and distance from the East that membership of Europe offers. When in 1993 Latvia's Parliament came under criticism from both the OSCE and the Council of Europe over the stringent natural-isation quotas it sought to impose, and this threatened to jeopardise its application to join the Council of Europe, the Latvian President, Guntis Ulmanis, intervened, and returned the law to Parliament for reconsideration. As a consequence, Latvia was able to follow the other two Baltic states into the Council of Europe in 1995. Similarly, OSCE criticism of Estonia's draft Aliens Law in June 1993 resulted in President Meri's returning it to Parliament and the enactment the following month of more moderate legislation. More recently, in the wake of the 1997 Luxembourg summit, which set out conditions for Estonia's membership of the European Union, the Estonian government agreed to extend citizenship to all stateless children born in the republic since 1992. This extension can be attributed in part to pressure from the EU, which specifically recommended that Estonia 'consider means to enable stateless children born in Estonia to be naturalised more easily'.[19]

The diaspora and the politics of multiple identities

There is no doubt that the Russian minorities feel that their codification by the nationalising regimes is socially unjust, and this is reflected in a strong sense of grievance towards those in power. One survey found that well over four-fifths of the diaspora in both Estonia and Latvia felt that the requirements for citizenship were unjust.[20] Yet this sense of grievance has not been translated into a mass exodus or mass collective action. The number of Russians who have taken up the option of return migration has been low. Between 1991 and 1998, only about 100,000 Russians (including other Russian-speakers) have returned to their erstwhile homelands (Fig. 4.2). It may well be, therefore, that despite the difficulties of negotiating the boundaries of citizenship, most Russian-era settlers have decided to remain in the Baltic states because of the higher living standards that their economically more successful regimes can offer compared with those of their erstwhile homeland, Russia. Similarly, when demonstrations have occurred, most notably during the first half of 1998 amongst Russians in Latvia, they have tended to attract at most only a few hundred participants.[21]

There is little doubt that the ability of the diaspora to engage in collective action has been constrained by a number of factors, not least by a political system that has purposely limited the political opportunities available to engage in collective action.[22] Besides choosing return migration as a response to their marginalisation, three other notable strategies have been pursued by the diaspora, each associated with a particular form of home-land politics.

The first strategy relates to those within the diaspora whose identity is still bound up with the Soviet homeland (*Sovetskaya rodina*). Initially, this form of identification was reflected in the emergence, beginning in 1988, of pro-Soviet groups in response to the rising tide of Baltic separatist-nationalism.

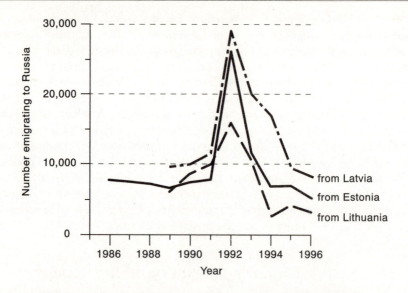

Figure 4.2   Emigration from the Baltic states to Russia, 1986–96.
Sources: *Citizenship and Immigration Departments of the Respective Baltic States*
(Tallinn, 1997; Riga, 1997; and Vilnius, 1996); (Moscow, Goskomstat, 1996 and
1997).

Organised in the form of counter-movements, or the so-called Inter-Fronts,
these movements were led by well-placed Communist Party functionaries
drawn from the party apparatus, factory managers and administrators,
whose interests and identities were bound up with safeguarding the neo-
Soviet vision of homeland. Their support base was particularly strong in
localities where they were able to mobilise constituents around an unreconstructed politics of 'class' and 'ethnicity', most notably in north-eastern
Estonia, where ethnic Russian and urban working-class identities overlap.

However, two developments in particular have weakened support for this
form since 1993. First, the formal limiting by the Estonian and Latvian governments of the political opportunities to engage in collective action, including the banning of the Communist Party, has deprived neo-Sovietism of its
institutional supports. Second, despite Moscow's relentless rhetoric concerning its support for the Baltic Russians, there has been a growing feeling
amongst Soviet-era settlers that their erstwhile homeland has abandoned
them. More pressure, it has been argued, could have been exerted in linking
the eventual agreement in 1994 to withdraw Russian troops from the Baltic
states to Russia's declared aim of standing up for diasporic interests.[23]

Since 1993, it is within a particular stratum of Baltic Russians, made up
primarily of an older generation of urban-industrial workers, who constitute less rooted and more recent migrants with little or no command of the
new state languages, that support for *Sovetskaya rodina* has remained

significant. It is also this element of the diaspora that has fallen back on Russia's offer of extra-territorial citizenship as a strategy of survival and security. By the late 1990s, some 113,000 residents of Estonia and just over 65,000 in Latvia had opted for Russian citizenship.[24] Indeed, their decision to take Russian citizenship may be as much the result of a lack of other options as of a strong commitment to the restitution of *Sovetskaya rodina*. When asked in a 1996 survey in Estonia if they preferred life under the Soviet period to that of the present day, well over two-thirds of Russians who had taken out Russian citizenship indicated that they preferred the Soviet period (Fig. 4.3). This new urban underclass is not prepared to learn a new language, remains nostalgic for socialist values (such as the extensive welfare state and full employment) and continues to be suspicious of market liberalisation. The results of recent Russian parliamentary and presidential elections show that Russian citizenship translates into strong support for the Communist Party. In the 1996 presidential elections, Russians in both Estonia and Latvia voted overwhelmingly for the Communist Party candidate, Gennadii Zyuganov, rather than for the centre candidate (Boris Yeltsin) or the nationalist right (Aleksandr Lebed or Vladimir Zhirinovsky). Indeed, of the Russians in the 'near abroad' who took part in the poll, only those in the Baltic states overwhelmingly endorsed Zyuganov (Table 4.1).

Table 4.1   Voting in the borderland states in the second round of the 1996 Russian presidential elections

	Number of voters	Turnout (%)	Yeltsin (% of the votes)	Zyuganov (% of the votes)	Opposed to both candidates (% of the votes)
Baltic states					
Estonia	74,046	29	21	77	2
Latvia	65,182	13	23	75	2
Lithuania	16,196	28	33	63	3
South-western borderlands					
Ukraine	43,223	88	62	31	6
Belarus	4,947	91	78	18	3
Moldova	30,249	61	45	51	4
Transcaucasia					
Georgia	16,604	94	67	25	7
Armenia	10,240	61	63	32	5
Azerbaijan	1,444	83	54	40	6
Central Asia					
Kazakhstan	42,624	70	69	23	8
Uzbekistan	4,118	52	68	29	3
Turkmenistan	6,852	58	48	50	2
Tajikistan	9,050	97	53	36	9
Kyrgyzstan	3,901	67	59	35	5

Source: *Vybory prezidenta Rossiiskoi Federatsii 1996. Elektoral'naya statistika* (Moscow, Ves' mir, 1996), p. 147.

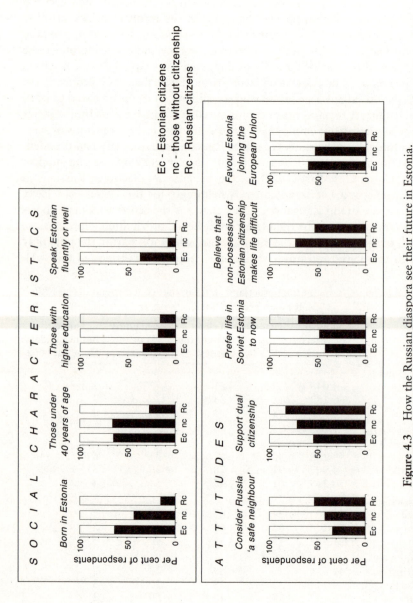

Figure 4.3 How the Russian diaspora see their future in Estonia.

Source: Tartu Ulikooli Turu-uurimisruhm, *Kirde-Eestii Linnaelanike Suhtumine Eesti Reformidesse Ja Sotsiaalpolitikasse* (Tartu, 1997).

However, the derisory turnout in the second round of the elections in both Estonia and Latvia (29 per cent and 13 per cent, respectively) suggests that those who have opted for Russian citizenship prefer to minimise their engagement in any form of political expression. Only one major demonstration has occurred since 1993 in either Baltic state involving Russian citizens. In March 1998, over 1,000 mainly elderly Russians in Riga protested against the high cost of public utilities, the shortage of jobs, insufficient pensions and a lack of clarity over the citizenship issue.[25]

The second strategy is bound up with learning the state languages. There is, in other words, a recognition, especially among the more pragmatic and the younger generation, that self-empowerment will come only by crossing the social boundaries of citizenship, which means giving priority to acquiring a knowledge of the language of the homeland-nation. This is what Laitin calls 'competitive assimilation'.[26] He hypothesises that large numbers of the diaspora respond as rational actors by recognising that learning the language of the homeland-nation is fundamental to securing a niche in the upwardly mobile and increasingly competitive middle-class labour market. The only likely brake on this trend is if cultural elites among the diaspora can raise the status of those who refuse to learn the language, a trend which has not been sufficient to secure a reversal of fortune in any of the Baltic states. Accordingly, as rational individuals, many ethnic Russians will accept, within the all-important arena of language, the nationalising state's citizenship rules provided that they can see longer-term economic and social benefits accruing as a result of becoming full members of the citizen-homeland. This may explain why many within the diaspora have chosen to invest their time and resources in qualifying for citizenship rather than engaging in a politics of collective action. The growth in attendance among Russianspeakers at Estonian and Latvian language classes indicates that many of the diaspora are keen to exploit such avenues to becoming citizens.[27]

However, it should not necessarily be assumed that the willingness of this stratum to learn the state language will lead to the depoliticisation of diasporic identities, particularly if time-investment is not matched by social expectations. Indeed, Russians are already finding it difficult to compete with a younger generation of Estonians and Latvians who are busily learning English, which is increasingly important as the language agenda is being reshaped by such globalising processes as the establishment in the Baltic states of transnational companies and by a state bureaucracy adjusting to the prospect of membership of the European Union. Paradoxically, it may well be that the willingness of particularly the younger diaspora to embrace the logic that the nationalising state demands, of devoting time to learning the state language, may also make them less equipped in the more immediate future to compete in the new global linguistic division of labour with native Estonian or Latvian speakers.[28]

Finally, there is a stratum of the diaspora, drawn primarily from a small but active cultural intelligentsia, who accept that their future lies within the

homeland of Estonia or Latvia and who identify with their countries of residence, but who at the same time want to preserve and advance diasporic
interests by engaging in limited collective action. This group is composed primarily of those who took an active role in supporting Baltic statehood in the
1988–91 period. The majority have become citizens of Estonia or Latvia and
have taken advantage of the political opportunities accrued through citizenship to advocate the creation of a polity that is more accommodating of multicultural communities. So far, however, this type of collective action has met
with little success in terms of liberalising citizenship laws or securing cultural
and linguistic autonomy for the countries' minorities. In part, this is due to
political factionalism. Although in the 1995 general election in Estonia, for
instance, Russians mobilised sufficiently around the political faction Our
Home Is Estonia (*Mei Kodu on Eestimaa*) to secure six of the 101 parliamentary seats, the group's effectiveness has been weakened by a lack of political consensus and by divisive personality politics. When Estonia's Russians,
in a 1995 survey, were asked which of the diasporic political parties they
supported, around half of those sampled (which included non-citizens) either
could not say or had not heard of them.[29] In short, citizen activists possess
limited unity of purpose to engage in effective collective action.

Central Asia: homeland politics and return migration

The situation of the diaspora in the states of post-Soviet Central Asia differs
from that of the Baltic states. According to Tishkov, 'the most painful mani-
festations of this problem [of Russians finding themselves living outside
Russia] have occurred in Central Asia, where internal instability and greater
cultural distances have caused a massive exodus of Russians'.[30] Of the 9.5
million Russians residing in the five Central Asian states at the time of the
1989 Soviet census, estimates suggest that more than 1.6 million left
between 1989 and 1996.[31] Thus, most of the exodus that has taken place
from the post-Soviet borderland states to Russia has been of ethnic Russians
from Central Asia (Table 4.2). This exodus has affected all the Central
Asian states, but notably Tajikistan. According to the more alarmist scenarios, this exodus will continue, leading to a further mass reduction in the size
of the diasporic community and raising questions about the future of the
Russian communities in some of the states of Central Asia, especially
Tajikistan. Following the years of fighting there, only a small fraction of the
Russian community remains.

This diasporic exodus needs to be considered in relation to the changing
nature of the homeland identities of the titular Central Asian nationalities.
There is little doubt that, for the peoples of Central Asia, adjusting to
post-colonial status and finding an identity to fit the new historical conditions of independent statehood have not been easy. As Shahrani, a Central
Asian scholar puts it, 'post-Soviet Central Asian societies are facing a seri-

Table 4.2   Net migration to and from CIS countries, 1990–96

	1990	1991	1992	1993	1994	1995	1996
Russia	164,000	51,600	176,100	430,100	810,000	502,200	343,600
South-western borderlands							
Ukraine	79,300	148,400	288,100	49,600	–143,200	–	–131,100
Belarus	–32,000	3,000	53,800	32,400	–3,300	–	–11,700
Moldova	–29,800	–33,700	–36,800	–15,100	–14,800	–17,100	–16,500
Transcaucasus							
Armenia	1,100	20,000	28,000	–12,300	–13,200	–11,200	–
Azerbaijan	–86,200	–40,200	–61,300	–57,900	–49,000	–44,600	–
Georgia	–39,000	–44,000	–45,000	–30,300	–32,300	–	–11,700
Central Asia							
Kazakhstan	–130,900	–48,900	–179,200	–203,300	–409,100	–243,300	–207,500
Uzbekistan	–179,600	–95,900	–74,700	–54,000	–138,900	–89,000	–50,300
Kyrgyzstan	–40,900	–36,600	–77,400	–120,600	–51,100	–18,900	–11,700
Tajikistan	–60,300	19,000	–142,300	–2,200	–51,800	–	–
Turkmenistan	–7,300	–4,800	342,700	7,800	–9,200	–	–17,400

Source: CIS Interstate Statistical Committee, *Official Statistics of the Countries of the CIS, 1997–2* [CD-ROM] (Moscow, CIS Interstate Statistical Committee, 1998).

ous spiritual crisis and are desperately in search of meaning and a moral compass'.[32] In contrast with the Baltic peoples, Central Asians did not aspire to sovereign statehood in 1991. Throughout the late 1980s, there was no mass engagement in secessionist, nationalist, religious or other forms of protest or collective action.[33] Rather, independent statehood was thrust upon Central Asia. Moreover, it has been doubly difficult for Central Asians to establish a sense of post-colonial identity because the imagined sense of national community – of what it means to be Tajik, Turkmen, Kazakh, Kyrgyz or Uzbek – was created and developed during the Soviet period. Indeed, it was the early Soviet state, in pursuing a policy of divide and rule, that geographically partitioned the region into five nationality-based Union republics, which led to the creation of homeland-nation identities amongst people whose sense of nation-ness had hitherto been either weakly developed or non-existent. Having had no previous experience of sovereignty to define the contours of national identity, Central Asians have had to define their conception of the sovereign homeland as part of an ongoing post-colonial search for national redefinition and symbol-building. In the development of statehood and national identity, three factors – citizenship, Islam and form of governance – have emerged as particularly important.

In contrast with Estonia and Latvia, all five Central Asian states granted citizenship to all those residing within the homeland-territory at the moment of independent statehood. Yet, from the outset, a tension existed between establishing a citizen-polity in which all individuals were to be treated equally, and the role that was envisaged for the titular nation within the socio-economic and political life of the citizen-homeland. On the one hand, opting for inclusive citizenship was linked to ensuring that the Russian diaspora – which throughout the Soviet period occupied a central role within the managerial, technical and administrative social structure of Central Asia – would continue to play a vital part in the running of the economy. Although the privileged position that ethnic Russians occupied within Central Asia was due primarily to their ability to usurp less qualified Central Asians, to a lesser extent it was also due to the tendency of the titular nationality to avoid certain occupations such as production-related employment because of the lower status such posts were accorded in traditional Central Asian society. So even in Kazakhstan, where the titular nation was demographically in the minority on the eve of independence, there was no prolonged debate or concerted effort on the part of Central Asians to exclude the Russian diaspora from membership of the citizen-homeland. Moreover, two states – Turkmenistan and Tajikistan – granted Russians the right to hold dual citizenship, in part motivated by a desire to furnish them with a greater sense of geopolitical security. There is also evidence to suggest that, in the case of Kazakhstan and Kyrgyzstan, attempts have been made to persuade ethnic Russians to remain in order to prevent the collapse of large sections of the national economies. As early as 1991,

Kyrgyzstan's president, Askar Akaev, refused to endorse a law which proclaimed that land was the property of 'the Kyrgyz people', instead decreeing it to be the property of all citizens of the republic. A year later the Kyrgyz state opened a Slavic University in the republic, the first of its kind in the region.[34] In a similar attempt to appease Kazakhstan's Russians, the Kazakh constitution of 1995 upgraded the status of Russian to an official language, although there is little evidence to suggest that such a policy is being fully implemented.[35] In all, it would seem that attempts to include the diaspora within the citizen-polity are bound up with a recognition of their importance to the modernisation of the Central Asian economy as well as reflecting the closer economic and geopolitical relations that most of the states of Central Asia – especially Kazakhstan, Tajikistan and Kyrgyzstan – continue to have with their northern neighbour.

Yet this attempt to accommodate members of the diaspora within Central Asia masks and is in tension with by far the more important set of state-building processes at work, namely those connected with promoting the idea of the nationalising state. Such practices include what Bohr prefers to label 'nationalisation by stealth'. In connection with policies of affirmative action, members of the titular nation are being privileged and rewarded within public sector employment and administration to the detriment of Russians and other minorities.[36] Such nationalising practices include elevating the titular language to that of the state language while the language of the redesignated coloniser is consigned to a secondary role within public life. The goal of reversing the linguistic Russification of the Soviet period has had especially far-reaching consequences for Central Asia's ethnic Russians, primarily because diasporic knowledge of the indigenous languages is very low. In Uzbekistan, for example, under 5 per cent of Russians in 1989 had a command of the new state language, whereas nearly two-fifths of Lithuania's Russians knew Lithuanian. As a consequence of their limited linguistic qualifications, ethnic Russians in professional and public sector employment in particular have complained that they are either losing their jobs or being passed over for promotion by less qualified members of the titular nation. In a 1996 survey, 26.3 per cent of Kazakhstan's ethnic Russians felt that they were being discriminated against because of their lack of knowledge of Kazakh.[37] Such marginalisation is not limited to the economic and social sphere of citizenship. Within the sphere of political representation, a process of ethnification is also well under way. Most notably, this includes the disproportionate over-representation of members of the titular nation within their respective parliaments. In Kazakhstan, for instance, where Kazakhs comprise 28 per cent of the citizen-electorate, the Kazakh share of representation in Parliament grew from 53 per cent in 1990 to 65 per cent in 1995, whereas in the same period Slavic representation fell from 37.5 per cent to 33 per cent.[38] Both space and time have also been appropriated and reinvented to meet the requirements of the nationalising state. In the case of Kazakhstan, the fear of regional secession amongst the

Russian diaspora concentrated in the northern borderland area was one of the main reasons for moving the capital from Almaty in the extreme south of the country to Astana, a windswept and remote town in the Russian-dominated northern steppe, in an attempt both to recentralise the peripheral north and to repopulate it with Kazakhs from the south. Similarly, re-inventing pre-colonial national histories by elevating particular epochs or past heroes of the pre-Soviet period and creating 'golden ages' in order to provide symbolic links and continuities with the post-colonial present have also become a notable feature of nation-building. Thus, Uzbekistani state symbol-builders look back to the supposed halcyon age of the fourteenth-century ruler Tamerlane, whose greatness is reimagined as part of the Uzbek struggle to secure their people's homelands against an encroaching and bar-baric north.

The second major ingredient of identity reformation is bound up with the re-emergence of Islam. For many Central Asian nation-builders, the twenti-eth-century history of their region represents a dichotomous struggle for cultural hegemony between two competing ideologies: the secular atheistic mission of the colonising Soviet north and the religious faith of the colonised Muslim south. In its commitment to creating an atheistic society, the Soviet state undoubtedly imposed limits on religious practices in the region's socio-political life. At certain times during Soviet rule, religion was confined solely to the private sphere of 'the self' and 'household'. Until the 1950s in particular, all public forms of Islamic worship, prayers, education and rituals were prohibited and places of worship (the mosques) and edu-cation (*maktabs*) were either closed down or turned into ethnographic museums. In the latter half of Soviet rule, however, Moscow put greater faith in the idea that Soviet-style modernity would lead to the weakening of religion; Soviet-engineered urbanisation, in particular, was given the role of social seculariser. With the region's urban and industrial transformation, combined with the supportive role that the Communist Party would con-tinue to play in promoting atheistic socialisation, Moscow envisaged that Islamic identities and cultural practices would eventually wither away. Confident that social change would facilitate the eventual creation of the atheistic citizen, the state was willing to permit Islam to be practised as long as it exerted control over the appointment of religious leaders. By co-opting a Muslim leadership into the services of the state, Moscow could not only more effectively monitor and thereby facilitate regional stability but could also use those leaders as emissaries in promoting its foreign policy goals in the Islamic Third World.[39] For urbanised Central Asians in particular, the idea of combining a Muslim identity with that of Soviet citizen was not nec-essarily in tension. On the one hand, Soviet-engineered urban modernity did have an impact on cultural practices, especially in the cities. By the late 1970s, in urban areas, the participation rates of Islamic women in the labour force were closer to those of other non-Muslim Soviet republics than to those of rural Central Asia. In addition, social changes were also having an impact on altering traditional Muslim attitudes towards large families.[40] On the other hand, Islam continued to have a major impact on cultural practices in both town and country, especially with regard to so-called 'life-cycle traditions' such as ceremonies of births, marriages and deaths.[41] In short, for many Central Asians, being 'Soviet' and 'Muslim' did not necessarily conflict. As Shahrani observes, 'the most significant achievements of Soviet rule in Central Asia may be the extent of its success in "colonising" the minds and consciousness of the peoples of Central Asia'.[42]

Since the early 1990s, however, Islam has emerged to become a central and celebrated component of public life. This is reflected in the re-opening of mosques, and in the renewed importance of religious rituals and ceremonies in the social life of both the cities and the countryside. However, it is important to acknowledge the diversity of this Islamic revival. Although Central Asians share a common Sunni faith, what is happening in the 1990s is not the revival of Islam, but of Islams, of a variety of sects, movements, parties and forms of identity politics. For the region's state-builders, especially their political leaders, what is particularly crucial is the simultaneous use and control of Islam, on the one hand to emphasise Islam as a unifying and coherent force in society but on the other hand to draw and exaggerate distinctions within the world of Islam, especially between the political leadership's normative conception of Islam and those fundamentalist identities which, it is argued, threaten the region's geopolitical stability and social welfare. Thus, political elites want to appropriate Islam and use it to their benefit in such a way as to ensure their popularity and continuance in power. In presidential inauguration ceremonies, therefore, some incumbents, in swearing an oath of allegiance to the new state, rest one hand on the Koran, while the other is placed on a copy of the state constitution. Similarly, while certain Central Asian leaders have embarked upon the highly symbolic pilgrimage to Mecca (the haj), a journey that any self-respecting Muslim is expected to undertake, they have also been careful to ensure that the haj has been 'taken out of season' lest too much emphasis be placed on its significance. Political leaderships also attempt to sell their regimes as modern, cosmopolitan and even Western-looking in orientation – Uzbekistan, for instance, attempted to claim a newly found modernity in its unsuccessful bid to secure the 2004 Olympic Games for the capital, Tashkent. But they also turn a blind eye to the impact of Islamic practices on gender issues, and women have come under increasing social and political pressure to give up the workplace for the home. Similarly, the Central Asian regimes are keen to capitalise upon their new geopolitical location within the Muslim world in order to re-establish favourable trading and political relations with fundamentalist Iran and Afghanistan, but at the same time they seek to make the most of Western and Russian Islamophobia in order to secure economic support and legitimacy by presenting themselves as the only form of governance capable of delivering both economic prosperity and geopolitical stability to the region.

Not surprisingly, these regimes have been anxious to curb those aspects of Islam that question their power base and authority. What is feared is that the 1992–93 civil war in Tajikistan, in which the Iranian and Afghan-backed Islamic movement attempted to seize state power, could occur elsewhere in the region. Thus, most of the Central Asian states repress religious activism, including Islamic political parties and social movements. Only in Tajikistan does religion remain a powerful political force, and even there the Islamic opposition claims to have no time for Iranian-style fundamentalism. The most significant challenger to state power is the Movement for the Islamic Revival of Tajikistan (MIRT), unique on the political map of Central Asia in that it is the only religious party that calls itself a party for all Central Asia's Muslims. Yet its support base is limited to locally organised informal groups in parts of the Central Asian countryside and in the more provincial towns.

Finally, nation-building has involved repackaging the idea that strong governance is central to the well-being of the homeland polity, based in particular on the notion that it is only through strong political leadership that both material prosperity and geopolitical stability will be secured. Indeed, the Central Asian regimes might best be described as being led by 'authoritarian modernisers'. Each regime, with the possible exception of Kyrgyzstan's, is dominated by an authoritarian-style and highly charismatic presidential ruler. Turkmenistan's President Niyazov has even adopted the title Turkmenbashi ('leader of the Turkmen'), thereby ushering in his own personality cult. This style of rule is combined with limited respect for the civil liberties of citizens. In one comparative study of state commitments to the protection of civil and political rights in the post-Soviet states, four Central Asian republics – Kazakhstan, Tajikistan, Turkmenistan and Uzbekistan – were deemed to have performed the least well since 1991.[43] The only exception to a modicum of engagement with democracy is Kyrgyzstan, although even that regime has, particularly since 1997, begun to show signs of slipping back towards a repressive police state. Yet Central Asia's political leaders recognise that transformation is necessary if their states are to become synchronised with the global economy and they are to attain the type of modernity to which they aspire. To this end they sell their regimes within the global market place as politically stable, natural-resource-rich republics that are worthy of outside Western investment. At the same time the presidential leaderships are able to tell their people that economic growth is possible only through strong governance, the continuation of outside investment and short-term social austerity.

Such visions of homeland have become increasingly problematic for Central Asia's Russians. Not only have they been marginalised in the reconstituted labour force and state bureaucracy, but they have also had to come to terms with a political system that provides few, if any, opportunities to articulate their demands. Thus, it would seem reasonable to assume that the reason why ethnic Russians are leaving Central Asia is linked to institutional practices of social closure and the fears many have for their future well-being in the region. Yet it is not entirely clear what has been motivating Russians to leave in such large numbers – whether this outmigration is voluntary or involuntary. The most common thesis holds that Russians have left primarily because of ethnic tension and violence. Yet ethnic violence, when it has occurred, has tended to be directed by Central Asians against Central Asians. There is little, if any, evidence to suggest that Russians have been on the receiving end of racially motivated attacks. Moreover, even though perception of inter-ethnic tension can be an important motivating factor for leaving, return migration was already well under way by the mid-1970s, long before ethnic tensions came to the fore.[44] Thus, from being a net recipient of Russian immigration, Central Asia began to experience a net outflow. This suggests that economic motives might have been more significant, as individuals made choices about whether, especially in a period of general economic decline, they were just as likely to be able to improve their living standards back home as in their place of settlement. Given that most post-Soviet return migration, as that from the Baltic states, has tended to be of well-qualified and younger Russians, it could be argued that economic motives continue to be of paramount importance. Indeed, as a number of commentators have suggested, the dramatic increase in the exit of ethnic Russians from Central Asia since the early 1990s has been due in part to the changing socio-economic status of Russians vis-à-vis the titular Central Asians, with the former losing their competitive advantage compared with the titular nationalities.[45]

Yet while the exit of Russians from Central Asia follows a chain-like or sequential migration, in which the able-bodied and younger males tend to constitute the first wave of migration, one study found a particularly large number of women and dependants – particularly children – in the migrant population.[46] As Pilkington notes, 'where people leave generally peaceful situations, dependent children are a de-motivating factor but where there is ethnic or social tension they become a reason to migrate'.[47] In a study in the mid-1990s of returnees in the Orel region of Russia, among the reasons given for leaving the post-Soviet south were poor inter-ethnic relations (38 per cent), discrimination against Russians (27 per cent), general socio-economic situation (13 per cent) and the growth of Islam (12 per cent). However, over 70 per cent cited the 'future of their children' as their reason for leaving, making it by far the most common response. Thus,

> while generally the presence of family dependants – children – is considered to be a de-motivating factor in migration decisions, since they must be properly housed and provided for in education, in the current migration of Russians ... the presence of young children ... is a motivating factor in the migration decisions.[48]

Although this study does not claim to be representative of Russians leaving Central Asia, these findings suggest that the migration flows from the region represent more an involuntary exit than one of choice.

Conclusions

This chapter has explored some of the multiple ways in which ethnic Russians in the post-Soviet borderlands have responded to the nationalising regimes. In the case of the Baltic states and Central Asia, diasporic responses have been conditioned by the available political opportunities, political resources and survival strategies. While in the case of Central Asia this has been expressed in a politics of exit, in Estonia and Latvia a desire to remain in the place of settlement has dominated but responses have still varied greatly, with some accepting that the only way to secure future prosperity is through negotiating the boundaries of citizenship by learning the state languages. While many ethnic Russians in the post-Soviet borderlands display some of the features of a diaspora, most notably in still envisaging Russia as a place of refuge and/or as a homeland of cultural affinity, many also display the features of what Cohen labels 'a stranded minority' whose collective sense of identity and willingness to engage in collective action remain limited. However, identities are rarely static, and much will depend upon the ways in which the politics of the diaspora continue to be played out between the borderland regimes and Russia, and on the way in which the Russian minorities themselves redefine their sense of identity in relation to both Russia and the borderlands.

Notes to Chapter 4

1 R. Brubaker, *Nationalism Reframed. Nationhood and the National Question in the New Europe* (Cambridge, Cambridge University Press, 1996), p. 103.
2 G. Smith, V. Law, A. Wilson, A. Bohr and E. Allworth, *Nation-Building in the Post-Soviet Borderlands. The Politics of National Identities* (Cambridge, Cambridge University Press, 1998).
3 A. Motyl, 'After Empire. Competing Discourses and Inter-state Conflict in Post-imperial Eastern Europe', in B. Rubin and J. Snyder (eds), *Post-Soviet Political Order. Conflict and State-Building* (London, Routledge, 1998), p. 16.
4 P. Kolstoe (ed.), *Nationbuilding and Ethnic Integration in Bipolar Societies. The Cases of Latvia and Kazakstan* (Oslo, University of Oslo, 1998); N. Melvin, *Russians Beyond Russia. The Politics of National Identity* (London, Royal Institute of International Affairs, 1995); J. Chinn and R. Kaiser, *Russians as the New Minority. Ethnicity and Nationalism in the Soviet Successor States* (Boulder, CO, Westview Press, 1996).
5 R. Cohen, *Global Diasporas. An Introduction* (London, Routledge, 1997).
6 G. Smith and A. Wilson, 'Rethinking Russia's post-Soviet diaspora. The potential for political mobilisation in eastern Ukraine and north-east Estonia', *Europe–Asia Studies*, 49(5), 1997, pp. 845–64.
7 G. Smith, 'The ethnic democracy thesis and the citizenship question in Estonia and Latvia', *Nationalities Papers*, 24(2), 1996, pp. 199–216.
8 R. Rose and W. Maley, 'Nationalities in the Baltic States. A Survey Study', *Centre for Public Policy*, no. 222 (Glasgow, University of Strathclyde, 1994).
9 G. Smith (ed.), *The Baltic States. The National Self-determination of Estonia,*

Latvia and Lithuania (London, Macmillan Press, and New York, St. Martin's Press, 1994).

10 *Atmoda,* 22 June 1989.

11 A. Steen, *Between Past and Future. Elites, Democracy and the State in Post-Communist Countries. A Comparison of Estonia, Latvia and Lithuania* (Ashgate, Aldershot, 1997).

12 E. Andersen, 'The legal status of Russians in Estonia's privatisation', *Europe–Asia Studies,* 49(2), 1997, pp. 303–16.

13 A. Hanneman, 'Independence and group rights in the Baltic states. A double minority problem', *Virginia Journal of International Law,* 32(2), 1995, p. 512.

14 Naturalisation Board of the Republic of Latvia, *On Naturalisation in Latvia* (Riga, 1997), pp. 56–63.

15 *Panorama Latvii,* 20 January 1993.

16 *Diena,* 23 June 1998

17 *Diena,* 5 October 1998.

18 R. Keohane, 'The institutionalisation of the new world order', *Relazioni Internazionali,* 1990, p. 10.

19 Estonian Government, *Roadmap to Reform. Estonia's Future Plans in the field of European Integration* (Tallinn, 1997), p. 5.

20 Smith (ed.), *The Baltic States.*

21 *Diena,* 14 May 1998.

22 For a fuller discussion of the role that limiting political opportunities can have in influencing the nature and form of collective action, see Smith and Wilson, 'Rethinking Russia's post-Soviet diaspora'.

23 Smith (ed.), *The Baltic States.*

24 *Molodezh Estonii,* 10 August 1996, p. 1; *Vybory presidenta Rossiiskoi Federatsii 1996. Elektoral'naya statistika* (Moscow, Ves' mir, 1996), p. 147.

25 *Diena,* 4 March 1998.

26 D. Laitin, 'Language and nationalism in the post-Soviet republics', *Post-Soviet Affairs,* 12(1), 1996, pp. 4–24.

27 *Diena,* 20 February 1995.

28 D. Trenin, *Baltiiskii shans. Strany Baltii, Rossiya i zapad v skladyvayushcheisya bolshoi Evrope* (Moscow, Carnegie Endowment for International Peace, 1997).

29 Tartu Ulikooli Turu-uurimisruhm, *Kirde-Eestii Linnaelanike Suhtumine Eesti Reformidesse Ja Sotsiaalpolitikasse* (Tallinn, 1997).

30 V. Tishkov, *Ethnicity, Nationalism and Conflict in and after the Soviet Union. The Mind Aflame* (Oslo, Prio, and London, Sage, 1997), p. 116.

31 Smith *et al., Nation-Building in the Post-Soviet Borderlands,* p. 206.

32 M. N. Shahrani, 'Islam and the Political Culture of "Scientific Atheism" in Post-Soviet Central Asia', in N. Bordeaux (ed.), *The Politics of Religion in Russia and the New States of Eurasia* (Armonk, NY, M.E. Sharpe, 1995).

33 A major exception to this was the Uzbek Popular Front Movement, *Birlik,* which in a short period in the late 1980s was able to mobilise up to half a million people.

34 Tishkov, *Ethnicity, Nationalism and Conflict in and after the Soviet Union.*

35 Kolstoe (ed.), *Nationbuilding and Ethnic Integration in Bipolar Societies.*

36 Smith et al., *Nation-Building in the Post-Soviet Borderlands,* p. 142.

37 *Kazakhstanskaya Pravda,* 29 November 1996.

38 Kolstoe (ed.), *Nationbuilding and Ethnic Integration in Bipolar Societies.*

39 K. Dawisha and B. Parrot, *Conflict, Cleavage and Change in Central Asia and the Caucasus* (Cambridge, Cambridge University Press, 1997).

40 D. Heer and N. Youssef, 'Female status among Soviet Central Asian nationalities. The melding of Islam and Marxism and its implications for population increase', *Population Studies,* 31(1), 1977, pp. 155–73.

41 S. Akiner, 'Melting pot, salad bowl or caldron? Manipulation and mobilisation

of ethnic and religious identities in Central Asia', *Ethnic and Racial Studies*, 20(2), 1997, pp. 362–98.

42 Shahrani, 'Islam and the Political Culture of "Scientific Atheism"', p. 277.

43 J. E. Lane and S. Ersson, *Comparative Politics* (Cambridge, Polity Press, 1997), p. 226.

44 Yu. V. Arutynian *et al.*, *Russkie. Etnosotsiologicheskie ocherki* (Moscow, Nauka, 1992).

45 J. Dunlop, 'Russia. In Search of an Identity?', in I. Bremmer and R. Taras (eds), *New States. New Politics. Building the Post-Soviet Nations* (Cambridge, Cambridge University Press, 1997), pp. 29–95.

46 H. Pilkington, *Migration, Displacement and Identity in Post-Soviet Russia* (London, Routledge, 1998).

47 Pilkington, *Migration, Displacement and Identity*, pp. 122–3.

48 Pilkington, *Migration, Displacement and Identity*, p. 122.

PART

II

Experimenting with democracy

|5|

Limits to democracy

By the late 1990s, few observers would describe Russia or many of the other post-Soviet states as proto-democracies. Indeed, the post-Soviet states, like many other states elsewhere in the world that have emerged from totalitarian, authoritarian or semi-authoritarian rule in the 1990s, have shown a tendency to develop into illiberal democracies – regimes that are democratically elected but routinely ignore constitutional limits on their power and deprive their citizens of basic civil, political and economic rights. In such illiberal regimes, the rule of law is tenuous. Moreover, as one commentator has noted, 'far from being a temporary or transitional stage, it appears that many countries are settling into a form of government that mixes a substantial degree of democracy with a substantial degree of illiberalism'.[1] As Roeder points out in relation to the post-Soviet states, 'the most important political development in many of the 15 successor states has been the retreat from previous gains of democratisation and the consolidation of new forms of authoritarianism'.[2] Although contested elections have been held, a variety of authoritarian tendencies can be identified. Roeder's analysis suggests three types of polity: *autocracies*, in which power is concentrated in a strong presidency and elected representatives have only limited influence in the political decision-making process; *oligarchies*, in which policy makers are the agents of a broader set of interests or cliques who operate outside the central executive, notably within the state bureaucracy, but also in relation to the interests of powerful business leaders or clans who are not necessarily part of the state apparatus; and *exclusive republics*, in which policy makers are accountable to a restricted social stratum such as the titular nation. By the late 1990s, most of the Central Asian states and Belarus had fallen into the first category, Georgia and Tajikistan into the second, and Estonia and Latvia (as ethnic democracies) into the third category.

This chapter explores three aspects of post-Soviet Russian society that help explain the limitations on the development of a civil society and democracy, particularly at the local level. The first section examines the changing nature and role of grassroots social movements in Russia. While social movements initially seized the political opportunities created by Gorbachev's *glasnost'* and *perestroika* to mobilise citizens to engage in collective action, following the collapse of the Soviet Union the role of social movements in the political life of the successor states and in advancing the frontiers of democracy diminished. I focus on two of the most prominent contemporary social movements, those representing the interests of labour and the environmental lobby, and look at the problems they face in their attempts to articulate opposition to the new political order. The second section focuses on the closest point of contact between civil society and the state – local governance. It examines the way in which local urban government has been affected by the political transition, and explores the difficulties that citizens still face in securing a meaningful voice in the running of their cities. The final section examines one of the most powerful challenges to democracy, the growth of organised crime. It considers the reasons for the explosion in organised crime since the early 1990s, and the uphill battle the state faces at the local, regional and national level to maintain its monopoly over the rule of law – an essential component of a sustainable democracy.

Democratic challenges: the role of social movements

The existence of social movements, the sorts of causes they espouse and groups they represent, as well as their relationship with the state, reveals much about the nature and extent of the post-Soviet democratic transition.[3] While political theorists generally consider a social movement to be a group promoting a particular form of organised collective action, Foweraker's understanding of a social movement is particularly germane to the post-Soviet experience: 'In the ... context of partial democracy', he writes, 'the best working definition of a social movement is a popular organisation which can make plausible claims to exercise a perceptible impact on the extension and exercise of the rights of citizenship'.[4] There is little doubt that the emergence of social movements in the late 1980s – which mobilised whole localities into collective action, from the Union republics through to the industrial coalfields and cities – played a key role in challenging Soviet power and extending the social boundaries of citizenship. But now power has changed hands it is not so certain that the political projects these movements espoused – including greater citizen participation, decentralisation and social justice – are still on course to be realised.[5] Moreover, compared with the late 1980s, social movements now play only a marginal role in political life. Such a development is not uncommon in transitional polities because social movements often decline or die out once a cycle of protest activity has passed.[6] For Toraine, however, this decline has been especially dramatic in post-communist countries. He argues that 'consciousness, politics and social movements play a marginal role in the tumultuous changes that are taking place, while economic changes have absolute priority. The market is replacing the party-state as the absolute master of society'.[7] It would therefore seem that citizens have become merely spectators who vote. As Bahry and Way note, Russia's citizens tend to confine their political participation solely to elections.[8]

Within social movement theory, two approaches are particularly useful to facilitate understanding of the changing role of social movements in the post-Soviet states. The first, associated with resource mobilisation theory, focuses both on the political opportunities for collective action and on the resources a movement has for mobilising constituent support (including movement aims, organisation, financial resources and leadership). As Jenkins and Klandermans note, 'social movements develop in a context defined by the state and the representative system, which affords opportunities for mobilisation and sets limits on the effectiveness of movement strategies'.[9] Thus, democratisation furnishes social movements with greater political opportunities to articulate the public's demands. Not surprisingly, social movements tend to be more evident in those post-Soviet states, such as the Baltic republics, Ukraine and Russia, where democratisation has gone furthest, and least evident in places such as Uzbekistan and Belarus, where they are openly repressed by the state. Yet paradoxically, the very channels that are opened up as a result of democratisation may also lead to the decline of social movements because multiparty elections and other means of access to the political process provide citizens with new channels for articulating social demands. Thus, in transitional polities, social movements are often replaced by political parties or turn into parties themselves. In some of the post-Soviet states, the environmental and women's movements have made this transition, assuming the status of parties. Similarly, the emergence of new social cleavages and political issues following independent statehood can also result in the fragmentation of movements previously united by a common cause. As Lane observes in relation to democratising states more generally,

> once the transition [to democracy] has been accomplished, the people are no longer univocally represented in civil society *versus* the state. Instead, democracy invites a proliferation of interest groups which fill the space of 'a civil society' – but are not necessarily linked to a political conscience in the way civil society theorists would like.[10]

In contrast, the identity-oriented approach explores social movements from the point of view of the political identities and collectivities they wish to defend. Manuel Castells, the doyen of this approach, is concerned primarily with the way in which identity mediates social movement activity.[11] For him, a movement's self-identification – what the social movement is and on behalf of whom it speaks – is of paramount importance. But he also looks at the movement's adversary, a principal enemy identified explicitly by the movement, and the movement's goals, the kind of social order it wishes to attain. This chapter looks at the labour and environmental movements in Russia using a combination of the *resource mobilisation* and *identity-oriented* approaches. Overall, it is suggested that the appearance of new political opportunities has reshaped the nature of the movements' activities as well as the strategies available to them, while a broader range of political identities are evident within these movements as a consequence of the new contexts in which they find themselves.

The labour movement

Despite its high profile, one of the features of the labour movement in the late 1990s compared with the early years of political transition is the more limited scope and intensity of its engagement in collective action, most notably through the use of the strike weapon. This may seem surprising given the dramatic fall in workers' real wages and the concomitant decline in urban living standards in the 1990s. However, there are a number of reasons for this trend. First, a type of social partnership appears to have been struck up between government and the new capitalist elite on the one hand and representatives of labour, namely the trade union movement, on the other hand. According to Schmitter's classic argument, such a corporatist approach is likely to produce less protest from labour than non-corporatist politics, because corporatist interest mediation contributes to narrowing the gap between societal claims for improved economic performance and social equity and the capacity of the state to satisfy these claims.[12] In the case of Russia, most trade union leaders seem to believe that, in the present stage of economic transition, it is in the interests of their members to work with the state and capital in order to secure the conditions for economic growth. Consequently, post-Soviet Russia's union leaders have not espoused a traditional class-based approach. Rather, calls for collective action, when they occur, are based upon defending the rights and general well-being of workers within the contextual limits of a state working towards maximising market-based economic growth.

While corporatist politics have played an important part in limiting opportunities for citizen-worker activism, fear of unemployment has also dampened enthusiasm for collective action. Although unemployment, even by the standards of late modern democracies, is relatively low and wage levels in some sectors are comparable with those in Third World countries, its consequences are still greatly feared by a labour force used to decades of full employment. Anxiety is further compounded by the low level of unemployment benefit paid to claimants. In short, fear of unemployment discourages what is generally the main form of collective social protest taken by a labour movement – strike action – which in turn favours corporatist politics and undermines the bargaining role of the unions.[13] As a consequence, rather than engaging in social movement activity, workers tend to prefer to spend their time supplementing their low incomes by working on their private plots or in the shadow economy.

While levels of unionisation remain high within the labour force, as was the case in Soviet times workers generally perceive unions to be remote, largely ineffective and untrustworthy. Their fragmentation into two types of union has also had major ramifications for worker solidarity. Although both espouse an identity based on defending workers' interests, the tactics they employ differ, which in turn affects the adversarial character of each. The best established and by far the largest of the union organizations is the Federation of Independent Trade Unions of Russia (FNPR), an umbrella group with a membership of about 40 million. The FNPR is the successor to the old Soviet trade union body and retained its mass membership, substantial funds and property. It has been critical of the government's stance on economic restructuring and privatisation, but has also often retained a special relationship with enterprise managers, reminiscent of the close ties that existed between local trade union officials and economic management during Soviet times. As a consequence, as Morvant and Rutland note, the FNPR is 'better suited to work with management to exact concessions from a third party, such as the government, than to defend workers against management'.[14] The other major union group, the so-called free or new trade unions, which include the Association of Social Trade Unions (or Sotsprof) and the Independent Miners' Union, emerged in the late 1980s. Membership of these unions is far smaller, and their organisational and financial resources are limited compared with those of the FNPR. While generally more supportive of the government and its market reforms than the FNPR, the new trade unions have pursued a different strategy of collective action by focusing their energies on defending workers against economic management. The similarities and differences between the two, using Castells's threefold typology of identity, adversary and goal, are shown in Table 5.1.

Table 5.1 The labour movement in Russia

Type	Identity	Principal adversary	Vision/goal
Established labour movement (FNPR)	Workers	Central government	National economic growth; defending rights in the workplace; safeguarding and securing improved living standards for members
Independent labour movement	Workers	Local authorities and enterprise managers	National economic growth; safeguarding and defending rights in the work place; safeguarding and securing improved living standards for members

For both types of union, one issue has been the main focus of social protest since the mid-1990s: the slow- or non-payment of wages to members. Indeed, for many workers, the non-payment of wages has become an only too painful alternative to mass unemployment during the period of economic reform.[15] According to official sources, between 1995 and 1997, about 70 per cent of workers have experienced irregular wage payments; in about a quarter of cases, such delays have exceeded one month.[16] A geography of wage arrears is also notable: arrears tend to be especially high in localities administered by poorer local authorities, which cannot afford to pay public sector workers such as teachers, and where workers are concentrated in the least competitive and traditional manufacturing sectors still reliant upon state subsidies, such as the defence industry. Although relatively well-off, one of the hardest hit regions has been Kemerovo *oblast'*, where in 1995–97 delays in the payment of workers' wages were double the one-month national average and were nearly three times as high in the region's major industry, coal mining.[17] Wage arrears have led to collective action, mainly strikes. As Table 5.2 shows, nearly two-thirds of Russia's provinces have been affected by strike action. Although the average strike has lasted less than 1 week, such collective action has done considerable damage to the economy. In May 1998, for example, strike action by coalminers in southern Siberia led to the blockading of the Trans-Siberian railroad, bringing havoc to the country's transport system.[18]

Table 5.2   The strike movement in Russia, 1995–96

	1995	1996
Number of regions in which strikes were recorded[a]	55	62
Number of strikes where strikes lasted longer than a single shift	8,856	8,278
Total participants in strikes (thousands of people)	489	663.9
Loss of work caused by strikes (thousands of worker days)	1,400	4,009.4
Average length of strike (in days)	2.8	6

[a] Out of 89 federal regions/ethnorepublics.
Source: A. Katsva, *Alternativy*, 2, 1997, pp. 36–7.

The strategies and tactics adopted by the two main union groups have frequently differed. The FNPR has tended to focus its energies on the government as adversary, in effect working with employers and local and regional authorities in order to secure rectificatory justice. The union remains suspicious of the state's claim that enterprise managers and local authorities are largely responsible for wage delays because of economic mismanagement and corruption. Because of the organisational resources at its disposal and a larger membership, the FNPR has been able to organise nationwide strikes, as it did in both 1996 and 1997. However, the response to strike calls has varied considerably from region to region, and the majority of industrial action has been localised. Moreover, such tactics have exacted only limited, short-term concessions from the state rather than a serious commitment to tackling the structural nature of the problem.

In contrast, the new trade unions have focused on local economic management as the adversary. Moreover, rather than engaging in strike action, these unions have concentrated on taking legal action against enterprise managers for wage delays on a case-by-case basis using Article 96 of Russia's Labour Code, which states that wages must be paid no more than 2 weeks in arrears. This strategy of supporting individual workers willing to take their employers to court has met with some success. However, its impact has been limited to bringing about a change in policy within individual workplaces or under the jurisdiction of a particular city council or occasionally a regional authority.

The environmental movement

The environmental movement has also proven to be amongst the most resilient of Russia's social movements. It was the first to emerge in the mid-1980s and remained at the centre of social protest throughout the late Soviet period. In contrast with the labour and nationalist movements, it was able to take early advantage of a reforming state that did not regard the issues it highlighted as a challenge to the legitimacy of state socialism. As a consequence, the environmental movement became a platform for bringing together and mobilising other forms of social protest that were united in their commitment to challenging the Soviet State. As Yanitsky notes,

> Even at the start of perestroika, when hundreds of thousands of people could be mobilised to take part in mass protest campaigns, this mass mobilisation was a result of a general readiness of the population to take part in *any* protest act ....[19]

Nonetheless, this did not mean that environmental issues were an unimportant motive for collective action. Environmental degradation affected whole communities in very direct and visible ways, and concerns about pollution from chemical plants or the consequences of large-scale development projects proposed by the state mobilised whole communities into collective action.[20] More than any other event, it was the catastrophe at the Chernobyl nuclear power plant in Ukraine in April 1986 that put the environment on the agenda. The far-reaching social and economic ramifications, including the devastating effects of radiation contamination and the creation of ecological refugees, raised the profile of environmental issues well beyond the local communities whose health and livelihoods were directly affected by the disaster, and did more than any other single event to expose the myth that, through socialist planning, Soviet socialism had secured the foundations for the safe management of the environment.[21]

Since the early 1990s, the environmental movement has become more diverse and fragmented in its aims and activities. From local communities engaging in collective action, it has become more global in scope as environmental groups have seized upon the opportunities to reframe their identity politics and to internationalise their networks of social support. The state and its polluting industries, the focus of early environmental protest, are no longer the only grievance. As the state has relinquished control over large parts of the space-economy and as Russia and the other post-Soviet states have opened up to the global capitalist economy, so new sites of protest have emerged. In sum, new, refined boundaries of protest and resistance have emerged within the environmental movement, espousing a variety of aims, adversarial politics and identities. These are encapsulated in the fivefold categorisation of environmental groups set out in Table 5.3.

Table 5.3   The environmental movement in Russia

Type	Identity	Principal adversary	Vision/goal
Green politics	Global	Uncontrolled global and local development	Sustainable restructuring
Alternativists	The green self	Marketisation	Decentralised communities based on 'ecologically sound places'
Eco-patriots/ eco-nationalists	Homeland-nation	Scale and speed of marketisation, polluters, centralisation	Territorial power
Defence of local space	Local, urban or regional community	Polluters, centralisation	Quality of local life
Environmental conservationists	Nature lovers	Uncontrolled development	Environmental preservation

Source: adaptation of the more general schema of Castells (1997) and applied to Russia.

The self-styled 'alternativists' share some of the beliefs of the so-called 'Green groups'. The underlying philosophy and aims of both are based on securing an appropriate balance between the material well-being of the communities they seek to represent and harmony with nature. To varying degrees, both groups draw their inspiration from the writings of eco-socialists such as the German philosopher Rudolph Bahro and from Germany's Green movement. Some of the more radical alternativists also draw their inspiration from the ideas of the late nineteenth-century Russian anarchist and geographer Peter Kropotkin and his utopian vision of ecologically balanced communities, in which mutual aid was seen as the chief force for survival, protection and progress.[22] Initially, such groups had close connections with the late 1980s peace movement. The Ukrainian Ecological Association, for example, grew out of Ukraine's Peace Movement. Since then, however, important differences have emerged between the alternativists and the Greens. The former embrace a more utopian politics, central to which is the idea of 'the green self', and include such groups as Ecopolis Cosino, which takes its inspiration from the works of Kavtaradze, a Russian writer whose vision of a post-material world is based on the notion of creating 'ecologically sound places' or ecopolises that should replace the deteriorating environments or megalopolises such as Moscow and St. Petersburg.[23] In contrast, the 'Green groups' tend to focus on the health and living conditions of citizens affected by environmental devastation. Like Greens in the West, they advocate policies of sustainable development, or, more place-specifically, sustainable restructuring, meaning liberalising the space-economy so that it does not adversely affect the environment. They include groups such as the Socio-Ecological Union in Russia, an organisation with branches nationwide whose origins date back to the mid-1980s, and, of more recent vintage, Greenpeace Russia – set up with support from Greenpeace International – which tends to focus on opposing large-scale projects of national or global significance. Seizing upon the opportunities created by the post-Soviet pluralist electoral system to promote environmental concerns, some of these Green groups have transformed themselves into political parties. Their appeal, however, is largely confined to the more educated social strata whose social values are less preoccupied with economic growth than with more general quality of life issues.

In contrast, eco-nationalists or eco-patriots are concerned primarily with prioritising the interests of their particular national homelands rather than with the appropriate universal relationship of society to nature. Two particular variants of such a homeland eco-nationalism can be identified. First, there are groups inspired by nineteenth-century Slavophilism and the importance of preserving something of the supposedly simple rural life of the pre-industrial Russian peasant. This grouping is opposed to large-scale industrialisation or urban growth, is highly suspicious of Westernisation and is supportive of a regulated market. Not surprisingly, it is associated with Russian neo-nationalism. The other variant comprises environmental groups which identify the environment with their people's cultural self-preservation. Many of these groups are linked to the indigenous people of the Russian far north, who are concerned about the way in which their traditional cultures and economic livelihoods are being threatened or even destroyed by the economic and social restructuring of their communities.

Like eco-patriot groups, there are also a plethora of localised environmental groups whose priority is to defend their own spaces from environmental harm, be it their neighbourhood, city or regional community. These groups tend to be more spontaneous and reliant on the support of other environmental organisations, and the duration of their activity is limited, focusing on the environmental consequences of a pollutant or development project.

Finally, there are the environmental or nature conservation groups. During the previous regime, it was this form of environmental concern, primarily because of its focus on what the authorities deemed to be a relatively harmless, romanticised view of nature protection, which was the most tolerated. The conservationist movement, however, has learned much from the strategies of other environmental groups and today pursues similar tactics, although its successes have also been limited. One example concerns opposition to plans to build Russia's first high-speed rail link between St. Petersburg and Moscow, a project that involved construction in the Valdai National Park, one of Russia's most beautiful and unspoilt nature reserves.[24]

Despite the limited successes of the environmental movement, there is no doubt that the political opportunities that have opened up have provided scope for more effective collective action. Decentralisation and the federal form of governance have created multiple access points. Most notably, social movements have the opportunity to influence the political process through local referendums. A federal law on referendums says that citizens have the right to call such a vote in their region if it is supported by a petition signed by at least 2 per cent of the local electorate. The referendum strategy has been pursued by a number of environmental groups. The first and most successful case was in Kostroma. In this region, anti-nuclear activists, led by a local environmental group 'In the Name of Life', succeeded in collecting 36,000 signatories, well above the 10,000 required by law, in support of a referendum calling for work on a nuclear power station to be halted. This was despite the impact the abandonment of the project would have on regional employment. Construction of the plant had begun in 1981, was suspended temporarily in 1990 in the wake of the Chernobyl disaster, but got under way again 2 years later. In the regional referendum in December 1996, 87 per cent of those who voted were opposed to the plant's completion; turnout was relatively high, at 59 per cent.[25] This outcome encouraged other environmental groups to pursue similar strategies, though they have had less success. In Krasnoyarsk, environmental groups secured well over the required number of signatures to hold a referendum on the construction of a nuclear waste processing plant, but the regional authorites refused to hold the poll, agreeing instead to a special enquiry by ecological experts into the health and safety implications of the project – a decision interpreted by the region's environmental lobby as no more than a delaying tactic.[26] In another region, Rostov, the anti-nuclear movement, led by the so-called Rainbow Keepers, a nationwide environmental group, has been protesting against the completion of a nuclear power plant near

Volgodonsk. Their campaign has been hampered by the regional authorities' insistence that the signatures of a daunting 10 per cent of the electorate must be gathered in order to force a referendum.[27]

The environmental movement has had only limited opportunities to boost its standing by winning the support of Green political parties or other parties sympathetic to environmental concerns. Although Green parties exist, they have been unable to win enough votes to gain parliamentary representation. Moreover, tension between environmental groups and Green parties, particularly over what party leaders see as the less orthodox activities and tactics pursued by some of the more radical local groups, has weakened the effectiveness of the environmental lobby. Some environmental groups, notably Greenpeace Russia, have tended to put their energies into building links with other like-minded groups, both in the neighbouring post-Soviet states and in the West. But although Greenpeace Russia has benefited from its connections with a well-funded organisation such as Greenpeace International, most environmental groups lack the basic financial or organisational supports necessary to run a successful social movement. Indeed, although environmental groups can draw upon the resources of a well-educated leadership, including eco-specialists, 'their intellectual capacity does not compensate for their lack of material resources'.[28] These limitations are compounded by the attitude of the mass media, which have increasingly moved away from covering, and thus politicising, environmental issues. On many occasions, the media have been downright hostile to environmental groups. The globalisation of local Green politics, for example, has been represented by some of the Russian media as unacceptable meddling by Western social movements in Russia's internal affairs. Local protesters opposing the building of the nuclear power plant in the Rostov region were represented uncompromisingly as 'unpatriotic' and even as the agents of 'foreign sources'.[29]

From the comparative perspective, there are important differences between the environmental and labour movements in Russia, particularly in the nature of their identity politics and in the aims and strategies that each has followed. However, parallels can be drawn between the features displayed by these two movements and those generally attributed to 'traditional' and 'new' social movements in late modern democracies.

1. The labour movement in Russia, like traditional social movements in the West, has a clearer social support base and identity, whereas Russia's environmental movement, like new social movements in the West, has a less clear appeal to one social group.
2. Russia's labour movement has a developed formal organisation, seeks political integration with the state and focuses on political rights in similar ways to its equivalents in the West. In contrast, Russia's environmental movement is similar to new social movements elsewhere, in that it is more concerned with changing societal values, attitudes and behaviour

than with direct interaction with the state. It aims to refuse power rather than take it.
3. The labour movement in Russia is more reactive and defensive, whereas the environmental movement, as in the West, tends to be more proactive.

Whither local democracy?

One of the main indicators of the success of any democratic transition is the extent to which political power has been decentralised and the say local communities have in governing their own affairs. Given that in Russia, and in most of the other post-Soviet states, citizens are now fully urbanised, it is the city and its political institutions that offer vital clues to developments in local democracy. During the early 1990s, a range of urban social movements, typically organised under the umbrella of a local movement for democracy, won political power in a number of Russia's major cities. Yet despite those political changes, debate continues on whether the form of urban governance now in place facilitates genuine local democracy. One school of thought holds that political transition has resulted in the meaningful devolution of political power and that urban municipalities and their locally elected representatives are playing a key part in building local democracy.[30] In contrast, it is also suggested that, despite regime change, there is a remarkable continuity in the way cities are governed. They argue that rather than becoming more autonomous and democratic, urban political institutions are in practice becoming more constrained by the centre and less accountable to their citizenry.[31]

There is, however, a consensus that, before the late 1980s, it was the centralised party-state, in effect the Communist Party, and not the local town council (or urban soviets), which governed the city. While the soviets were envisaged by early Bolshevik theorists as the political institution through which the local community would participate in the running of its affairs (as captured in the Bolshevik slogan 'All power to the Soviets'), such a system quickly became contrary to the requirements of the Stalinist State, which needed a highly centralised system and an obedient urban citizenry in order to plan and execute the country's transformation into a powerful urban-industrial machine. Although from the mid-1950s city soviets were granted some leeway to administer their municipalities (even a highly centralised state requires urban authorities to carry out certain localised functions and tasks), their autonomy remained heavily circumscribed. The urban authorities were delegated responsibilities in two main areas. First, they were given jurisdiction over collective urban consumption, i.e. in the provision of local public goods and services. This included administering such public services as housing, education, culture, health and the retail system. Urban soviets were not, however, given control over city budgets, and they had little scope to move capital from one budget sector to another. Local industrial enterprises shared the responsibility for housing workers, but housing policy was not always well co-ordinated between the two chief providers in a polity where accountability to the central institutions predominated. Second, the town soviet was given responsibility for the supervision and implementation of central policy regulations concerning a range of urban functions, from environmental pollution to urban-industrial development, through to monitoring zoning laws. It did not, however, have any power to legislate on local urban affairs.

Political representation within urban soviets was also circumscribed by the centre, which undermined the city's capacity to represent and reflect the interests of its local citizenry. So while representatives of the urban soviet were elected every two and a half years by local residents, the Communist Party played a key role in the nomination of those who were eventually permitted to stand for election. Without party approval, a candidate's name could not appear on the ballot paper. However, centrally imposed guidelines did facilitate the political representation of certain social groups – of women, old and young people, ethnic minorities and industrial workers – reflecting a policy of affirmative action designed to make the composition of locally elected representatives reflect the heterogeneity of urban society. Because citizens had a duty to vote and well over 90 per cent of the local electorate regularly turned out to do so for the only candidate standing in their neighbourhood or workplace, local election day itself was little more than a ritualised occasion for registering the supposed unity of the party-state and its citizenry. However, because the city's elected representatives were drawn from the local community, they were not immune to advancing local interests, but the degree to which they were willing to do so depended on their sense of civic consciousness and responsibility to the urban community. Occasionally, therefore, urban soviets came into conflict with both the local party machine and the centre.

Democratising municipal politics by institutional change was envisaged by the *perestroika* reformers as crucial to the more general democratisation of political life. This local dimension to the democratic transition came to the fore in 1988 when the Gorbachev administration signalled that local soviets were to become genuinely accountable to their citizens. Multiparty and multicandidate elections were held in 1990, ending 7 decades of Communist Party monopoly over local affairs. Local soviets were also given more responsibility for running cities, including greater control over budgets. With the 1991 local government reforms, local autonomy was further extended, enabling the soviet to be finally 'transformed from a rubber stamp to a deliberate policy making body by free elections and the demise of the Communist Party'.[32]

The question that then emerged was how to create a set of political institutions commensurate with the conduct of democratic and responsive local politics. The problems associated with such a gargantuan task are well illustrated by the experiences of Russia's second city, St. Petersburg. With a population of over five million, St. Petersburg is an influential city with a radical liberal tradition reflected in its history of being in the vanguard of support for political change.[33] In the 1990 city election, Leningrad (as St. Petersburg then was) saw its leading social movements progress from political opposition to political power. The city's Popular Front, a popular movement that embraced a plurality of democratic-based social interests, won two-thirds of the seats on the city council. Besides the Popular Front, other social movements also won political representation, including the Democratic Forum, human rights organisations and the Green movement. Not surprisingly, the institutionalisation of social movements resulted in a radical change in the roles of their leaders and activists[34] – a transformation not without its problems. As Duka goes on to note,

> the consequence of obtaining the majority of PetroSoviet [city council] seats had not been discussed nor was it expected. [The leadership's] inability to handle urban community problems was all too evident. There was a hysterical fear of winning. The question of readiness had not been raised. The focus was only on running for election.[35]

Besides having an unclear vision of what local democratisation should entail and a lack of experience in running a democratic city, on taking office the pro-reformers, once the leadership of the urban social movements, became increasingly distant and alienated from their social support base. Between 1991 and 1996, under the city's elected but increasingly controversial mayor, Anatolii Sobchak, local residents displayed an increasingly apathetic attitude towards local politics, as demonstrated by low voter turnout in local elections and poor attendance at public meetings. In part, this was a product of a decision by the Yeltsin administration to grant more powers to urban executives in order to counter-balance the continued presence of, if not control by, the Communist Party in many urban soviets, and to ensure that urban executives would be loyal both to the central administration and to the president personally. As mayor, Sobchak was given considerable powers, which brought him into conflict with the city soviet. From 1991 to 1993, there was gridlock that prevented agreement being reached on a coherent set of policies for the city. This was especially true with regard to housing. As a market reformer, Sobchak wanted to move fast on the privatisation of housing, a policy fervently resisted by the city soviet. Importantly, both the mayor and soviet lacked an institutional mechanism for resolving their differences. Each repeatedly declared the actions of the other to be illegal. In March 1992, a vote of no confidence in the mayor was passed by the city soviet. Sobchak, however, was offered a way out in October 1993. In line with the increasing centralisation of the Yeltsin administration following the crackdown on the Russian Parliament, local government was again reformed. This time the local soviets, seen by the Yeltsin administration as hotbeds of Communist Party support, were abolished and replaced by new local councils. St. Petersburg's 400-strong soviet was therefore abolished, and in the process of rewriting the city charter

Sobchak took many legislative responsibilities for himself. As the mayor of one of Russia's two cities with federal status (the other being Moscow), he enjoyed powers comparable to those of the governors of large Russian regions. As Yeltsin had decreed that governors and their equivalents could interpret rules governing local elections, Sobchak proposed that those who had not been resident in the city for at least 5 years be excluded from the right to vote in city elections. This in effect disenfranchised about one-fifth of St. Petersburg's adult population. Moreover, borrowing from a 1993 general election decree, he declared that turnout at local elections had to exceed 25 per cent of eligible voters before local elections could be valid.

In the 1994 St. Petersburg local elections, 75 per cent of the electorate did not participate, reflecting both confusion over who ran the city and the record of past urban mismanagement. Because only 25 of the 50 seats in the renamed city assembly were filled, the legislative branch could not meet until further elections secured the necessary two-thirds quorum, and urban government therefore collapsed. As Mellor notes, 'this electoral fiasco meant that there was no democratic forum for the city throughout 1994'.[36] Until November, when fresh elections were held, the mayor ruled the city unchallenged. In the subsequent mayoral elections of May 1996, however, Sobchak was defeated. Not only had his style of rule alienated local democratic groups and much of the local electorate, he had also come into conflict with the Yeltsin administration.[37] His administration was also the subject of widespread allegations of corruption, particularly in relation to housing privatisation.[38]

Thus, the process of urban democratisation, as illustrated by the experience of St. Petersburg, has been inhibited by the nature and slow speed of institutional change. As Mellor notes with regard to urban politics more generally, with the exception of the period from 1990, when city soviets were elected, to their abrupt abolition in October 1993, there is considerable continuity with the Soviet regime, the only major difference being the absence of the centre's monopoly over city politics through the Communist Party.[39] Democratic input has been minimal and there has been local subjugation to central directives, while local administrations have had low priority in the allocation of state funds. Urban political power has also been far from transparent. In a major survey of the St. Petersburg electorate conducted in 1995 and 1996, when asked who governed the city, respondents were divided almost equally among the city soviet, capital and organised crime.[40]

Yet urban government has also had some success in alleviating the negative consequences of central government policies in the sphere of collective consumption. Local governments have shown themselves to be more sensitive to the needs of their communities, particularly the vulnerable and disadvantaged. Most cities have to contend with a growing urban underclass – the poor, elderly, unemployed and poorly paid state-sector workers – who have either not shared in the benefits of market-led reform or have ended up as its victims. Some city authorities have attempted to assist the local poor, through wage compensation, assistance to families with children or invalids and by continuing to control prices of housing, public transport, retail services, leisure activities and funerals.

City policies in these spheres, particularly housing privatisation, have brought them into conflict with the centre. In 1991, the Russian government launched a far-reaching programme to transfer public housing to the market sector. It was, as Yeltsin put it, linked to creating a middle class of property owners who would support the rapid transition to a market economy. This policy began a major debate over whether the public sector should continue to provide housing for Russia's citizenry. As a large proportion of state housing is municipally controlled and managed, the issue for urban local authorities was how much privatisation should be carried out and to what timetable. There have also been disputes within city authorities on such issues. Fast-track privatisers, keen to generate capital, and urban budget officials concerned about reducing the spiralling cost of maintaining public housing have come into conflict with departments and other agencies concerned with social needs. Yaroslavl, a city with a population of just over 600,000, is probably typical of the way in which cities have approached these problems.[41] As part of Russia's privatisation policy, the city authorities began calculating initial land values in 12 zones of the city. These rates varied from a proposed land rent of 55,000 rubles per hectare in the city outskirts to 92,000 rubles in the more desirable city centre. Apartments smaller than or equal to the norm were to be transferred free of charge to private ownership. Special local provisions were introduced to expedite the free transfer of title deeds to the families of military officials and survivors of the Chernobyl nuclear disaster. These were more generous than those recommended by the central government. Residents of larger apartments were to pay an additional fee of 698 rubles per square metre of housing space above the city norm. Once the deeds had been obtained, a resident was able to rent or resell his or her apartment. Not surprisingly, privatisation proceeded fastest in the more desirable districts. But the opportunity was also taken up in many less desirable parts of the city as a result in no small measure of the mayor's encouraging Yaroslavl's citizens through a local publicity campaign to 'pass a valuable resource on to their offspring'. When Moscow decided to speed up privatisation in early 1993 and allow all residents to receive deeds at no charge irrespective of the size of their apartments, the Yaroslavl authorities were obliged to follow accordingly. But for a brief period at least, city authorities were able to demonstrate civic responsibility by a form of distributive justice that favoured the least advantaged within public sector housing.

The urban democratic process has also been hampered by the limited control the municipalities exercise over city budgets. According to Mildner, 'the centralist nature of local government finance in Russia, the lingering Soviet mentality governing the expenditure driven budget process, and the powerful position of regional administrations have so far crushed any

Table 5.4   Sources of revenue for selected provincial Russian cities, 1994

	Gatchina	Sosnovyi Bor	Vyborg	Voronezh	Syktyvkar
Federal tax shares	90.5	97.1	87.5	62.4	86.0
Central grants	NA	NA	NA	15.8	11.5
Local taxes	9.4	2.6	12.0	20.9	2.5
Privatisation	0.2	0.3	0.5	0.9	1.0

Figures given in per cent.
NA, data not available.
Source: adapted from K. Mildner, 'Underfunding democracy', *Transition*, 1(9), 1995, p. 51.

attempt at establishing local self-government or local democracy'.[42] So although urban authorities do enjoy greater control over urban spending than they used to, and the centre has legislated that higher levels of government are not to interfere in the urban budgetary process, in practice the amount of fiscal autonomy that the city has at its disposal is limited, and it remains highly dependent on both central and regional government. The cities' limited room for manoeuvre is evident in the way in which urban governments obtain their revenue. Although differences in the exact composition of revenue funding exist among cities (particularly between Moscow and St. Petersburg and cities with a lower status), there is also a remarkable degree of similarity, as Table 5.4 shows. Funding comes from the following four main sources:

1. *Federal taxes*. These account for as much as 90 per cent of municipal revenue. How much is allocated to the municipality is at the discretion of regional governments. No laws are yet in place about how much should be allocated to the cities. Consequently, how well cities fair tends to depend upon political discretion, the financial resources available to a regional authority, and the effectiveness of the city authority in annual bargaining rounds.
2. *Central grants*. These are intended to make up for shortfalls in urban government expenditures. Some of these central grants are intended for specific local capital investment projects or social programmes.
3. *Local taxes*. This revenue source, which comes from personal and corporate income tax, usually accounts for under 10 per cent of local revenues. Much of this tax accrues from new privately owned small and medium-sized enterprises. Municipalities with a higher proportion of small and medium-sized enterprises therefore tend to fair better. In contrast, cities dominated by one large state-controlled industry tend to generate the least local capital.
4. *Local privatisation*. This is from the sale of municipal property, including the privatisation of some urban services.

Cities therefore lack economic autonomy and are highly dependent in particular on other governmental authorities for generating revenue. The centre is also able to use federal taxes and the allocation of central grants as political leverage to influence municipal policy on spending. Despite this dependency on the centre, there is little incentive to seek alternative sources of income. If an urban authority succeeds in attracting external revenue, it then attracts less revenue from either federal taxes or in the form of grants. Yet urban public spending continues to fall far short of local consumption needs. Out of their meagre budgets, city authorities have to continue to provide basic service utilities (notably water, gas and electricity), nearly all welfare services (including education and health care), and the upkeep of housing stock, much of which is still in public ownership (see Table 5.5). Local authorities also have to finance the wages of large numbers of public sector workers. Consequently, most municipalities are faced with an ongoing financial crisis. Rather than providing relief, central government adds to their difficulties. First, the wage rates of municipal employees are fixed by the centre, although wages have to be paid out of local budgets. Second, central government continues to intervene with regard to policy on public sector housing and communal services. At one point ceilings imposed by the centre on rent increases prevented urban authorities from generating additional income by increasing rents. However, the artificially low prices maintained during the early post-Soviet period are being gradually liberalised, allowing urban authorities more room for manoeuvre.

Table 5.5   Privatisation of housing in selected Russian cities and regions, 1990–95

	1990		1995	
	Privatised apartments	Percentage of all apartments	Privatised apartments	Percentage of all apartments
Moscow city	2,800	0.10	1,199,000	41
St. Petersburg	200	0.01	361,000	29
Nizhnii Novgorod oblast	300	0.04	282,000	33
Novosibirsk oblast	200	0.03	283,000	35
Sakha (Yakutia)	300	0.13	47,000	19
Sverdlovsk oblast	500	0.04	513,000	39
Tatarstan	900	0.12	191,000	25
Ulyanovsk oblast	100	0.02	62,000	22
Yaroslavl oblast	200	0.05	120,000	32
Russian Federation	53,300	0.16	12,495,000	36

Source: Goskomstat Rossii, *Regiony Rossii 1997*, vol. 2 (Moscow, Goskomstat, 1997), pp. 460–2.

Challenges to democracy: the dual state

One of the major issues linked to democratisation in Russia and the other post-Soviet states is ensuring control over the rule of law throughout a state's territory – one of the basic functions of a democratic state. Since the early 1990s, Russia has increasingly taken on the features of a dual state, that is, a polity in which many aspects of economic, social and political life operate within the rule of law, but where a parallel or alternative state also exists outside the administrative and judicial structures of the sovereign state and where the rule of law is flouted or does not apply. This is the world of organised crime and corruption, which threatens to undermine the fragile foundations of democracy and the emergence of a civil society. According to a variety of accounts, this world is on the increase. One highly respected recent Western survey reported that corruption in the post-Soviet states was now the highest of any region in the world.[43] Russia, in particular, has emerged as a major centre of organised crime. By 1997, more than 9,000 criminal groups with an estimated 100,000 members existed in Russia alone.[44] Organised crime is not a phenomenon restricted to the largest cities. In Ryazan province, for instance, it was recently reported that a local 'mafia' (organised crime) group had successfully penetrated local law enforcement agencies, private businesses and the local authorities, and had been involved in more than 70 contract killings, large-scale extortion rackets and bombings of local businesses, resulting in the death of more than 100 people in the region.[45] Crime has multiplied within the countryside too. In isolated rural areas in Kemerovo and Penza *oblast's*, for example, armed racketeers have demanded protection money to prevent the theft of livestock and the destruction and looting of crops.[46]

What has emerged in Russia is an anarcho-capitalist society, one which is characterised by the growth of an entrepreneurial and dynamic market economy but where the rule of law is precarious and large-scale disorder is not far below the surface. While many observers acknowledge that there is a link between the growth of the market economy and the explosion in organised crime,[47] there have been few comprehensive attempts to theorise the relationship between economic transition and organised crime; one of these has been provided by Varese.[48] Drawing his inspiration from the classic works of Gambetta on organised crime in such transitional societies as Sicily and Italy,[49] Varese constructs a seven-stage causal-developmental model, which is summarised below:

1. If a (state) monopoly over property exists, there is no scope for the emergence of private suppliers of protection.
2. The end of monopoly over private property produces an increase in the number of people that own assets.
3. The number of transactions in which individual agents with property rights engage will grow substantially.
4. A demand for trust in whoever enforces property rights will emerge.
5. This demand will not necessarily be entirely met by the state, or at least not efficiently or quickly enough.

6. There will be scope for the private supply of protection as a substitute for trust.
7. A potential supply of private suppliers of protection is present.

Accordingly,

> Russia is undergoing a transition to the market which is in some crucial respects similar to the one experienced by Sicily in the nineteenth century. The spread of property has not been matched by clear property rights legislation, administrative or financial codes of practice, and the authorities seem ill-equipped to enforce them when they exist. Such a situation reduces trust in the state and fosters a demand for alternative sources of protection.[50]

Varese's thesis may be further elucidated and qualified.

Despite possessing a monopoly over the ownership of property during the Soviet period, the state was not in total control of its space-economy. As was noted in Chapter 2, a large non-state or second economy existed throughout the Soviet era. Existing in tandem with the socialist planned economy, the so-called 'shadow' or 'second' economy covered a vast and varied set of economic activities, ranging from those that were technically legal but outside the structure of the socialist planned economy to the outright illegal (involving drug trafficking, money-laundering and the pilfering of state property from the workplace). While organised crime groups did exist, composed in particular of small-scale Georgian, Armenian and Chechen 'blood Mafia', the most developed and sophisticated networks of corruption and organised crime were located amongst sections of the Communist Party itself, the *nomenklatura*, who were responsible for administering the economy and state bureaucracy. By virtue of their positions, the *nomenklatura* had the opportunity to become embroiled in various scams, including embezzling through falsifying or padding local, regional or sectoral production schedules, engaging in the illicit sale of goods and services, and even on occasion profiting from connections with drug trafficking and prostitution. One of the most notorious and highly publicised scandals during the Brezhnev years involved cotton production in Uzbekistan. There, high ranking members of the Uzbek Communist Party, including party secretary Sharaf Rashidov, were involved in falsifying the region's cotton production figures. They claimed billions of rubles from Moscow in exchange for 'virtual cotton', that is, cotton that existed only on paper. In what is probably the most insightful account of organised crime during the Soviet period, Arkadii Vaksburg recounts how easy it was for the Uzbek leadership to embezzle from the state:

> Cotton, produced almost entirely by sweated peasant labour without modern implements, brought these Mafiosi officials enormous profits. And who would refuse to increase his earnings by up to ten times if it cost no effort whatever to do so? One only had to add a nought here

or two or three noughts there to the records. One nought on paper was worth millions of rubles – the possibilities were enough to make the head swim.[51]

It was, however, the end of the state's monopoly on property ownership and the introduction in Russia of a large-scale programme of economic liberalisation and privatisation that created the opportunities for organised crime to flourish on a vast, unprecedented scale. In what has been dubbed the sale of the century, thousands of state enterprises and other state property were sold off. This was a largely uncontrolled and poorly regulated sale of state assets at bargain-basement prices to anyone who had money and power; thus it not only created a new stratum of property owners but also boosted the standing both of corrupt party officials and of organised crime. The sale of public property, in particular, provided considerable room for corruption. In Moscow in 1993, for example, the city authorities sold the rights to a large public building to five well-connected private companies for 1.5 million rubles in an auction closed to outsiders. A few weeks later, a second auction took place, this time open to the public, in which, following an exchange of bribes, the property was sold for 250 million rubles. The property was then put on the open market and sold for 1.5 billion rubles. In just 2 months, the property had increased in value a thousand-fold.[52]

Owing to the piecemeal way in which legislation over property rights has unfolded, there is considerable ambiguity in the field of ownership of land and housing, as well as in many other spheres of social and economic life where legislation has not kept pace with market reforms. The long absence of a copyright law is one example. Despite the ready market for bootlegged videos, musical recordings and so on, the state failed to produce a law to adjudicate on copyright. A 1994 study, for example, estimated that more than 95 per cent of all computer software distributed in the post-Soviet states was pirated.[53] Non-existent, incomplete and conflicting legislation has meant there is little public trust in the state's capacity to make effective, enforceable laws. Also, shortcomings in economic legislation make it easier to bypass the law.

The state's inability to protect private property or its owners' personal safety has weakened popular trust. The perception among citizens is that the state is no longer in control. Even everyday crime – even if it is not linked to organised syndicates – is considered a symptom of what Russians call *bespredel* (a state of lawlessness). As Table 5.6 shows, serious crime, notably violent crime, has grown dramatically in Russia and all the post-Soviet states. In the absence of effective legislation to protect property and the individual, individual offences and organised crime have therefore flourished. The average urban citizen in Russia is more than five times as likely to die a violent death than his or her counterpart in the UK or France. Kidnappings, arson attacks on businesses, gang shoot-outs and contract killings are now commonplace occurrences in Russia's major cities.

Table 5.6 Recorded violent crime in CIS countries, 1991 and 1996

	Number of recorded crimes		Recorded crimes (per 100,000 population)		Premeditated murder and attempted murder		Assault causing GBH		Rape and attempted rape	
	1991	1996	1991	1996	1991	1996	1991	1996	1991	1996
Russian Federation	2,167,964	2,625,081	1,463	1,780	16,122	29,406	41,195	53,417	14,073	10,888
South-western borderlands										
Ukraine	405,516	617,262	780	1,231	2,902	4,896	6,850	8,429	2,351	1,752
Belarus	81,346	127,232	792	1,238	546	1,130	1,258	1,895	706	555
Moldova[a]	44,530	44,485	1,021	1,030	290	523	517	630	347	322
Transcaucasus										
Armenia	13,109	12,479	363	330	220	160	253	179	48	38
Azerbaijan	15,617	17,528	216	232	489	545	397	350	48	73
Georgia	21,982	14,483	–	267	524	405	383	291	100	73
Central Asia										
Kazakhstan	173,858	183,977	1,030	1,151	1,732	2,625	3,667	4,059	1,654	2,025
Uzbekistan	88,630	65,980	423	282	1,062	1,153	1,342	946	568	808
Kyrgyzstan	32,061	39,623	699	836	366	519	568	522	352	362
Tajikistan	18,477	13,388	338	224	148	482	260	222	103	74
Turkmenistan	19,268	14,784	512	336	306	334	329	241	165	98

[a] CIS Statistical Committee estimate.
Sources: Data based on Russian Federation Ministry of Internal Affairs, Russian Federation Justice Ministry, CIS Statistical Committee, *Prestupnost' i pravonarusheniya (1991–1995). Statisticheskii sbornik* (Moscow, 1996); *Official Statistics of the Countries of the CIS, 1997–2* [CD-ROM] (Moscow, CIS Interstate Statistical Committee, 1998).

According to the Russian Interior Ministry, there were an estimated 450 contract killings in 1996 alone, only 60 of which were solved.[54]

The lack of trust in the state has created a vacuum that has quickly been filled by the mafia. Gambetta's observations concerning the role that organised crime can play in such situations are as relevant to Russia as they are to Sicily: 'The most specific activity of mafiosi', he notes, 'consists in producing and selling a very special commodity, intangible, yet indispensable in the majority of economic transactions. Rather than producing cars, beer, nuts and bolts, or books, they produce and sell trust'.[55] In short, the crime syndicates in Russia, as elsewhere, provide a kind of 'privatised Leviathan' by offering protection and security against chaos and disorder.[56] Choosing to obtain organised protection under such circumstances can hardly be considered irrational.

A flourishing private industry in personal and property security has developed because of the state's inability to fulfil its responsibilities to protect citizens. A number of urban municipalities, notably Moscow, have even responded to the high incidence of organised crime against property by offering 'extra police protection at a price' to guard businesses and their employees, while many law-enforcement personnel, attracted by the prospect of boosting their meagre salaries, are involved in moonlighting. The monetary incentives on offer mean that there is a readily available supply of highly specialised labour willing to make the transition to employment in organised crime. Many such criminals used to belong to the KGB or the Red Army, or were sporting figures. They range from former KGB code crackers to computer experts from the former military–industrial complex, and their skills are put to use in a vast number of illegal ventures, ranging from extortion to the growing 'cybercrime' industry. The equipment needed for protection rackets is also readily available, pilfered or bought from KGB, military and police units.

The mafia, organised crime and its globalisation

The above model, however, captures only part of the picture. Russia's integration into the global market-place has also resulted in organised crime's traversing its sovereign borders to become truly transnational in scope. Organised crime has in effect seized upon the opportunities opened up by Russia's more porous national borders to become global in its operations. So just as the legal Russian economy has gone global, so has its criminal economy. There are various dimensions to these activities. They include drug trafficking, with Russia emerging not only as a major transit route from Asian suppliers to markets in western Europe but also as a centre for the production and illegal export of manufactured drugs, such as amphetamines. The parlous state of the armed forces has also resulted in a lucrative trade in arms dealing and even in nuclear material. A lucrative industry has also developed in the smuggling out of precious raw materials, money laundering and trafficking in human beings.

Russian criminal groups also constitute part of a co-ordinated global network of crime syndicates. Russian mafia organisations now connect up with a variety of regional crime syndicates: the Italian, Sicilian, US (Gambinos) and Japanese (Yakuza) mafiosi; the Central Asian, Chinese (Sun Yee) and Columbian (Cali) drug cartels; as well as the Albanian and Turkish drugs traffickers. In November 1994, for instance, it seems that a meeting of the world's leading mafia organisations took place in the French town of Beaune: Russian mafia groups were welcomed by other representatives of an elite global club of organised crime syndicates to discuss carving up the market in western Europe for drugs, prostitution, smuggling and extortion rackets, and to consider greater co-operation and to pool expertise.[57]

Thus, democracy in Russia and the other post-Soviet states is being challenged not only from within but also by the global nature of organised crime. Organised crime is playing a part in shaping the economic fortunes of Russia and the other post-Soviet states. In Latvia, for instance, money laundering involving criminal groups from Russia and Ukraine has emerged as a major destabilising factor. Laws against the free exchange of the ruble and hryvna into hard currency in Russia and Ukraine has meant that banks in Latvia, where there were no exchange controls, have become one of the major destinations for mafia-capital from the East. According to one study, 70 per cent of Latvian bank deposits in 1993 originated in part or in whole from illegal activities.[58] While such financial transactions represent a major flow of foreign capital into Latvia, which could be passed on as credit and share holdings to legal private businesses, thereby aiding the transition to a market economy, at the same time, Latvia's capital city, Riga, has begun to earn the reputation as a centre for mafia banking, which has reduced the city's attractiveness to more legitimate inward capital investment. In Russia, foreign investment, which is crucial for economic recovery, has also been put off by the prevalence of extortion and racketeering. Organised criminal groups have emerged as 'national gatekeepers', offering foreign companies their protection services. It is estimated that by the mid-1990s, about half of Western businesses in Russia had to deal with such problems. The global nature of organised crime has also facilitated capital flight, which has done much to weaken post-Soviet economies, in particular the Russian economy.

The globalisation of crime has also shaped the nature of relations among states as the criminal economy, and attempts to police its activities, take on international proportions. Concern over the discovery of radioactive materials from Russia in Germany, for example, spurred closer co-operation between the intelligence services of the two countries, while Hungary and other European countries have shown increasing concern over Ukrainian and Russian crime syndicates' involvement in drugs, prostitution and protection rackets in their cities.[59] Russia and Switzerland have focused on ways to combat money laundering. According to the Swiss authorities, suspiciously large Russian deposits in Swiss banks, totalling some 3.2 billion dollars, were made in 1996 alone, a large proportion of which were thought to emanate from organised crime.[60]

Notes to Chapter 5

1 F. Zakaria, 'The rise of illiberal democracy', *Foreign Affairs*, 76(6), 1997, p. 24.
2 P. Roeder, 'Varieties of post-Soviet authoritarian regimes', *Post-Soviet Affairs*, 10(1), 1994, p. 61. For a fuller discussion, see K. Dawisha and B. Parrot, *Democratic Changes and Authoritarian Reactions in Russia, Ukraine, Belarus and Moldova* (Cambridge, Cambridge University Press, 1997).
3 G. Diligenskii, 'Chto my znaem o demokratii i grazhdanskom obshchestve?', *Pro et Contra*, 2(4), 1997, pp. 5–21; A. Zubov, 'Sovremennoe russkoe obshchestvo i "civil society": granitsy nalozheniya', *Pro et Contra*, 2(4), 1997, pp. 22–37.
4 J. Foweraker, *Theorising Social Movements* (London, Pluto Press, 1995), p. 114.
5 B. Kagarlitsky, *Restoration in Russia. Why Capitalism Failed* (London, Verso, 1995).
6 S. Tarrow, *Power in Movement. Social Movements and Contentious Politics* (Cambridge, Cambridge University Press, 1998).
7 A. Toraine, *What is Democracy?* (Polity Press, Oxford, 1996), p. 175.
8 D. Bahry and L. Way, 'Citizen activism in the Russian transition', *Post-Soviet Affairs*, 10(4), 1994, pp. 330–66.
9 J. Jenkins and B. Klandermans (eds), *The Politics of Social Protest. Comparative Perspectives on States and Social Movements* (London, University of London Press, 1995), p. 7.
10 M. Lane, 'Tom Paine and civil society', *New Left Review*, 214, 1997, p. 44.
11 M. Castells, *The Power of Identity* (Oxford, Basil Blackwell, 1997).
12 P. Schmitter, 'Still the century of corporatism?', *Review of Politics*, 36(1), 1974.
13 L. Holmes, *Post-Communism* (Oxford, Polity Press, 1997), p. 278.
14 P. Morvant and P. Rutland, 'Russian workers face the market', *Transition*, 2(13), 1996, p. 11.
15 S. Clarke, P. Fairbrother and V. Borisov, *The Workers' Movement in Russia* (Aldershot, Edward Elgar, 1995).
16 A. Katsva, *Alternativy*, 2, 1997, pp. 36–7; see also A. Buzgalin and A. Kolganov, 'Russia's trade union movement today', *Prism*, 3(16), 1997.
17 Katsva, *Alternativy*, pp. 36–7.
18 *Segodnya*, 10 July 1998, p. 5
19 O.N. Yanitsky, 'The ecological movement in post-totalitarian Russia. Some conceptual issues', *Society and Natural Resources*, 9(1), 1996, p. 72.
20 P. Pryde, *Environmental Management in the Soviet Union* (Cambridge, Cambridge University Press, 1991).
21 Pryde, *Environmental Management in the Soviet Union*.
22 P. Kropotkin, *Mutual Aid* (London, Heinemann, 1902).
23 K. Pickvance, 'Social movements in Hungary and Russia. The case of environmental movements', *European Sociological Review*, 13(1), 1997, pp. 35–54.
24 *Delovoi Peterburg*, 30 June 1997.
25 *Nezavisimaya gazeta*, 20 November 1997.
26 *Nezavisimaya gazeta*, 20 November 1997.

27 *Nezavisimaya gazeta*, 20 November 1997.
28 Pickvance, 'Social movements in Hungary and Russia'.
29 *Segodnya*, 7 August 1997.
30 See, for example, B. Ruble, *Money Sings. The Changing Politics of Urban Space in Post-Soviet Yaroslavl* (Cambridge, Cambridge University Press, 1995); B. Michnik, 'An assessment of the growing local economic development function of local authorities in Russia', *Economic Geography*, 1995, pp. 150–70.
31 H. Hinton, 'Urban administration in post-Soviet Russia. Continuity and change in St. Petersburg', *Environment and Planning C. Government and Policy*, 13, 1995, pp. 379–93; K. Mildner, 'Underfunding democracy', *Transition*, 1(9), 1995, pp. 50–4; R. Mellor, 'Through a glass darkly. Investigating the St. Petersburg administration', *International Journal of Urban and Regional Research*, 21(3), 1997, pp. 481–503.
32 Hinton, 'Urban administration in post-Soviet Russia', p. 381.
33 L. Trautmann, 'Fuhrungswechsel an der Newa. Burgermeister- und Prasidentenwahlen in St. Petersburg', *Osteuropa,* 46(11), 1996, pp. 1124–405; Hinton, 'Urban administration in post-Soviet Russia'.
34 A. Duka, 'Transformation of local power elites. Institutionalisation of social movements in St. Petersburg', *International Journal of Urban Regional Research*, 21(3), 1997, p. 433; see also R. Orttung, *From Leningrad to St. Petersburg. Democratisation in a Russian City* (London, Macmillan Press, 1995).
35 Duka, 'Transformation of local power elites', p. 436.
36 Mellor, 'Through a glass darkly', p. 495.
37 *Rossiiskaya gazeta,* 7 February 1996.
38 Trautmann, 'Fuhrungswechsel an der Newa. Burgermeister- und Prasidentenwahlen in St. Petersburg'.
39 Mellor, 'Through a glass darkly'.
40 V. Golofast, T. Protassenko and O. Bozhkov, 'The elite of St. Petersburg as seen by the city inhabitants', *International Journal of Urban and Regional Research*, 21(3), 1997, pp. 406–24.
41 Ruble, *Money Sings*.
42 K. Mildner, 'Underfunding democracy'.
43 A. Brunetti *et al.*, 'Institutional obstacles to doing business. Region-by-region results from a worldwide survey of the private sector', *World Bank Policy Research Paper,* no. 1759, 1997.
44 *Rossiiskaya gazeta*, 13 June 1997.
45 According to a 1997 Interior Ministry Report of Russia, as reported in *Rossiiskaya gazeta*, 3 December 1997.
46 F. Varese, 'Is Sicily the future of Russia? Private protection and the rise of the Russian mafia', *Archives Européennes de Sociologie*, 35(2), 1994, pp. 224–58.
47 M. Goldman, 'Why is the Mafia so dominant in Russia?' *Challenge*, January–February, 1996, pp. 39–47; J. Millar, 'What's Wrong with the Mafia Anyway? An Analysis of the Economics of Organised Crime in Russia', in B. Kaminski (ed.), *Economic Transition in Russia and the New States of Eurasia* (Boulder, CO, Westview Press, 1997), pp. 206–19; see also G. Fiorentini and S. Pelzman (eds), *The Economics of Organised Crime* (Cambridge, Cambridge University Press, 1997).
48 Varese, 'Is Sicily the future of Russia?'.
49 D. Gambetta, 'Fragments of an economic theory of the mafia', *European Journal of Sociology,* 29, 1988, pp. 127–45; D. Gambetta, *The Origins of the Mafias* (Cambridge, mimeo, 1991)
50 Varese, 'Is Sicily the future of Russia?'.
51 A. Vaksburg, *The Soviet Mafia* (London, Weidenfeld and Nicolson, 1991), p. 114.

52 *Forbes Magazine*, 27 September 1993.
53 Varese, 'Is Sicily the future of Russia?'.
54 RFE/RL on-line report, 20 January 1997.
55 Gambetta, 'Fragments of an economic theory of the mafia', p. 128.
56 R. Putnam, *Making Democracy Work. Civic Traditions in Modern Italy* (Princeton, Princeton University Press, 1993).
57 *The Sunday Times*, 29 March 1998.
58 N. Dale, 'The globalisation of the Latvian economy since 1991', *International Politics*, 33(1), 1996, pp. 97–108.
59 On the Hungarian case, see K. Schelter, 'Bedrohung durch die russische Mafia', *Internationale Politik*, 52(1), 1997, pp. 31–6.
60 ITAR-TASS, 30 January 1997.

6

Multiculturalism, federalism and democracy

Because all the post-Soviet states constitute multicultural societies – societies which include a variety of national and ethnic groups – managing multiculturalism has had to form an integral part of each polity's project of governance. While some of the more democratised states have experimented with accommodationalist strategies towards their minorities, the governing elites of other polities tend to equate the dominant nation with the state and have shown little sympathy towards minority demands. Consequently, as Gurr notes, 'efforts at so-called nation-building led by a dominant group almost invariably threaten minorities who regard themselves as separate people'.[1] Neither the scale nor range of minority demands for recognition shows signs of abating as minorities seek ways of redefining their political status in relation to the way in which they are governed and with whom they are governed. Minority demands continue to take a multiplicity of forms. At one end of the spectrum are minorities that reject membership of the political space to which they currently belong and engage in secessionist struggles, either to create their own national political space or to be reunited with co-nationals in another common political homeland (Fig. 6.1). At the other end of the spectrum are minorities that aspire to their own autonomous political spaces (e.g. the Crimean Tatars in Ukraine and the Gagauz in Moldova) or, in the case of minorities that are not settled in a compact area, seek alternative institutional means of securing political representation and support for the preservation of their languages, cultures and way of life (e.g. Poles in Lithuania, Ukrainians in Russia, Roma in Moldova).

That such a politics of multiculturalism remains so important raises two key questions about the nature of political transition. The first concerns the strategies of governance that have been adopted to manage multiculturalism and their relative success in reducing ethnic tension and violence. The second concerns the extent to which such forms of governance can be regarded as commensurate with interpretations of a socially just polity, in which the political aspirations of the majority and minority alike are represented and

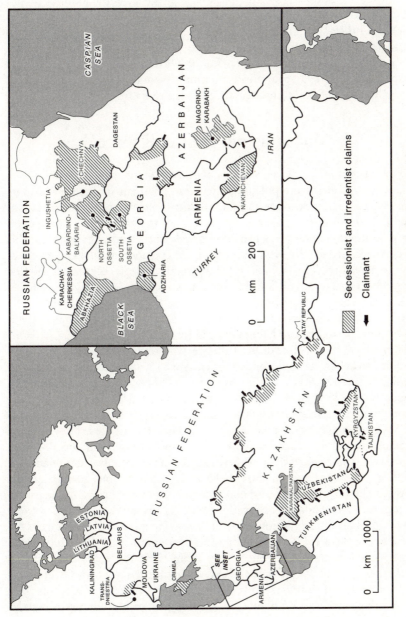

Figure 6.1 Secessionist and irredentist claims in the post-Soviet states.

respected. This chapter explores these themes. First, it identifies and examines the range of strategies of multicultural governance adopted by the post-Soviet states. It then goes on to look more closely at one of those strategies, federalism, as adopted by the largest post-Soviet multicultural polity, Russia. It explores the making of post-Soviet federal Russia and the way in which the process of federalisation has responded to multicultural politics and then examines attempts since 1996 to develop a more coherent federal policy. Finally, it considers the question of whether a democratic federation can provide an effective antidote to minority and majority nationalism, which threatens to destabilise Russia and lead to its fragmentation.

Managing multicultural space

To govern multicultural space, the post-Soviet states have drawn upon a variety of strategies, from policies designed to eliminate multiculturalism by creating a more homogenous national political space to those aimed at managing the phenomenon. A useful taxonomy of methods of conflict regulation in multiethnic polities is provided by McGarry and O'Leary,[2] and this has been adapted to provide a framework for considering the experiences of the post-Soviet world (Table 6.1). Of the eight strategies identified, the first four seek to end multicultural differences, while the remaining four aim to manage the consequences of multiculturalism. More than one strategy may have been used simultaneously, while others may have been pursued for only a short period before being replaced by another policy.

Eliminating multiculturalism is in one way or another associated with attempts to make national and political space geographically congruent. The most extreme variant of this involves acts of genocide: 'the intention to destroy physically a whole or substantive part of a group because they are members of that group and whose membership is defined by the perpetrator'.[3] While no part of the post-Soviet world has experienced the systematic genocide or ethnic cleansing which has characterised the break-up of Yugoslavia, and none of the post-Soviet states has officially sanctioned such a policy, acts of genocide have been committed by one group against another. The most notable case concerns the disputed enclave of Nagorno-Karabakh in Azerbaijan. Large numbers of the enclave's Armenian settlers had to flee their homeland for Armenia following a series of pogroms in the region in the early 1990s. Another strategy for eliminating multiculturalism is the forced migration of one group from their place of settlement to another. Also in the Caucasus, the exit of Ingush from North Ossetia was bound up with the desire of many Ossetians to reclaim the republic as their exclusive and undisputed homeland following Ingush attempts to reclaim areas that had belonged to their autonomous republic prior to World War II. Since October 1991, some 34,000 to 64,000 Ingush settlers have been forced to flee the republic for neighbouring Ingushetia as a result of clashes

Table 6.1   Methods for eliminating and managing multicultural space

Type	Examples
1. Methods for eliminating multicultural space	
(a) *Genocide*	Pogroms in Nagorno-Karabakh (early 1990s)
(b) *Forced-population transfers*	Ingush from North Ossetia (1992 and 1996) Georgians from Abkhazia (1992–93)
(c) *Territorial self-determination*	Trans-Dniestria from Moldova; Abkhazia (1992–93) and South Ossetia attempt to break away from Georgia; Chechnya' s secession from Russia, (1990–96)
(d) *Integration and/or assimilation*	Ukrainophone Russians
2. Methods for managing multicultural space	
(a) *Nationalising state practices*	To varying degrees, all the post-Soviet states (one particular variant of this is *ethnic democracy*, applicable to Estonia and Latvia)
(b) *Arbitration (third party intervention)*	Russia's intervention in Tajikistan, Trans-Dniestria and Georgia; OSCE mediation in Estonia, Latvia, Georgia, Crimea and Chechnya
(c) *Consociationalism or power-sharing*	A form of limited pseudo-consociationalism in Ukraine since 1994, limited to elite consultation between Ukrainians and Russians
(d) *Federalisation*	Russia (following the introduction of its 1993 federal constitution)

between the two communities, in which more than 600 people have been killed.[4] However, cases of ethnic violence have been restricted largely to the post-Soviet south and were more common during the chaotic early rather than the later period of political transition.

The number of cases of territorial self-determination through the creation or reorganisation of polities in the post-Soviet states – the third strategy of eliminating multicultural space – has been less widespread than was originally predicted, although secessionist demands by ethnoregional groups continue to loom large on the political agenda in a number of states, including Azerbaijan (Nagorno-Karabakh), Ukraine (Crimea) and Georgia (South

Ossetia and Abkhazia). In at least two cases, however, Chechnya (Russia) and Trans-Dniestria (Moldova), such demands have resulted in the emergence of new *de facto* sovereign borders, although in neither case has this led to the *de jure* establishment of new sovereign political spaces.[5] Although the Russian military fought in vain for 2 years to keep the breakaway republic of Chechnya within the Russian Federation, the republic has not won *de jure* independence or foreign recognition. For the small, predominantly Slavic enclave of Trans-Dniestria, whose already poor economy has suffered as a consequence of conflict with the Moldovan government, it seems that some form of compromise will eventually be agreed whereby the region is granted a form of regional autonomy but formally remains within the Moldovan state.

The final strategy of eliminating multicultural difference, that of voluntary integration (or cultural assimilation), generally involves the creation of a common homeland identity that transcends ethnic or other forms of cultural difference. While many of the post-Soviet states proclaim their commitment to such a goal, there is little evidence to suggest that it has been realised in any of them. The chances for the success of this strategy are the greatest where ethnic differences have become depoliticised as a result of overlapping identities, as in the case of some ethnic Russian Ukrainophones in Ukraine, and where the incidence of inter-ethnic marriage is high, as in parts of Latvia and Lithuania. For the time being, however, numerous obstacles hinder the creation in the post-Soviet states of common homeland identities based on two-way multilingualism and fair access to political opportunities and employment for all ethnic groups.

Strategies for managing multiculturalism have been used more frequently. However, these are not necessarily commensurate with democratisation and democratic practices. As was seen in Chapter 4, nationalising state tendencies, the most widespread of the strategies for managing multiculturalism, may conflict with democratic practices. Political elites in the post-Soviet states have often responded to the challenge of multiculturalism by attempting to ensure the cultural and even political dominance of the homeland nation by giving them a predominant position in the political, administrative and coercive apparatus of the state, making it difficult for those who are not deemed to belong fully to the homeland polity to gain access to key socio-economic and political positions. Tension between a dominant nation and subordinate ethnic group as well as outright conflict has on occasion led to the adoption of the second strategy for managing ethnic difference – arbitration by a third party. Two mediators have played the role of arbiter in the post-Soviet states. Russia, in its self-designated role as Eurasia's policeman, has brokered peace deals in conflicts in Tajikistan, Moldova and Georgia. However, although Russian mediation has enjoyed some success in producing a greater degree of stability in the countries concerned, it has largely been perceived as an instrument for reasserting Russian control over the region.[6] The efforts of the other major external actor – the OSCE (the Organisation for Security and Co-operation in Europe) – have also met with some success in reducing inter-ethnic tension, for example in Georgia, Crimea, the Baltic states and Chechnya.

None of the above strategies, however, has laid the foundations for the coexistence of ethnic groups by institutionalising multicultural democracy. The remaining two strategies – consociationalism and federalism – are generally held to offer better prospects for stable coexistence. Multicultural management through consociationalism, or power-sharing between major ethnic groups, is usually seen as requiring the representation and accommodation of political elites from all the major ethnic groups within government; the right of each ethnic group to veto controversial legislation or policies; and the right of each ethnic group to cultural autonomy. While some Western-liberal theorists regard consociationalism as a possible solution to ethnic tension in societies such as Kazakhstan and Latvia, based on power-sharing between their two respective major ethnic groups,[7] the only state that has come close to adopting some elements of consociational politics is Ukraine. Sensitive to the ethnic divisions between the more Ukrainian and nationalist west and the predominantly Russophone, more conservative and communist-oriented east, Kiev has, since 1994, been keen to pursue more accommodationalist policies towards its eastern half. Though not institutionalised as part of a formal strategy, Ukrainian politics has entailed one aspect of power-sharing, i.e. bringing representatives of both the west and east into national coalition governments.[8] Following the March 1998 parliamentary elections in Ukraine, which saw the Communist Party gain the largest number of votes, this strategy of incorporating elites from the two major communities is likely to be increasingly important if the alienation of one or other community is to be avoided.[9]

The only post-Soviet state to use federalism to manage multiculturalism is Russia. With by far the largest number of ethnic groups (some 140), it faces the greatest multicultural challenge. Russia has the task of resolving a series of ethnic conflicts in Chechnya, North Ossetia, Dagestan and Ingushetia, where demands for minority recognition are being played out with often tragic consequences. Yet while Russia's experiment with federalism is generally interpreted as an attempt to ensure the successful transition to democracy while retaining the state's territorial integrity, doubts have been expressed over Russia's claim to constitute a federation based on democratic principles. The federal constitution adopted in December 1993 proclaimed (Chapter 1, Article 1) that 'Russia is a democratic federative law-based state', but a state's claim to federal status must rest on more than an assertion that it constitutes a federation. The shift towards more authoritarian rule following the clash between the president and Parliament in autumn 1993, and the increased powers of the president vis-à-vis the new Federal Assembly and regional and local government, cast doubts upon Russia's claim to democratic status.

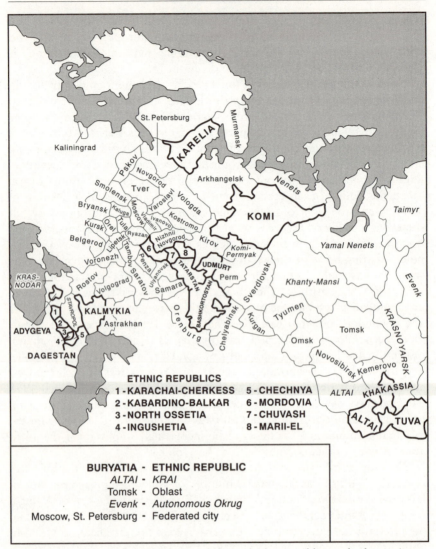

ETHNIC REPUBLICS
1 - KARACHAI-CHERKESS   5 - CHECHNYA
2 - KABARDINO-BALKAR   6 - MORDOVIA
3 - NORTH OSSETIA   7 - CHUVASH
4 - INGUSHETIA   8 - MARII-EL

BURYATIA - ETHNIC REPUBLIC
ALTAI - *KRAI*
Tomsk - Oblast
Evenk - *Autonomous Okrug*
Moscow, St. Petersburg - Federated city

Figure 6.2   The Russian Federation: federated ethnorepublics and other regions.

Nonetheless, Russia does contain some of the features generally associated with a federation.[10]

1. Representation is preponderantly territorial. Russia comprises 89 'federal subjects': 21 higher-status ethnorepublics, formed on national-territorial lines, and 68 lower-level subjects, formed on territorial lines – 49 regions (*oblast's*), 6 territories (*krais*), 10 autonomous districts (*okrugs*), the Jewish autonomous *oblast'*, and 2 'federal' cities (Moscow and St. Petersburg). (See Fig. 6.2.)

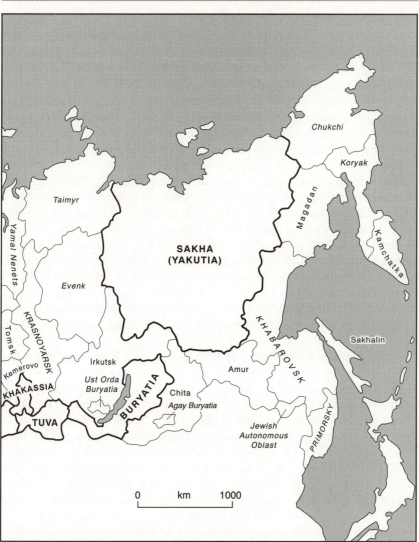

Figure 6.2 *continued*

2. Territorial representation is secured on at least two sub-national levels: namely 'local self-government' and 'regional government'.
3. Constituent units are incorporated into the decision-making process of the federal centre by representation in both the upper chamber of the Federal Assembly (the Council of the Federation) and the lower house (the State Duma). The 178-member-strong Federation Council comprises *ex officio* the heads of state of the ethnorepublics and regional governors, all of whom following a 1996 decree are popularly elected, and the heads of the regional legislatures.

The question of whether a multiethnic federation that seeks to accommodate some of its minorities by granting them ethnorepublican status will succeed in securing stability and social justice is hotly debated. Those who defend this policy hold that such an arrangement provides a means of managing inter-group conflicts that might otherwise develop into violence and lead to the proliferation of secessionist demands for independent statehood. Hence, the argument goes, the introduction of such a form of spatial governance has helped to weaken the drive for secession amongst minorities by providing an institutional alternative to nation-statehood. Furthermore, it is argued, federalism can be defended as a means of accommodating minority demands on the basis of the social value of group liberty. On the grounds that minority cultural self-preservation (as well as political representation) is of fundamental importance for individuals, because belonging to a minority culture provides a meaningful context for choice, the retention of group rights through federal supports is defended as a counterweight to majority group (Russian) cultural assimilation. Any conception of citizen entitlement should therefore be extended to protecting the right of minorities to be culturally different. Such an arrangement is justified, it is contended, so long as the basic rights of citizens who have different identity commitments to those of the titular ethnorepublic nation, or no such commitments at all, are protected.[11]

Those opposed to federalism on national minority lines argue that it promotes an exclusivist-nationalism, which increases the likelihood of inter-ethnic violence and even the prospects of regional secession.[12] Not only do such arrangements tend to solidify and make what might be temporary or partial group identities permanent, they also allow key policy areas to be hijacked by partisan ethnorepublican elites, and thus increase the probability of tyranny by the minority, in relation to federal politics in general as well as within the ethnorepublic, where in most cases the titular nation constitutes a demographic minority (Table 6.2). As Fedorov notes, such ethnorepublican elites have a tendency to use their status to obtain special privileges and rights through bargaining and political deals with the centre.[13] Thus, they are in a position to ignore basic federal obligations, which results in disproportionate contributions to the federal budget which are detrimental to the interests of both the federation and its poorer constituent units. Second, it is argued that, by empowering particular ethnorepublican minorities, the Russian federal arrangement imposes limits on genuinely pluralist interests because the demands and concerns of other forms of identity politics are downgraded or marginalised. Thus the capacity of the federal system to represent forms of collective identity other than those of the dominant ethnorepublican minority is invariably disadvantaged. In short, for proponents of a more liberal variant of federalism, it is of uppermost concern to counter domination by either nationalist-minded minorities or the majority national group (Russians) by prioritising the individual rights of citizens regardless of their ethnic or national affiliations. It is deemed best

Table 6.2   Ethnic composition of Russia's ethnorepublics

	Population (1989 census)	Titular nationality (%)	Russians (%)
Central Russia			
Bashkortostan	3,940,000	22	39
Chuvashia	1,340,000	68	27
Karelia	790,000	10	74
Komi	1,250,000	23	58
Marii-El	750,000	43	48
Mordovia	960,000	33	61
Tatarstan	3,640,000	49	43
Udmurtia	1,610,000	31	59
North Caucasus			
Adygeya	430,000	22	68
Chechnya[a]	1,270,000 (865,000)	(66)	(25)
Dagestan	1,800,000	80[b]	9
Ingushetia[a]	(300,000)	(75)	(13)
Kabardino-Balkaria	750,000	48 (Kabardins) 9 (Balkars)	39
Kalmykia	320,000	45	38
Karachai-Cherkessia	415,000	31 (Karachais) 10 (Cherkess)	42
North Ossetia	630,000	53	30
Siberia			
Altai	190,000	31	60
Buryatia	1,040,000	24	70
Khakassia	570,000	11	79
Sakha	1,090,000	33	50
Tuva	309,000	64	32

[a] The population of Checheno-Ingushetia was 1.27 million at the time of the 1989 census. The figures in parentheses are population data for Chechnya and Ingushetia on 1 January 1994. The nationality breakdown of the two republics is estimated on the basis of 1989 census data.
[b] The indigenous category includes Avars (28 per cent), Dargins (16 per cent), Kumyks (13 per cent), Lezgins (11 per cent), Laks (5 per cent), Tabasarans (4 per cent), Nogais (2 per cent), Rutuls (1 per cent), Aguls (1 per cent) and Tsakhurs (0.3 per cent).
Sources: *Demograficheskii yezhegodnik Rossiiskoi Federatsii 1993* (Moscow, Goskomstat, 1995); Goskomstat Rossii, *Regiony Rossii, 1997* (Moscow, Goskomstat, 1997).

therefore to confine ethnic or national identification to the private sphere. It should not be the function of the federal state, it is argued, to permit discrimination against the individual citizen by granting special privileges to particular national or ethnic groups.

Having sketched out the nature of the multicultural problem facing Russia, this chapter will now look at whether Russian federalism, driven in part by a commitment to minority representation, is likely to be successful in the long term, or whether Russia is adopting self-defeating structures vulnerable to the very centrifugal forces it is trying to manage.

Multiethnic politics and the federal process

Post-Soviet Russia's federal system has been shaped by three main tensions. First, conflict over the appropriate designation of powers between the centre and the ethnorepublics during the process of refederalising Russia, that is, during the construction of the present federal system after the collapse of the USSR. Second, tension arising from federal asymmetry – the unequal distribution of powers among Russia's ethnorepublics, on the one hand, and its regions, on the other – which raises questions concerning equality between the federation's constituent units. Third, the political debates within the Russian Federation and its constituent units on the issue of whether the federation should be structured on the basis of individual or ethnic group rights for its citizens.

Refederalisation: the politics of conflict

The problems multicultural Russia now faces are primarily a product of the way in which federal politics has evolved since 1990. Following the collapse of the Soviet federation and Russia's declaration of state sovereignty in 1990, attempts at refederalising Russia have been shaped largely by tensions between efforts to preserve Russia's territorial integrity and the ethnorepublics' drive for self-empowerment. The question of how best to divide powers between the centre and Russia's constituent units, especially the more vocal ethnorepublics, was one that the Yeltsin administration faced right from the outset. The Russian leader initially offered the ethnorepublics 'as much sovereignty as you can stomach',[14] a strategy motivated in part by his desire to secure a political power base in the republics during his battles with Gorbachev. The first attempt to provide a building block for refederalisation was the so-called Federal Treaty of March 1992, signed by 18 of the then 20 republics. Only Checheno-Ingushetia (which officially became two separate republics later that year) and Tatarstan refused to participate. The treaty permitted the ethnorepublics to adopt their own constitutions and laws, elect their own legislatures and heads of state, appoint their own supreme courts, have their own symbols of statehood and control many of their own resources. While this treaty, which allowed the ethnorepublics a higher status than the other regions, did appease most of the ethnorepublics, it also encouraged them to enact legislation that brought them increasingly into conflict with Moscow. Indeed, the failure to reach a fully workable compromise was one of the factors that led Yeltsin in 1993 to dissolve the Russian

Parliament and to reclaim the initiative for the centre by putting a draft federal constitution, written by his supporters, to a national plebiscite.

The provisions contained in the Federal Treaty formed the basis of those parts of the new federal constitution adopted in December 1993 that dealt with the delimitation of powers between the ethnorepublics and the federal centre, although no mention of the treaty itself was made in the constitution.[15] However, the constitution fell short of providing the scale of sovereignty many of the ethnorepublics had envisaged. Although it accepts the principle of national self-determination, it does not confer the right to secede. Chapter 1, Article 4, states that the Russian Federation 'ensures the integrity and inviolability of its territory'. This omission strikes at the heart of centre – ethnorepublican tensions. Some of the constitution's drafters viewed the right of the ethnorepublics to secede as a violation of Russia's status as an integral 'primordial-territorial' entity. The ethnorepublics, however, regarded the failure to include such a provision as the denial of a nation's right to self-determination. The 1993 constitution also contravenes a basic given in late modern democracies that central authorities may not unilaterally redefine the powers of its constituent units. In the Russian constitution, the president has been given both powers of judicial review (i.e. the right to suspend acts issued by the executive bodies in Russia's provinces) and of arbitration between federal and local bodies or between constituent members of the federation.

Several ethnorepublics felt that the constitution violated many of the autonomous rights previously embodied in the Federal Treaty. In the referendum, held on 12 December 1993, the constitution received support from only nine of the 21 republics. A majority of voters in seven republics rejected the constitution (Adygeya, Bashkortostan, Chuvashia, Dagestan, Karachai-Cherkessia, Mordovia and Tuva); the plebiscite was declared invalid in Tatarstan, where less than 14 per cent of the electorate voted; and Chechnya did not participate at all.[16] Despite protests from a number of the ethnorepublics that their consent had not been given to this pro-presidential constitutional variant, Deputy Prime Minister Sergei Shakrai was adamant that its introduction was legitimate because it had been endorsed by 58.4 per cent of those who voted: 'The constitution has been approved by citizens, not by the components. As citizens have approved it, the Constitution is now in force in all constituent parts of the Russian Federation'.[17]

With all 21 ethnorepublics introducing their own constitutions, a 'war of sovereignties' was waged between the republics and the federal centre. According to the Yeltsin administration, by late 1996 no fewer than 19 of the 21 ethnorepublican constitutions were in breach of the federal constitution.[18] Violations included declaring the republic a subject of international law, establishing illegal taxes and dues, and proclaiming the right to decide questions of war and peace and the right to grant citizenship. In an attempt to reclaim the initiative, and prompted by fears that the pro-independence policies of the Chechen government would spur on other republics to push for secession, Moscow began to negotiate a series of bilateral power-sharing treaties while continuing to claim that the federation was based on equality between its constituent parts.

Asymmetric federalism: the politics of differentiation

The evolution in Russia of an asymmetric federation is far from unique. As in Spain and Canada, developments in Russia demonstrate that federalisation may involve 'a post-constitutional process of reaching important agreements as much as it may rely on an original compact'.[19] Thus, as in Spain, expanding constituent governance has continued as part of an ongoing, fluctuating process in which an asymmetric federal construction has gradually unfolded, although in Russia the process has been less planned or systematically thought through than in Spain's transition to an *estado de las autonomies* (a state made up of autonomies). What also distinguishes Russia from other such experiments is the sheer extent of federal asymmetry: by March 1999, about 50 of its constituent units had successfully negotiated varying degrees of privileged status, with 'work in progress' on a dozen or so more.

Not surprisingly, considerable controversy has surrounded the question of whether the federation should be based on equality or differentiation of federal subjects. Initially, many federalists had supported the idea of the so-called 'republicanisation' of Russia, in which Russia's constituent units, following the recommendations of a parliamentary commission in November 1990, would be based on 50 or so non-ethnic-based constituent units similar to the German Länder. Under this scheme, the Russian *oblast's* were to be transformed into republics, which ensured that citizens, irrespective of their place of residence, would be entitled to equal rights. In the event, the proposals adopted by the presidium of Russia's Supreme Soviet in January 1992 won the day: a distinction was drawn between the ethnorepublics and the regions, with the autonomy of the latter more restricted than that of the former. The regions, for example, were allowed to adopt charters, while the republics had the right to their own constitutions. Although initially envisaged as a stop-gap measure, this system, which was clearly designed to appease the more bellicose ethnorepublics, formed the basis of the Federal Treaty and the constitution. Not surprisingly, it has attracted considerable opposition from the regions, which see it as creating two classes of citizens: those residing in the federation (the ethnorepublics) and those who have to abide by the rules of a unitary state (the regions).[20] In an attempt to appease the regions (and secure their support in the 1996 presidential elections), Yeltsin finally granted them the right to hold direct elections to the position of regional governor, a post that had hitherto been appointed by the president. This brought the regions closer to the status of the ethnorepublics and enhanced their position *vis-à-vis* the centre.

The signing of bilateral power-sharing treaties – beginning in February 1994 with Tatarstan, followed by agreements with a number of the other ethnorepublics and, from 1996, with several regions – has reinforced differentiation between the federation's constituent units. Designed to build bridges and in effect to rectify what the ethnorepublics, in particular, saw as the inadequacies of the 1993 constitution, the process has resulted in greater differentiation between individual ethnorepublics, but at the same time it has blurred the distinction between the ethnorepublics and some of the regions. Inter-republican differentiation is reflected in the language used in codifying the individual treaties. Tatarstan led the way in securing significantly more powers, concessions and advantages than the other subjects of the federation. The treaty it signed recognised the republic as a constituent member of the federation, but did not acknowledge the primacy of the federal constitution or Article 4 of that document (the inviolability of Russia and the superior status of the federal constitution and federal laws).[21] In contrast with Tatarstan, which is recognised as 'a state joined with the Russian federation', neighbouring Bashkortostan is 'a sovereign state within the Russian federation'. Kabardino-Balkaria is described as only 'a state within the Russian Federation', while Udmurtia is merely deemed to be 'a republic'.[22]

Rather than reflecting a decision to treat the ethnorepublics distinctively as part of a coherent nationalities policy, federal asymmetry appears mainly to mirror the anarchy of the political market place. The greater bargaining power of some ethnorepublics and regions compared with others, especially the resource-rich republics and regions, has been particularly evident in influencing political outcomes.[23] In short, developments since 1996 have done much to fuel demands amongst Russia's regions to extend the rights of the federation's constituent units by equalising their status relative to that of the ethnorepublics. This scramble to create a more symmetrical federation, however, has not been without its problems. As Valentei notes,

> everyone knows what separating one's children into favourites and others can result in. The effect has been analogous [in relation to the Russian Federation], a total lack of respect on the part of the children towards the parents and towards each other.[24]

Individual versus group rights: the politics of tension

The federal process has also straddled an uneasy compromise concerning the question of minority rights, of whether the citizen as an individually or group-constituted subject offers the better prospects for realising a democratised and stable federation. While elements of group rights have been incorporated into and recognised by both constitution- and treaty-framers, individual rights have taken priority on the basis of the premise that the rights of minorities can best be safeguarded through promoting individual liberties. This principle is reflected in both the 1992 Federal Treaty, which emphasised above all the rights and liberties of individuals as paramount, and the constitution, which is unequivocal in prioritising the equality of all people and subjects of the Russian Federation. Thus, the constitutional right to use a native language is informed largely by such liberal thinking. On the other hand, the federalising process reflects important collectivist principles with regard to ethnic minorities, not least the right of both sub-units and peoples to self-determination.

There are a number of probable reasons for framing minority rights in this way. In their desire to democratise, especially during the formative period in state formation (1990–93), liberals in post-Soviet Russia held up the Western-liberal model as the only proven antidote to the former state ideology, which in both institutionalising and practising collectivism had suppressed individualism and stifled individual freedoms. This meant embracing a conception of liberal democracy that entailed replacing what was deemed to be the repressive, as well as economically and socially sti-fling, collectivism of socialism with the economic freedoms of the market place. It also implied creating a non-ethnic secular state in which individual citizens, for the first time in Russia's history, could participate directly in the polity irrespective of their ethnicity, which it was felt should now be relegated to the private sphere. However, for Russian nationalists, liberal-individualism has also been used as a convenient smoke screen for promot-ing and safeguarding a majority nationalism that seeks to relegate expressions of minority ethnicity to the private sphere but to promote Russian ethnicity in the public sphere, on the basis of restoring the pur-ported dignity of the Russian people and the spirituality of the Russian nation.[25] Thus, for Russian nationalists, the rejection of group rights and the promotion of individual rights is also bound up with reclaiming their national homeland of Russia from a Soviet regime that was perceived as promoting the territorial rights of national minorities to the detriment of Russians. In short, many Russians felt that Soviet nationalities policy had made them an underprivileged majority in the Russian republic (RSFSR), their own national homeland. This was also reinforced by a widely held fear that the continuation and expansion of such preferential treatment for minorities would result in discrimination against Russians both nationally and especially in the ethnorepublics. Finally, for Moscow's federation-builders, there is the recurring fear that support for minority group rights promotes geopolitical chaos and fragmentation. In order to contain the envisaged anarchy of secessionist demands, the centre has shown a willing-ness to entertain granting concessionary rights only to the presently consti-tuted ethnorepublic federal units, in an attempt to thwart further group demands. It is a strategy which has also received a receptive hearing amongst ethnorepublican elites concerned about ensuring the hegemony of their own titular nations in areas where they are not in a demographic majority. In only five of the 21 republics does one titular nation constitute a clear majority: in Chechnya, Chuvashia, Ingushetia, Tuva and North Ossetia (Table 6.2).

In actuality, then, multicultural politics has been largely caught up with promoting the rights of either the majority or minority national group. As the Russian government's minister responsible for ethnic relations noted,

> today, collectivist values are as much part of Russia's culture as liberalism is in the West: today, collective rights for the people of Russia have not less but probably more meaning than individual rights, although the priority of the latter could be realised in the future. At least in Russia, individual rights will not become an absolute value as in the West, where this was achieved through the elimination of whole peoples and tribes notwithstanding 'sacred devotion' to humanistic values. Thank goodness that the Russian nation has historically been lacking such western hypocrisy.[26]

A Eurasianist vision of multicultural federalism

Despite legitimate claims that Russia has still to perfect a coherent and viable nationalities policy, a series of laws and decrees have been introduced since 1996 that constitute an attempt to rethink the relationship between federation and diversity. The most important and wide-ranging of these was a presidential decree (No. 909) issued in June 1996 approving the concept of the state nationalities policy of the Russian Federation.[27] Although a legally non-binding document, it represents the outcome of a compromise between the centre and constituent subjects on the most appropriate way of effecting a fairer and more equitable form of federal justice. Rather than simply looking towards a Western-liberal model or nationalist solutions, it is an attempt to develop a conception of distributive justice that encapsulates a variety of principles and solutions reflecting what might be more appropriately labelled as Russia's efforts to find 'a third way'.[28] In addressing both equality and difference among the federation's subjects and in attempting to stake the federation's future on what might be best described as a mixed-rights perspective on national minorities, it lays out a more integrated approach, albeit a schema which one political commentator interprets as 'a hybrid, an eclectic mixture of values'.[29]

One powerful normative conception of Russia that the decree proposes is the construction of the federation around a Eurasianist vision.[30] As Russia occupies a special and unique place within northern Eurasia, it is held that Russia must find its own particular niche and solutions to its cultural diversity. Accordingly, the goal of a multiethnic Russia is to ensure 'the cultural self-preservation and further development of national traditions and co-operation of Slavic, Turkic, Caucasian, Finno-Ugric, Mongolian and other peoples of Russia within the framework of Eurasian national-cultural space'.[31] Both European and Asian experiments with state-building are therefore rejected as inappropriate to what is deemed to be a more viable Eurasian way of 'harmonising the development of nationalities'. No doubt reflecting a concession to the majority culture, what is more problematic is the part ascribed to the Russians in this process:

> thanks to the unifying role of the Russian (*russkii*) people . . . , a unique unity and diversity and spiritual community and union of various peoples have been maintained. . . . Inter-ethnic relations in the Russian Federation will in large part be determined by the general national situation of the Russian people, a buttress of Russian Federation statehood.

Embedded in the ambiguity of Eurasianism are two conflicting normative interpretations of a multicultural Russia. One reading conveys a sense of federation working towards multicultural coexistence. Here the centuries-long intermingling of European and Asian cultures is seen as a positive, beneficial and enriching force, providing the potential for national coexistence on a variety of spatial scales – from the federal to the neighbourhood – based upon mutual recognition of the equal value of all national and ethnic cultures. It is an interpretation which within the public sphere at least is generally supported by the political leaders of the ethnorepublics.[32] The other reading, which gives ethnic Russians 'a leading role', is more problematic. In its more extreme form, it ascribes a special mission and identity to the Russian nation within post-Soviet Eurasian space. Herein lies much of the problem in reviving the conception of Eurasianism, which at least in terms of its original formulation holds that Russia's mission should be to promote the Russian language, culture and values as well as to reallocate a special role for the Russian Orthodox Church. This reading also reflects a crisis of national identity, of what it means to be an ethnic Russian in a territorially reduced and redesignated multicultural homeland. Thus, just as Soviet nationalities policy discouraged institutional, ethnic Russian nation-building within Russia proper (RSFSR) – with Russians instead being encouraged to think of the Soviet Union as their national homeland – so too is there a widespread feeling that Russia's post-Soviet federation has marginalised Russians and is designed exclusively to bolster minority nation-building institutions. Moreover, as noted in Chapter 3, for many ethnic Russians Eurasianism again raises the spectre of imperialist ambitions, of where the true boundaries of Russia should lie.

Besides emphasising the federation's commitment to the preservation and national self-determination of the ethnorepublics, the decree also offers the prospect for further regions to enter into power-sharing agreements with the centre, thus coming closer to Spain's model of offering autonomy to all constituent units that desire greater control over their affairs. This, however, it is made clear, 'does not mean that the aim is the "gubernization" [creating regions modelled on Tsarist guberniyas] of the republics or the "republican-isation" of the regions (*oblast's*) and districts (*krais*)'. Rather, the goal is to recognise 'the striving of peoples for self-determination and objective processes of integration into a Russian federated (*rossiiskoe*) society'.[33] It is a statement reminiscent of the dialectical policy of the Soviet regime, which envisaged both the flourishing (*rastsvet*) of the national cultures of its eth-norepublics through federal institutional supports and at the same time their moving closer together (*sblizhenie*) through the federation's commitment to greater socio-economic equalisation between its constituent parts. The decree thus emphasises the importance of 'equalising the level of socio-economic development of federation subjects', of allocating resources according to need and developing measures to boost the economy of depressed regions, notably of central Russia and the North Caucasus. Thus, federation is about promoting the redistribution of wealth, in a manner reminiscent of the way in which the policy of *sblizhenie* purportedly functioned during the Soviet period.

The goal of rectifying socio-economic inequalities embedded in this vision of federation raises an important issue that has become marginalised in Western discussions of the politics of multiculturalism. As Fraser argues, with regard to questions of social justice in late modern democracies, the dislodging of material inequalities from considerations of group rights has impoverished any coherent understanding of distributive justice; rather, 'justice today requires both redistribution and recognition'.[34] Hence, in any consideration of multicultural federation, it is argued that group rights should be rethought so that attention is paid not only to the right to be culturally different but also to ensuring that such a politics of recognition does not exclude considerations of the economically and socially disadvantaged. This is in effect where Walzer's proposition falls down:

> If some sort of union – federation or confederation – is our goal, the best way to reach it is to abandon coercion and allow the tribes to separate and then to negotiate their own voluntary and gradual, even if only partial, adherence to some new community of interest.[35]

Within the Russian context, such advice is an invitation to the economically powerful and more advantaged ethnorepublics to effectively renegotiate and reshape the fiscal framework of federation to their own advantage and so to the detriment of other less powerful and more economically disadvantaged constituent units. Moreover, while some of the poorest constituent units are ethnorepublics, many of the regions also suffer from severe economic impoverishment (such as Kostroma, Ivanovo and Pskov).[36] As a number of federalists in Russia have argued, any understanding of federal distributive justice should not lose sight of such inequalities; to do otherwise is likely to weaken support amongst the poorer ethnorepublics and Russian regions for recognition of the equal value of a multicultural federation.

The decree also attempts to broaden the remit of those who qualify for self-determination by addressing itself to those ethnic minorities who either do not possess their own administrative homeland or live outside the home-land claimed by their co-nationals (e.g. Tatars living outside Tatarstan). The authors in effect broaden the concept of federation by recognising 'multiple forms of national self-determination', including acknowledging the rights of those not represented as constituent federal subjects to national-cultural autonomy. This concept draws inspiration from the ideas of the late nine-teenth-century Austrian Social Democrats Karl Renner and Otto Bauer, who proposed a schema for the recognition of the group rights of the terri-torially non-represented. Thus, the decree acknowledges that the national minorities and especially 'the small scattered peoples' of the far north should be able to decide questions concerning 'the preservation and devel-opment of their customs, language, education, culture'. Accordingly, the federal authorities proposed setting up an Assembly of the Peoples of Russia, which would include representatives of dispersed minorities. In addition, in proposing a form of cultural subsidiarity within the localities, national-cultural autonomy signals not only the potential role that local government might play in 'directly reflecting residents'' interests and allow-ing a more flexible response to national needs, but also the participatory role that minorities and diasporas are encouraged to perform in creating 'self-governing public organisations in places of compact settlement' and in promoting their own 'local language media', which, it is intended, would be buttressed through state financial support. So far, however, the idea of national-cultural autonomy has had little success in capturing the imagina-tion of the territorially dispersed. The minority that has perhaps enjoyed the greatest success in attracting resources to promote cultural autonomy and local self-government are the Germans, who are scattered throughout cen-tral Russia and southern Siberia. Two such culturally autonomous districts have been set up in the Omsk and Altai regions, for example.[37]

While Decree 909 has generated a variety of debates concerning the bal-ance to be struck between competing visions of a multicultural federation, a more recent government resolution, concerning the abolition of nationality from the new internal passports, has rekindled tension between liberalism and nationalism. In arguably the most significant development in the federal nationalities policy since the introduction of the federal constitution in December 1993, a July 1997 government resolution, following a presiden-tial decree issued 4 months earlier, caused a storm of controversy by remov-ing the nationality entry – 'line 5' (*pyatyi punkt*) – from new internal passports to be introduced beginning in late 1997.[38] Its aim was to bring the new passports into line with the federal constitution, which states that citi-zens should not be obliged to define or declare their nationality. In purport-ing to resecure the importance of individual over group rights, it has been hailed especially by supporters of a more liberalising federation as refocus-ing on the importance of the individual over collective rights, and as central to weakening the manipulation of multiculturalism by nationalistically minded ethnorepublican elites.[39] This argument is developed further by

Starovoitova, who argues that 'line 5' is unnecessary in a civil society, where individuals should be equal regardless of nationality and that to retain such a designation would facilitate further discrimination within the ethnorepublics against the non-titular nationality.[40] Opposition, not surprisingly, has come from a number of the ethnorepublics, especially Tatarstan, whose State Council adopted a resolution in October 1997 halting issuance of the new documents in the republic. Regarded as a culturally assimilating resolution by Moscow, it has been widely interpreted in the republic as 'depriving ethnic groups of their identity' and as intending to 'destroy ethnic harmony'. In addition, it is also seen as representing yet another victory for those federalists who wish to replace the ethnorepublics with the 'gubernisation of Russia'.[41] While compatible with the universal practice in other multiethnic federations, opposition to the proposed reform reflects the continued significance that many ethnorepublican leaders give to the importance of 'line 5' as ensuring the formal reproduction of collective identities.

Federation, the ethnorepublics and social justice

The ethnorepublics display many of the features of 'nationalising regimes' of the sort that have emerged in the post-Soviet borderland states, despite the fact that they may frame their declarations of sovereignty in non-ethnic terms. The Sakha constitution, for example, opens, 'We, the multinational (*mnogonatsionalnyi*) people of the Republic of Sakha . . . .'[42] Political elites therefore have a tendency to equate their homelands with a national rather than a multicultural understanding of political space, where homeland-markers are culturally essentialised and taken as absolute, where there is little or no room for recognition of those individuals with overlapping or multiple senses of identity, and where the dominant nation claims monopoly rights over what is deemed to be the historic ethnic homeland. Such exclusivist claims imply, for example, that Russians who arrived in the ethnorepublics during recent decades should have their political rights restricted because they inhabited the region at a later period than the ancestors of the so-called homeland-nation. For those who hold with exclusionist principles, promoting expulsion, limiting immigration or assimilating co-nationals is often 'tactics' bound up with ensuring the pre-eminence of the homeland-nation within its political space. As such practices infringe upon the liberties of others, they cannot be justified with reference to group rights.

One of the most effective means of weakening such exclusivism may well be through federation. For weakly developed democracies, Walzer's formula therefore seems apt: 'the best hope for restraint lies . . . in federal or confederal checks and balances and in international pressure'.[43] This is not an argument that denies the principle of the right of nations to independent statehood but rather one which acknowledges that there are grounds to suggest that nation-statehood would for the moment at least lead to the far greater infringement of the rights of others. Thus, if it can be shown that secession would be likely to limit the liberties of other minorities and individuals or, through certain cultural practices, even the liberties of some of its own peoples, then there may be an a priori case for not supporting secession.[44] There are two points that are important to make in this regard.

First, demands for secession are not widespread in Russia: only two republics, Chechnya and Tatarstan, have, since 1990, demanded independence from Moscow. The other ethnorepublics seek only greater autonomy.[45] Although no referenda on secession have been held to test the ethnorepublic constituent democratic will, the weakness of other indicators of majority support for secessionism, such as secessionist-nationalist organisations, would suggest that, like their political elites, most ethnorepublican constituents see their future best served as part of a federation, or in the case of some, notably Tatarstan and probably Sakha, through a confederal arrangement. The reasons why secession is so weakly developed include perceptions of economic unviability and the prospect of being materially worse off outside the federation. On the basis of rectifying a past injustice of involuntary incorporation into Russia, a criterion generally acknowledged as legitimate grounds for secession, only one ethnic republic, Tuva, would qualify. As a sovereign state between 1921 and 1944, it was incorporated into the Soviet Union without the consent of its constituent majority.[46] However, as one of the poorest republics of the federation, it is highly dependent on federal subsidies, one possible reason why secession has little support.

Second, the Chechen experience warrants consideration. Although Chechnya is not archetypal, its experiences before and after the war (1994–96) illustrate some problems of secessionism in illiberal polities. It is difficult to establish whether there was a democratic mandate for Chechnya's declaration of independence in November 1991: both rebel parliamentary and presidential elections did occur in October 1991, although some estimates suggest that turnout may even have been as low as 10–12 per cent.[47] Even before the war began in December 1994, about one-sixth of the population had fled the republic, primarily ethnic Russians whose individual and group rights had been violated. Now, after republican presidential and parliamentary elections in January 1997 and the signing of a peace treaty between Moscow and Chechnya in May 1997, in which the two sides agreed to postpone a resolution to the republic's status until 2001, neither individual nor group rights are widely respected. Although post-1996 human rights violations cannot be separated from the Chechen experiences of the 21-month war, in which the atrocities committed by Russian federal forces during the war are widely acknowledged,[48] nonetheless the scale and intensity of such violations cannot be ignored. Of particular concern to Western human rights organisations has been the recent introduction and use of the shariat criminal code, which 'allows for an alarming level of violent punishment, invasions of privacy, and violations of other basic, internationally recognised human rights'.[49] In August 1997, the Chechen

Parliament also passed a law making Chechen the republic's sole official language. It is the only ethnorepublic to have enacted such legislation. Of course, given the increasing impact of Islamic militancy on the making of post-war Chechnya, it is only too easy to fall into the trap of the liberal critique of minority ethnocentrism by defending the values of a secular federation that should be accepted by all minorities, without acknowledging that such a stance reflects the very image of fundamentalism that it perceives in minority leaders. But when such practices are conducted against those who do not share this culture (Chechnya's minorities) or who have not consented to the election of its representatives, then the issue becomes more complex and not easily resolved.

The question must therefore be asked of whether individual and group rights are more likely to be protected in a far from democratic federation than in an illiberal state. And in this regard there are a number of ways in which federalisation and federal politics can act as a counterweight to extremist nationalisms. First, there is the role that federal institutions can play in counteracting such practices. The Russian Constitutional Court, re-established in 1995, has provided a means of curbing or reversing exclusivist practices. In June 1997, for example, it ruled against the ethnorepublic of Khakassia for introducing a republican electoral law that required candidates to the republican legislature and the post of executive head to demonstrate a minimum of 5- and 7-year periods of residency in the republic respectively, while federal legislation stipulated that the minimum residency requirement could not exceed 1 year (all such residency requirements have now been outlawed by the centre). As part of its 1996 power-sharing agreement, Krasnodar krai managed to negotiate the right to regulate migration into its region.[50] Although not based on issues of cultural protection but grounded in the desire to introduce a local admissions policy in a district that has received a disproportionately large share of refugees from the North Caucasus, it has triggered a debate about the role the federal centre should play in providing resources and employment opportunities in localities of emigration, thereby pre-empting protectionist actions by local political elites, who treat membership of their ethnorepublic or region as a private club.

Second, negotiating bilateral power-sharing treaties with the centre has encouraged the promotion of a civic-territorial local identity rather than 'nationalising' practices by political elites. In other words, there is evidence to suggest that, within some ethnorepublics, identities are becoming more territorially rather than ethnically focused, with local citizens increasingly identifying with their ethnorepublic, irrespective of their ethnic affiliation. For example, in Tatarstan, where the titular nation comprises only some 49 per cent of the republic's population and where both Russians and Chuvash constitute sizeable minorities, 'the fact that political struggles have been framed as centre–periphery rivalries rather than inter-ethnic ones has contributed to a strong sense of Tatarstani civic identity'.[51] Thus, the Russian minority may feel as strong a sense of civic loyalty to Tatarstan as it does to the Russian (*Rossiiskii*) state. Other studies of civic identities also show that ethnicity is not necessarily the 'community of fate' that exclusivist-national-ists would wish to portray. In a survey of four ethnorepublics (Tatarstan, Sakha, North Ossetia and Tuva) it was found that most Russians saw their identities as lying equally with either the ethnorepublic and Russia or just with the ethnorepublic, and only a small proportion just with Russia.[52] Similarly, in another survey, in 19 of the 21 republics more respondents placed themselves in the category of citizen with equally shared loyalties (Russia and the republic) than in any other category.[53] Somewhat paradox-ically, the formation of such cross-cutting identities owes something to the legacy of the Soviet nationalities policy, which promoted an inter-commu-nal culture leading to high levels of inter-ethnic marriage and multilingual-ism.

Third, federation has required local elites to adopt a relatively balanced approach to language issues, especially between the titular nation and Russians. Most republics have endorsed both the titular language and Russian as official state languages (the latter as the language of 'federal com-munication'), as mandated by the federal constitution. In some ethno-republics, a special state programme exists outlining strategies for broadening the use of the titular language in political, economic and cul-tural life, a policy that is defensible on the grounds of cultural survival and in reversing linguistic colonialism. In this regard, from the standpoint of social justice and for practical everyday reasons, it would be morally right that Russians should speak the indigenous language, for despite high levels of multilingualism amongst the titular nations (according to the last, 1989, census, 70 per cent of the titular nations of the ethnorepublics could speak Russian), Russians' knowledge of other federation languages is poor. At the same time, the federation has helped to protect the linguistic needs and sen-sitivities of Russians. In one of the most multicultural republics, Bashkortostan, where Turkic-speaking Bashkirs make up 22 per cent of the population, Tatars 28 per cent and Russians 39 per cent, the authorities purposely put off a decision concerning what languages should be adopted, and encouraged a public debate. Consequently, ethnic group representatives agreed to promote what is labelled 'the cult of the native language' in which all vernaculars – not just the three major spoken languages – 'deserve equal protection and development under the law'. Moreover, while it is acknowl-edged that the state has a role to play in promoting the equal worth of some 13 languages, 'the cult of the native language' is also based on the assump-tion that the most vital work for linguistic revival should be delegated to the family, more specifically to the mother.[54] By moving the focus of language politics and obligation for all languages from the state to the private sphere, political elites have attempted to avoid making language a politically charged issue.

Finally, international pressures have also played an important part in shaping a more democratic and less ethnic- conflict-ridden federation. Global economic institutions, such as the European Bank for Reconstruction and Development (EBRD) and the World Bank, have played a direct role in linking aid and development to ensuring Russia protects its minorities and works towards a more democratic federalism. More specific human rights organisations, notably the OSCE and the Council of Europe, have played an important part as mediators in ethnic tensions and in ensuring that Russia complies with recognised international human rights norms, while the European Union has been effective in using punitive trade measures to insist that Russia allows the OSCE access to monitor the volatile situation in Chechnya. In short, the price of international recognition and trade is linked to minority accommodation.

Conclusions

For a democratic federation to be realised in Russia, few would therefore disagree that the usual components of a successful federation must be present – namely, toleration, respect, compromise and mutual recognition of the right to be different. In order to safeguard this right to be different it must be understood that a democratic and stable federation requires space for promoting individual liberties as well as accommodating group rights. As part of the federal process in Russia, group rights are being realised primarily through asymmetric federalism. Provided that the federal process offers the opportunity for all constituent units – ethnorepublics and others – to renegotiate their federal status, and that no autonomy claims are slighted, there is the prospect of ensuring fulfilment of both a politics of recognition and federal stability. Essential also for a democratic trajectory in Russia, as in the other post-Soviet states, is an acceptance that people have 'had little experience with political associations that normally provide important linkages or mediating networks for individuals in liberal societies and [have] had little or no opportunity to try out their interactive skills in the political arena'.[55] In short, if federation is to succeed in acting as a counterweight to exclusive nationalism of either the cultural majority or minority, it needs to provide the conditions for creating a plurality of identities and political actors based upon guarantees of free association and access to public forums of the sort that a civic society and economic liberalisation can help generate.

Moreover, by redefining national self-determination to include the right to national-cultural autonomy, the authors of Decree 909 create the prospect of a potentially more democratic and flexible policy, similar to what some Western political theorists have called elsewhere a culture-based non-territorial self-determination.[56] Particularly in the present period of social flux, in which identities are especially fluid, a federation needs to be flexible enough to devolve powers to smaller, autonomous national

groupings. It could well be that working towards such a democratic federalism, provided that it is not stillborn, may provide the best counterweight
to the perils of both Russian and minority nationalism.

Notes to Chapter 6

1 T. Gurr, *Minorities at Risk. A Global View of Ethnopolitical Conflicts*
(Washington DC, United States Institute of Peace Studies, 1993), p. 90.
2 J. McGarry and B. O'Leary, *The Politics of Ethnic Conflict Regulation* (London,
Routledge, 1993).
3 A. Palmer, 'Colonial and modern genocide. Explanations and categories', *Ethnic
and Racial Studies,* 21(1), 1998, p. 89.
4 I. Rotar, 'The Ingush-Ossetian crisis', *Prism,* 29 August 1997.
5 Other cases would include possibly the 'Karabakh republic', and the self-styled
'independent' republics of Abkhazia and South Ossetia. Alhough their 'host'
countries have not accepted their independence, the regions run most of their
own political affairs.
6 S. N. Macfarlane, 'On the front lines in the near abroad. The CIS and the OSCE
in Georgia's civil wars', *Third World Quarterly,* 18(3), 1997, pp. 509–25.
7 P. Kolstoe, *Nationbuilding and Ethnic Integration in Bipolar Societies. The
Cases of Latvia and Kazakstan* (Oslo, University of Olso, 1998).
8 A. Wilson, *The Ukraine. The Unexpected Nation* (Yale, Yale University Press,
1999).
9 *The Economist,* 4 April 1998, p. 46.
10 G. Smith (ed.), *Federalism. The Multiethnic Challenge* (London, Longman,
1995).
11 These debates can be found in the following: R. Abdulatipov, 'Dva tipa natsional'nogo samosoznaniya', *Nezavisimaya gazeta,* 18 April 1996, p. 5; V. Kolosov
and B. Treivish 'Etnicheskie arealy sovremennoi Rossii. Sravnitel'nyi analiz riska
natsional'nykh konfliktov', *Polis,* 2(32), 1996, pp. 47–55; S. Ya. Matveeva,
'Natsional'nye problemy Rossii. Sovremennye diskussii', *Obshchestvennye
nauki i sovremennost',* 1, 1997, pp. 52–62; N. Mikhaleva, 'Konstitutsionnye
reformy v respublikakh – sub"ektakh Rossiiskoi Federatsii', *Gosudarstvo i
pravo,* 4, 1995, pp. 3–10; V. Ivanov, I. Ladodo and M. Naraov, 'Sostoyanie
mezhnatsional'nykh otnoshenii v Rossiiskoi Federatsii (po rezul'tatam issledovanii v regionakh RF)', *Sotsial'no-politicheskii zhurnal,* 3, 1996, pp. 33–49;
V. Lysenko, 'Naskol'ko prochna dogovarnaya osnova federativnykh
otnoshenii', *Federalizm. Teoriya, praktika, istoriya,* 3, 1996, pp. 11–34;
S. Valentei, 'Rossiiskie reformy i rossiiskii federalizm', *Federalizm. Teoriya,
praktika, istoriya,* 2, 1996, pp. 23–36; G. T. Tavadov, 'Sovremennye federatsii i
ikh sub"ekty', *Sotsial'no-politicheskii zhurnal,* 1, 1997, pp. 38–45; V. Tishkov,
'Chto yest' Rossiya?' *Voprosy filosofii,* 2, 1995, pp. 3–17; V. Tishkov, *Ethnicity,
Nationalism and Conflict in and after the Soviet Union. The Mind Aflame*
(London, Sage, 1997); E. Stroev, 'Rossiiskii federalizm. Nuzhno idti dal'she
obshchikh formul', *Federalizm. Teoriya, praktika, istoriya,* 3, 1996, pp. 3–10;
'Sostoyanie perspektivy rossiiskogo federalizma: politika, pravo, ekonomika',
Sotsial'no-politicheskii zhurnal, 1, 1997, pp. 14–27.
12 Tavadov, 'Sovremennye federatsii i ikh sub"ekty', pp. 38–45.
13 B. Fedorov, *Chtokak budem delat'* (Moscow, 1994), p. 20.
14 *Literaturnaya gazeta,* 15 August 1990.
15 *Rossiiskaya gazeta,* 25 December 1993.

16 *Rossiiskie vesti*, 25 December 1993.
17 *Rossiya*, 19–25 January 1994, p. 3.
18 *Rossiiskaya gazeta*, 4 November 1996.
19 R. Agranoff, 'Federal evolution in Spain', *International Political Science Review*, 17(1), 1997, p. 390.
20 Stroev, 'Rossiiskii federalizm. Nuzhno idti dal'she obshchikh formul', pp. 3–10.
21 Lysenko, 'Naskol'ko prochna dogovarnaya osnova federativnykh otnoshenii', pp. 11–34.
22 J. Hughes, 'Moscow's bilateral treaties add to confusion', *Transition*, 2(19), 1996, pp. 39–44.
23 *Moskovskie novosti*, 6–12 June 1996.
24 Valentei, 'Rossiiskie reformy i rossiiskii federalizm', p. 30.
25 Matveeva, 'Natsional'nye problemy Rossii. Sovremennye diskussii', pp. 52–62.
26 R. Abdulatipov, *O federativnoi i natsional'noi politike Rossiiskogo gosudarstva* (Moscow, Slavyanskii dialog, 1995), p. 19.
27 *Rossiiskaya gazeta*, 10 July 1996, p. 5.
28 T. Resler, 'Dilemmas of democratisation. Safeguarding minorities in Russia, Ukraine and Lithuania', *Europe–Asia Studies*, 49(1), 1997, pp. 89–106.
29 Matveeva, 'Natsional'nye problemy Rossii. Sovremennye diskussii'.
30 E. Chinyaeva, 'A Eurasianist model of interethnic relations could help Russia find harmony', *Transition*, 1 November 1996, pp. 30–5.
31 *Rossiiskaya gazeta*, 10 July 1996, p. 5.
32 *Nezavisimaya gazeta*, 5 March 1996, p. 3.
33 *Rossiiskaya gazeta*, 10 July 1996, p. 5.
34 N. Fraser, *Justice Interruptus. Critical Reflections on the 'Postsocialist' Condition* (London, Routledge, 1997).
35 M. Walzer, 'The new tribalism. Notes on a difficult problem', *Dissent*, Spring 1992, p. 169.
36 M. Bradshaw and J. Palacin, *An Atlas of the Economic Performance of Russia's Regions* (Birmingham, University of Birmingham, 1996).
37 *Rossiiskaya gazeta*, 29 March–4 April 1997 (*Dom i otechestvo* supplement). It should also be noted that the Germans in these regions have been able to draw upon considerably more federal resources than many other groups, thanks in large part to support from Germany, which has sought to stem the inflow of Germans from the post-Soviet states after the collapse of communism.
38 *Rossiiskaya gazeta*, 16 July 1997, p. 5.
39 V. Tishkov, 'Demokraticheskoe gosudarstvo ne obyazano vmeshevat'sya v sugubo lechnyi vopros', *Izvestiya*, 4 November 1997, p. 5.
40 G. Starovoitova, *Argumenty i fakty*, 45, 1997, p. 5.
41 *Kommersant-Daily*, 18 October 1997, p. 3.
42 *Konstitutsiya (Osnovnoi Zakon) Respubliki Sakha* (Yakutiya), 1994.
43 Walzer, 'The new tribalism', p. 170.
44 A. Buchanan, *Secession. The Morality of Political Divorce from Port Sumter to Lithuania and Quebec* (Boulder, CO, Westview Press, 1991).
45 D. Treisman, 'Russia's "ethnic revival". The separatist activism of regional leaders in a postcommunist order', *World Politics*, 49(1), 1997, pp. 212–49.
46 T. Penter, 'Die Republik Tywa (Tiuwa). Nationale und kulturelle Wiedergeburt einer ehemaligen Sowjetkolonie', *Osteuropa*, 47(7), 1997, pp. 666–83.
47 Tishkov, *Ethnicity, Nationalism and Conflict in and after the Soviet Union*, p. 202. This, however, does not imply that the majority of Chechens were against independent statehood. According to one estimate, which draws upon public opinion surveys and other data, it is probable that in 1991 not less than 60 per cent of the population of Chechnya supported the rebel Chechen leader, General Dudaev. For discussion of this and other points concerning the 1991

elections in Chechnya, see J. Dunlop, *Russia Confronts Chechnya. Roots of a Separatist Conflict* (Cambridge, Cambridge University Press, 1998), pp. 113–15.

48 C. Gall and T. De Waal, *Chechnya. A Small Victorious War* (London, Pan, 1997).

49 R. Denbar, 'The legacy of abuse in Chechnya and OSCE intervention', *Helsinki Monitor*, 1, 1997, p. 71.

50 *Izvestiya,* 21 August 1997.

51 L. Hanauer, 'Tatarstan and the prospects for federalism in Russia. A Commentary', *Security Dialogue*, 27(1), 1996, p. 82.

52 L. Drobizheva (ed.), *Natsional'noe samosoznanie i natsionalizm v Rossiiskoi Federatsii nachala 1990-kh godov* (Moscow, IEA, 1994).

53 Tishkov, *Ethnicity, Nationalism and Conflict in and after the Soviet Union*, p. 262.

54 K. Graney, 'Bashkortostan. A case study on building national identity', *RFE/RL*, 26 August 1997.

55 J. Mostov, 'Democracy and the politics of national identity', *Studies in East European Thought,* 46, 1994, p. 22.

56 See in particular Y. Tamir, *Liberal Nationalism* (Princeton, Princeton University Press, 1993), p. 73.

PART III

Geopolitical economy, the market and privatisation

|7|

The geopolitical economy of the CIS

The transition from central planning to the market has been accompanied by attempts to preserve some form of economic union or regional trading bloc through the Commonwealth of Independent States (CIS). The CIS was set up on 8 December 1991 in Minsk by the Slavic states of Russia, Ukraine and Belarus, and membership was declared open to all the post-Soviet states that accepted its aims and principles. Under the Alma-Ata Declaration of 21 December 1991, the CIS was extended to include Armenia, Azerbaijan, Moldova and the five Central Asian states. Subsequently its membership fluctuated. Now, following Georgia's accession in December 1993, it includes all the post-Soviet states except the Baltic republics, which have remained resolutely opposed to joining. The CIS's initial aims were modestly formulated: to provide a forum for discussing and managing the economic and geopolitical problems bequeathed by the USSR's sudden fragmentation. These included defence issues, especially the safe management of the Soviet nuclear arsenal; the division of the USSR's assets and liabilities (including the Soviet debt to Western economic institutions); the creation of mechanisms to resolve armed conflicts, unstable borders and minority disputes; trade interdependency; and transfrontier pollution.

While the CIS was conceived as a transitional body, there was no clear consensus among its members regarding what it was in transition towards. Since September 1993, however, when the Treaty on the Creation of an Economic Union was signed, the commonwealth has been committed to a long-term policy of deepening integration through the establishment of 'a common CIS economic space', while at the same time preserving the newly won territorial independence of its members. Russia, Belarus and Kazakhstan have taken the vision of economic and political union the furthest, establishing a Customs Union in 1995. This has since been extended to include Kyrgyzstan (1996) and Tajikistan (1999).[1] There remains, however, considerable debate over the viability of the CIS, either in its present form or as a regional trading bloc comparable with the European Union (EU) or even the North American Free Trade Association (NAFTA). Some commentators have argued, primarily on the grounds of economic interdependency, that the CIS or a similar regional trading association is a practical necessity.[2] Within an increasingly regionalising global economy, they contend, such a union is essential to the economic and social welfare of both Russia and the other CIS countries. Others argue that, at most, the CIS is a geopolitical smokescreen aimed at preserving Russian security interests, despite the end of the Cold War. At minimum, it is a transitional body whose members share no more than a common geopolitical past that is increasingly irrelevant to their situation as market-driven and geopolitically realigning polities. As one early sceptic concluded, 'The CIS is the world's biggest fig leaf. It was created to cover the loss of an empire. Like all fig leaves, it will eventually wither and fall off'.[3]

This chapter examines the geopolitical economy of the CIS. First, it explores the changing nature of regional interdependence by applying what Keohane and Nye, in their classic work on the international political economy, describe as a phenomenon of complex interdependence.[4] This entails examining the ways in which inter-state linkages in trade, finance and resource dependency can play a crucial part in shaping the nature and politics of inter-state relations more generally. Though not formulated in relation to the post-Soviet states, the notion of complex interdependence is of value in understanding the impact of the legacy of Soviet centrally planned interdependent development on CIS inter-state relations and of the political choices open to the post-Soviet states as a consequence of such a legacy of dependent development. The second section of this chapter examines the differing relationships between Russia and the other CIS member states. It looks at the various stances that have emerged among the borderland states towards the development of the CIS and, in particular, the role of the regional hegemon, Russia. Third, the chapter considers the prospects for such a community by comparing the evolution of the CIS with that of its successful Western neighbour, the European Union. Finally, it turns to the outsiders in this regionalisation project, the Baltic republics, examining why these three countries have been the most successful of the post-Soviet states in reorienting their economies westwards.

Framing the CIS: shifts in complex interdependence

The legacy of Soviet centrally planned interdependent development has played an important part in framing the parameters of post-Soviet regional reintegration. The scale of this interdependence was recognised by Mikhail Gorbachev, who, in his last-ditch attempts to prevent the collapse of the Soviet Federation, emphasised that the 15 republics constituted one common and interdependent economic space, and warned of the dire economic consequences that would follow from geoeconomic fragmentation. In the Soviet era, interdependence was evident in many ways. Under central planning, the republics were developed as heavily specialised units of production. In effect, the command economy created huge sectoral economic agglomerations enjoying full or nearly full monopolies in the making of a wide range of products. Uzbekistan, for example, specialised in cotton production, Azerbaijan in oil industry equipment and Latvia in electronics. One plant manufacturing 90 per cent of a given product could thus give the republic in which it was located a virtual monopoly over the Soviet market. Regional specialisation contributed to a high degree of trading dependence among the republics. On the eve of Soviet fragmentation, exports to other republics accounted for a very high proportion of net material product or NMP (GNP minus services) in all the borderland republics, most notably in Belarus (69.9 per cent), Estonia (66.5 per cent), Latvia (64.1 per cent), Armenia (63.7 per cent), Moldova (62.1 per cent) and Lithuania (60.9 per cent). Only in Russia was the figure comparatively low, with inter-republican trade accounting for 18 per cent of its NMP.[5] Consequently, the economic welfare of the borderland republics in particular was bound up with the survival of some form of economic union. The republics' interdependence was further reinforced by Moscow's commitment to equalising regional differences by redistributing resources from the richer to the poorer republics. While falling far short of the utopianist redistribution of wealth envisaged by the Soviet Union's architects, this policy ensured that the less developed southern states in particular benefited from close economic integration. In the last 3 decades of Soviet rule, the southern republics were net recipients of direct transfers of capital from the federal budget, while the richer republics, specifically Russia, Ukraine and the Baltic republics, were its most significant donors. More controversially, there is the widely accepted claim that the system of Union republican turnover tax also furthered redistribution. The republics were responsible for collecting their own local taxes (including personal and sales taxes on specific consumables and services), a share of which was paid over to the centre. Consequently, it is contended, the more developed republics contributed a higher proportion of their tax revenue to Moscow than did the less developed south.[6] Hence, the redistribution of resources contributed significantly to the south's socio-economic development. However, at the same time, as Islamov's calculations suggest, such claims are deceptive, given that raw materials and semi-finished products were subject to a higher rate of turnover tax than manufacturing industry, which affected particularly the primary-producing Central Asian republics.[7] As Islamov notes, 'for many years the mechanism of turnover taxes provided a hidden instrument for pumping out big sums of value added from the less developed to the more developed republics'.[8] So while the Central Asian republics did benefit over the longer period from the reallocation of budgetary resources, it is important not to exaggerate the extent to which Central Asia was a net recipient of the Soviet command system of reallocation. While not eradicating the north–south gap, it allowed the southern republics to increase their spending on social welfare, partially offsetting the costs of their rapidly growing populations. Thanks to such benevolent colonialism, by the mid-1980s the southern Soviet republics enjoyed higher living standards and greater social welfare support than their non-Soviet Muslim neighbours, such as Pakistan, Afghanistan, Iraq and Iran.[9] Not surprisingly, therefore, the southern republics were the least keen to see the end of the Soviet Union and, in the early and mid-1990s at least, were among the most enthusiastic in their support for regional reintegration.

With the region's transition from a centrally planned economic federation to decentralised nation-statism, the nature of interdependence has altered. One of the most notable consequences of the readjustment has been a change in the geography of trade. Two trends are particularly discernible. First, there has been a dramatic decline in the value of total trade of CIS countries (Table 7.1). Between 1991 and 1994, the value of the total trade of the post-Soviet states (using official/commercial exchange rates) dropped dramatically, from about US$650 billion to some US$153 billion (excluding the Baltic states).[10] Even when exchange rates are adjusted to give a more realistic comparison between the Soviet and post-Soviet periods, the fall is still marked – from approximately $585 billion to $263 billion (including the Baltic states).[11] Equally revealing is the dramatic decline in the volume of trade in the early 1990s between Russia and the other CIS countries. By 1994, it had declined to an eighth of what it had been in 1991.[12]

Second, the proportion of intra-CIS trade relative to trade between the CIS and the outside world has also fallen (Table 7.2). Intra-Soviet/CIS exports as a proportion of total exports declined from about three-quarters in 1990 to about one-quarter by 1996. Similarly, intra-Soviet/CIS imports fell from just under three-quarters to two-fifths of total imports. Thus, trade has become more global and less regional in orientation since the early 1990s, as countries have, to varying degrees, reoriented their trade to countries outside the former Soviet Union. This trend is particularly evident in the Baltic states, especially Estonia, where by the mid-1990s three-quarters of total trade was with countries outside the CIS. Nevertheless, it must be remembered that trade with the rest of the world started from a low base and that intra-CIS trade remains important for most of the post-Soviet states.

The productivity and overall economic performance of all the post-Soviet states deteriorated sharply as a consequence of the USSR's collapse and the universal commitment of the successor states to their own individual, autarchic policies of economic liberalisation. This had a particularly damaging effect on the scale and nature of CIS trade. Between 1992 and 1996, the average annual decrease in GDP of the CIS countries was about 10 per cent (compared with an average growth of about 2 per cent in the EU in the same period).[13] Although all member states were affected, there was considerable variation. Decreases in GDP in Russia, Belarus, Kazakhstan and Uzbekistan were the least marked (Table 7.3). Indeed, by 1996 these four countries had GDPs comparable with those of the early 1980s; Ukraine, Armenia and Tajikistan had GDPs comparable with 1970s levels by 1996, while Moldova, Georgia and Azerbaijan were still at 1960s levels by the mid-1990s. It was only after 1996 that most of the CIS states began to register a real growth in GDP. In particular, local wars in Georgia, Moldova and Tajikistan have had a disastrous effect on national economic performances by destroying infrastructure, militarising a sizeable proportion of the workforce and frightening off potential foreign investors.

Collapse and transition also prompted a number of CIS countries initially to pursue overly protectionist policies with regard to other CIS members in order to safeguard their own local needs. Exports were often restricted, resulting in acute shortages of fuel, consumer goods and certain manufactured goods in most CIS countries, while the imports of certain commodities were also regulated in order to facilitate adjustment to market conditions in the short-term. The readjustment went hand in hand with the introduction of national currencies in place of the ruble, which also hampered intra-CIS economic co-operation. In 1992, only Ukraine and the Baltic states chose to leave the ruble zone and establish their own national currencies[14] – widely considered a hallmark of territorial sovereignty – but by 1994 most of the other CIS states had followed suit. Only Belarus and Tajikistan were attached to the Russian-dominated ruble area for longer. In the Belarusian case, Russia and Belarus agreed to work towards a common currency as part of the Russian–Belarusian Union, a body strongly promoted by pro-Russian President Alyaksandr Lukashenka, who was elected in July 1994. However, because of practical difficulties, monetary union was postponed indefinitely, and in January 1995 the Belarusian ruble became the country's sole legal tender. Civil-war-torn Tajikistan, where Russian military intervention in support of the incumbent government has given Moscow considerable leverage over economic affairs, continued to use the Soviet ruble until 1993 and negotiated re-entry into a new ruble zone in 1994. In May 1995, however, the Tajik ruble replaced the Russian ruble. The introduction of a permanent national currency, the somon, has been postponed indefinitely.

But despite success in finding suppliers and markets outside the CIS, the borderland states, with the notable exception of the Baltic republics, continue to display a high degree of dependence on Russia and hence 'a vulnerability to developments' there.[15] Dependence is most marked in relation to energy and other raw materials. For both geopolitical and economic reasons, Russia was prepared to subsidise the borderland states by supplying them with cheap oil and gas. For energy-deficient states like Belarus, Armenia, Moldova, Georgia and Kyrgyzstan, a dependable supply of oil at below world-market prices is central to economic survival. It has been estimated that, in 1992, Russia was subsidising the other CIS member states by underpricing exports of energy and raw materials to a sum equivalent to

Table 7.1 Geography of trade in the USSR/CIS, 1990–96 (in millions of US dollars)

	1990		1991		1994		1995		1996	
	Soviet Union	Rest of the world	Soviet Union	Rest of the world	CIS	Rest of the world	CIS	Rest of the world	CIS	Rest of the world
EXPORTS										
Russia	126,627	80,900	108,571	53,100	13,861	53,001	14,262	65,607	15,755	71,874
South-western borderlands										
Ukraine	64,947	13,390	49,598	8,500	5,619	4,653	6,960	6,168	7,361	6,970
Belarus	29,193	3,438	23,151	1,661	1,479	1,032	2,930	1,776	3,647	1,816
Moldova	9,920	405	6,190	180	406	160	467	279	546	256
Transcaucasia										
Armenia	5,810	109	3,823	70	158	58	167	104	128	162
Azerbaijan	10,347	723	9,091	487	275	378	285	353	290	341
Georgia	9,702	515	5,594	30	117	39	97	58	129	71
Central Asia										
Kazakhstan	14,310	1,777	14,285	1,183	1,874	1,357	2,632	2,343	3,472	2,758
Uzbekistan	13,846	1,390	13,761	1,257	1,583	966	1,110	1,712	890	3,321
Kyrgyzstan	4,144	89	5,163	23	223	117	269	140	393	112
Tajikistan	4,029	609	3,456	424	93	399	252	497	331	439
Turkmenistan	4,185	195	6,314	146	1,651	494	930	951	1,142	551
USSR/CIS total	320,910	104,721	268,022	67,581	27,339	62,654	30,361	79,988	34,084	88,671

IMPORTS

Russia	114,041	82,900	83,333	45,100	10,317	28,344	13,593	33,117	14,440	31,798
South-western borderlands										
Ukraine	66,083	15,907	61,217	11,300	7,838	2,908	9,996	5,488	11,106	6,518
Belarus	25,154	5,256	20,375	1,957	2,092	975	3,677	1,887	4,570	2,369
Moldova	8,461	1,432	5,525	656	476	183	569	272	664	415
Transcaucasia										
Armenia	5,946	855	4,686	830	206	188	334	340	278	578
Azerbaijan	7,198	1,413	7,013	1,248	486	292	228	440	340	621
Georgia	8,388	1,543	4,806	480	272	65	154	232	271	448
Central Asia										
Kazakhstan	24,261	3,250	16,949	2,546	2,179	1,384	2,609	1,172	2,964	1,298
Uzbekistan	20,108	2,217	14,100	2,048	1,401	1,202	1,118	1,630	1,517	3,195
Kyrgyzstan	5,388	1,298	4,293	785	210	108	354	169	487	351
Tajikistan	5,693	655	4,361	706	233	314	478	332	383	286
Turkmenistan	4,954	523	3,684	618	686	782	745	619	389	924
USSR/CIS total	319,444	121,026	243,954	69,431	26,396	36,745	33,855	45,698	37,409	48,801

Sources: Data for 1990 and 1991 are USSR official statistics, based on official and commercial exchange rates, cited in M.V. Belkindas and O.V. Ivanova (eds), 'Foreign trade', in *Statistics in the USSR and Successor States*, World Bank Studies of Economies in Transition, no. 18 (Washington DC, World Bank, November 1995). Data for 1994–96 are from CIS Interstate Statistical Committee, *Official Statistics of the Countries of the CIS, 1997–2* [CD-ROM] (Moscow, CIS Interstate Statistical Committee, 1998).

Table 7.2   Geography of trade in the USSR/CIS, 1990–96 (in percentages)

	1990		1991		1994		1995		1996	
	Soviet Union	Rest of the world	Soviet Union	Rest of the world	CIS	Rest of the world	CIS	Rest of the world	CIS	Rest of the world
EXPORTS										
Russia	61	39	67	33	21	79	18	82	18	82
South-western borderlands										
Ukraine	83	17	85	15	55	45	53	47	51	49
Belarus	90	10	93	7	59	41	62	38	68	32
Moldova	96	4	97	3	72	28	63	37	68	32
Transcaucasia										
Armenia	98	2	98	2	73	27	62	38	39	61
Azerbaijan	94	6	95	5	42	58	45	55	46	54
Georgia	95	5	99	1	75	25	63	37	65	35
Central Asia										
Kazakhstan	89	11	92	8	58	42	53	47	56	44
Uzbekistan	91	9	92	8	62	38	39	61	21	79
Kyrgyzstan	98	2	0.4	99.6	66	34	66	34	78	22
Tajikistan	87	13	89	11	23	77	34	66	43	57
Turkmenistan	95	5	98	2	77	23	49	51	67	33
USSR/CIS total	75.4	24.6	79.9	20.1	30.4	69.6	27.5	72.5	27.8	72.2

IMPORTS

Russia	58	42	65	35	27	73	29	71	31	69
South-western borderlands										
Ukraine	81	19	84	16	73	27	65	35	63	47
Belarus	83	17	91	9	68	32	66	34	66	34
Moldova	96	4	97	3	72	28	68	32	62	38
Transcaucasia										
Armenia	87	13	85	15	52	48	50	50	32	68
Azerbaijan	84	16	85	15	62	38	34	66	35	65
Georgia	84	16	91	9	81	19	40	60	38	62
Central Asia										
Kazakhstan	82	12	83	13	61	39	69	31	70	30
Uzbekistan	90	10	87	13	54	46	41	59	32	68
Kyrgyzstan	81	19	84	16	66	34	68	32	58	42
Tajikistan	90	10	86	14	43	57	59	41	57	43
Turkmenistan	90	10	86	14	47	53	55	45	30	70
USSR/CIS	**72.5**	**27.5**	**77.8**	**22.2**	**41.8**	**58.2**	**42.6**	**57.4**	**43.4**	**56.6**

Sources: As for Table 7.1.

Table 7.3   Gross domestic product of CIS member states, 1990–96 (in constant prices as a percentage of the previous year)

	1990	1991	1992	1993	1994	1995	1996
Russia	97.0	95.0	85.5	91.3	87.3	95.9	95.1
South-western borderlands							
Ukraine	–	91.3	90.1	85.8	77.1	87.8	90
Belarus	98.1	98.8	90.4	92.4	87.4	89.6	102.6
Moldova	97.6	82.5	71	98.8	69.1[a]	98.1[a]	92.0[a]
Transcaucasia							
Armenia	94.5	88.3	58.2	91.2	105.4	106.9	105.8
Azerbaijan	88.3	99.3	77.4	76.9	80.3	88.2	101.3
Georgia	84.9	78.9	55.1	70.7	108.7	103.3	111.2
Central Asia							
Kazakhstan	–	89.0	94.7	89.4	87.4	91.8	101.1
Uzbekistan	–	99.5	88.9	97.7	94.8	99.1	101.6
Kyrgyzstan	–	92.2	86.1	84.5	79.9	94.6	105.6
Tajikistan	–	–	–	82.7	87.3	87.6	83.3
Turkmenistan	–	–	–	101.5	82.9	90.0	100.1
CIS	–	**94**	**86.1**	**90.3**	**86**	**94.7**	**95.4**

[a] Excluding the Dniester left bank.
Sources: *Ekonomicheskie novosti Rossii i Sodruzhestva*, no. 21, 1997; CIS Interstate Statistical Committee, *Official Statistics of the Countries of the CIS, 1997–2* [CD-ROM] (Moscow, CIS Interstate Statistical Committee, 1998).

around one-seventh of the CIS's GDP.[16] In 1993, however, faced with dramatic falls in energy production and tempted by the more lucrative global market place, Russia introduced far-reaching increases in the price of its energy shipments to the borderland states. Another aspect of interdependence is the indebtedness of the borderland states to Russia. This is partly the result of Russia's decision to grant credits to maintain reciprocal trade turnover and partly due to the failure of the borderland republics to pay for goods delivered, particularly energy supplies. By mid-1995, all CIS borderland countries had amassed considerable debts to Russia, most notably Ukraine (11 trillion rubles), Belarus (2.5 trillion), Kazakhstan (1.4 trillion) and Moldova (1.3 trillion). While providing Moscow with economic and political leverage over individual countries and CIS affairs in general, such indebtedness also carries costs for Russia. In early 1997, one of the major debates in Moscow foreign policy circles was whether the process of renegotiating the restructuring of borderland debts should continue or whether Russia should adopt a more punitive policy with regard to non-payers, including the ultimate sanction of cutting off energy supplies.[17]

While the liberalisation of trade and other forms of economic activity has opened up the CIS borderland states to the global market place, new patterns of co-operation are also emerging within the CIS. One of the most notable concerns Russian trade with three of the largest states – Ukraine, Kazakhstan and Belarus – which increased from 70 per cent of all Russian exports to CIS countries in 1991 to 88 per cent by 1995. Among Russian imports from all CIS member states, the share of imports from these three states has also increased, from 60 per cent to 83 per cent over the same period. Thus, complex interdependence continues to ensure a powerful role for Russia in the region's economic reintegration. For the borderland states in particular, therefore, tension exists between the legacy of Soviet interdependence and the emergence of Russia as an economic hegemon, on the one hand, and the disintegrative effects of geopolitical fragmentation and the desire to connect up with the global market place, on the other.

View from the borderlands: Ukraine, Belarus and Georgia

There is little doubt that one of the main reasons for Russia's support of the CIS is its perception of the organisation as a means of protecting its economic and geopolitical interests in northern Eurasia. With its overwhelming military pre-eminence and large share of the CIS's GDP and total population, Russia has the credentials to play a powerful role as regional hegemon, and has been especially keen to promote the CIS as a military-defence organisation. Six CIS member states signed the 1992 Tashkent Collective Security Agreement, but at a CIS meeting in February 1995 most rejected Moscow's proposal on the joint defence of CIS borders. Russia is also keen to promote the CIS as a leading global institution in order to amplify Russia's influence and interests in world affairs. Finally, Russia has sought to use bilateral treaties to promote its own economic interests within the borderlands. One such treaty was an agreement with Turkmenistan designed to co-ordinate the development of the two countries' oil and gas complexes and to lead to the creation of a north–south transport corridor extending from European Russia through Pakistan to the Persian Gulf. As the two countries account for the lion's share of the CIS's gas reserves, the treaty had the potential to play a crucial part in the future prosperity of both countries.

Russia is not alone in promoting its economic interests through bilateral or multilateral treaties with other CIS member states, but not surprisingly when Moscow pursues such practices there is concern in the borderlands that they reflect a strategy of divide and rule within a union of unequal partners. Many of the borderland states believe that Moscow's policies show that it has not renounced the very imperialist economic and geopolitical ambitions from which they have been struggling to escape for at least a decade. With the Russian military still present in a number of member states, notably in Tajikistan and Georgia, most of the post-Soviet states remain suspicious of Russia's geopolitical intentions. In 1996, their unease was heightened when the lower house of the Russian Parliament voted in favour of repealing the Belavezha accords, which had finalised the end of the Soviet Union and led to acknowledgement of the territorial sovereignty of the post-Soviet states.

Yet the most striking feature of the borderland states is the diversity of their attitudes towards the CIS. Their stances are shaped in large part by their relations with and perceptions of Russia. Three factors appear crucial: first, the potential of each borderland state to escape complex interdependence; second, the nature and strength of homeland nationalism; and finally, geopolitical vulnerability to the regional hegemon. We can consider the impact of these factors in shaping the very different stances taken by Ukraine, Belarus and Georgia.

It was certainly the view of the original architects of the CIS that any regional co-operation beyond managing the end of the USSR would depend upon the establishment of cordial relations between Russia and Ukraine. Indeed, for many in Moscow, the initial reason for establishing the CIS was to preserve some sort of union between these two Slavic states. Ukraine's position, by contrast, has been shaped largely by its desire to avoid being dominated either geopolitically or economically by Russia. Yet although it initially took the view that the CIS should be little more than a mechanism for managing the dissolution of the Soviet Union, since 1994 Ukraine's position has mellowed. The change in Ukraine's relations with Russia was due in part to the election that year of Leonid Kuchma, who replaced the more Ukrainian-nationalist-minded Leonid Kravchuk as president.

Ukraine has been able to take a more critical stance on CIS integration than have some of the other borderland states because of its greater potential to escape complex interdependence. With a population of over 50 million, Ukraine is by far the largest and most influential of the borderland states. This does not mean, however, that Ukraine is not heavily locked into the CIS trading regime. The proportion of Ukrainian trade with the CIS remains relatively high. According to IMF direction of trade data, Ukrainian exports to Russia rose from 3.8 billion in 1994 to 6 billion a year later, while imports from Russia went up from 6 billion to 7.6 billion over the same period.[18] For Ukraine, trade with Russia therefore remains very significant, accounting for 39 per cent of Ukrainian exports and 48% of its imports in 1996.[19] Ukraine also remains the world's largest importer of Russian oil and gas. Yet Ukraine has shown that it has the ability to recast its economic relations within northern Eurasia, in particular to look westwards.

Ukraine's resistance to further political or military integration with the CIS, as evidenced by its leadership of the CIS non-aligned group (which also includes Georgia, Moldova and Azerbaijan), is linked to its desire to prevent encroachments upon its much-vaunted sovereignty. Indeed, it is the desire of Ukrainian nationalists, particularly in the country's western heartlands, to distance their homeland from Moscow that has done much to reshape relations between Kiev and Moscow. There are good reasons why Ukraine should adopt such a position. First, many in Moscow argue that the cultural distance between the two states is minimal. Owing to their common Slavic heritage, Ukraine's political leaders have been especially anxious to draw clearly demarcated political boundaries between their country and Russia. This desire has been reinforced by the presence within Ukraine of an 11-million-strong population of ethnic Russians, by far the largest such presence in any of the CIS borderland states. Initial fear in Kiev that a secessionist movement could develop in the eastern Donbas region, where the Russians are concentrated, has, however, been unfounded.[20] The second reason for Ukraine's cautious approach to integration is linked to its southern peninsula, Crimea. Transferred from Russia in 1954 to mark the 300th anniversary of the Pereyaslav Agreement uniting tsarist Russia with Ukraine, the peninsula has been the focus of territorial claims and counter-claims since the early 1990s. Caught in the middle have been the Crimean Tatars, who are as much opposed to rule from Kiev as from Moscow. Thus, a complex triadic politics has emerged, involving secessionists, integrationists and autonomists. Separatist calls by Russians in Crimea, bolstered by support from nationalists in Russia, have provoked stern resistance from the government in Kiev, which is anxious to ensure that Crimea remains an integral part of Ukraine. But for the time being at least, Kiev has managed to appease most factions within the peninsula by granting the region special autonomous status within a sovereign Ukraine. Finally, tension between Russia and Ukraine has also arisen over the division of the much-coveted Soviet Black Sea Fleet. But in 1997 an agreement on the division of the fleet and the naval port of Sevastopol was eventually reached and a friendship treaty signed.

Although aware that it has to tread very carefully in order not to antagonise its eastern neighbour, Ukraine has sought to minimise its perceived geopolitical vulnerability to Russia by gently pushing towards integration with the West. With NATO now approaching its western frontier, Ukraine appears to see closer co-operation with such a Western-based military-security system as necessary, although full NATO membership is unlikely in the foreseeable future. There are also many in Ukraine who visualise their country as part of the EU rather than as part of a Russian-dominated CIS, although realists in Kiev know that this is unlikely to happen until well into the next century. Ukraine also has aspirations of becoming a regional hegemon by acting as a bridge uniting West and East. But it has no wish to become 'a buffer zone' between a CIS military bloc and NATO. As Ukrainian President Kuchma put it, Ukraine is 'resolutely opposed to Europe's split into two camps'.[21] Ukraine's desire to serve as a conduit between East and West also reflects the country's search for a compromise compatible with its own internal political geography. As Mroz and Pavliuk note, 'just as it has combated anti-Russian sentiment in its western region, the Ukrainian government has done its best to avoid anti-NATO paranoia, present in other CIS countries, in its eastern half'.[22]

With by far the largest and potentially the most influential national economy between Russia and Germany, Ukraine is well placed to fulfil its aspiration of becoming an economic hegemon. It has been the most active of the CIS countries in promoting links with Central Europe, notably with the neighbouring Visegrad group (Poland, Hungary, the Czech Republic and Slovakia). But the Central European region offers only limited economic possibilities, particularly in regard to energy supplies. Thus, for its second regional strategy, Ukraine embarked in 1997 upon the formation of an alliance with three other CIS member states – Georgia, Azerbaijan and Moldova – in what is now dubbed the GUAM regional bloc. Initiated in partnership with Georgia, the bloc has been shaped by a common mistrust of Russia and a desire to benefit from the export of Azerbaijan's Caspian oil via Georgia and Ukraine. Looking south-eastwards towards Transcaucasia is not, however, a new phenomenon in Ukrainian geostrategic thinking. One of Ukraine's foremost geopolitical theorists of the 1940s, Yurii Lypa, called for Ukraine to centre itself on a geostrategic region mapped out by the dense network of rivers that would facilitate the supply of raw materials from Transcaucasia. This, he envisaged, would act as a counterweight to any possible interference from Russia.[23] The main reason for Ukraine's vulnerability to Russia is its continuing dependence on Russian energy supplies. Thus, refocusing on Transcaucasia offers Ukraine the prospect of finally weakening its age-old dependence on Moscow.

Belarus has taken a very different stance on CIS integration. Of all the member states, including Russia, it has been by far the most strident in its support for deeper regionalisation.[24] In April 1996, largely on the initiative of its president, Alyaksandr Lukashenka, Belarus signed a treaty with Russia 'On the Formation of a Community of Sovereign Republics'. This treaty signalled Belarus's desire not only to build a stronger and more integrated CIS but also to facilitate an eventual union with Russia. Less charitably, Starovoitova has described the motives of the Belarusian leadership as wanting to preserve a feudal *droit du seigneur* in its relations with Russia.[25] Although Russia was clearly willing to sign such a treaty, a move supported enthusiastically by both the country's Communist Party and its nationalists, Moscow's agenda differs from that of Belarus. As Markus notes: 'although Russia is often accused of harbouring imperial ambitions, in the case of Belarus it has been Moscow that has stalled on closer integration with Minsk'.[26] While Belarus's leadership wanted to create 'a real ... union treaty, without any ambiguities',[27] Yeltsin was adamant that such a treaty should not be interpreted as signalling the formation of a confederal bilateral state.

Symbols of a national homeland are weakly developed in Belarus, and the boundaries with their Slavic cousins, the Russians, are blurred and not easily distinguishable. But these are not the only reasons why Belarus has remained so supportive of the Russian–Belarusian Union and the CIS. Of all the borderland states, it is amongst the most dependent on Russia economically.[28] This reliance is reinforced by the glacial pace of internal economic and political reform, and by Belarus's limited efforts to become more Western in orientation. As late as 1996, the CIS accounted for 66 per cent of Belarus's total trade. Dependence on Russia is also reinforced by the legacy of the Cold War. Formerly the geopolitical epicentre of the Eastern bloc, Belarus still remains a virtual garrison state of Russia. For its part, Russia has not been insensitive to the continuing loyal support of Belarus. Thus, in 1996, Russia agreed to cancel Belarus's 1.276 billion dollar debt to Russia for gas and credits, in exchange for Belarus's cancellation of Russia's smaller debt of 914 billion dollars accrued primarily from Belarus's agreeing to the stationing of Russian troops on its territory. While Belarus continues to see Russia as its main patron in security matters, Russia sees Belarus as a potentially important ally in relation to its geosecurity interests in the Western borderlands. With NATO's expansion, which since March 1999 has included Poland, the Czech Republic and Hungary, Belarus may again emerge as an important front-line state, vital to the pre-empt of further NATO encroachment eastwards.

In contrast with both Ukraine and Belarus, security issues have been uppermost in shaping Georgia's relations with the CIS and Russia. Indeed, geopolitics has had a pervasive impact on Georgian statehood and its economic fortunes throughout the formative years of its independence. Wracked by civil war, Georgia was unable to attempt serious economic reform until the mid-1990s. Georgia's foreign policy has also been largely shaped by Russia's interests in the region and its role as mediator in ethnic disputes within the country.[29] While it may be overstating the case to say that as a consequence Georgia, like the other Transcaucasian states, enjoys 'only limited freedom in determining [its] foreign policy objectives',[30] Russia has accompanied its recognition of Georgia's territorial sovereignty with explicit demands for co-operation in what it sees as vital security matters in the region.

Russia's designation of Transcaucasia as 'a zone of vital influence'[31] explains its decision to embroil itself in Georgia's internal affairs. Russia has intervened in two ethnoregional secessionist struggles in Georgia. In 1992–93, it was accused by Tbilisi of lending support to Abkhazian separatists, and it has also played a mediating role in that conflict. In South Ossetia, which sought to unite with North Ossetia in the Russian Federation, it has also played a peacekeeping role. The continuing presence of Russian troops in the region also reflects Moscow's determination to safeguard Russia's broader geopolitical and economic interests in the Caucasus. Matters of concern include the growing interest shown by both Turkey and Western multinational companies in the energy-rich Caspian

Sea region. Given the heavy involvement of Russian oil and gas companies, Moscow is keen to keep the states of the region – especially strategically important oil- and gas-rich Azerbaijan – politically, militarily and economically dependent on Russia.[32]

Georgia's desire to protect its sovereignty has coexisted uneasily with Russian interventionism in the region, particularly in the early years of independent statehood.[33] Under the presidency of Zviad Gamsakhurdia and fuelled by Moscow's support of the Abkhazian separatists, Georgia underwent a brief period of distancing itself from what Georgian nationalists have long regarded as their nation's 'imperial other'. Following the election in 1992 of the more pragmatic Eduard Shevardnadze as leader, Georgia became a member of the CIS in late 1993. Georgia's distance from any Western regional security system makes it particularly vulnerable to its powerful northern neighbour and has forced it into a rapprochement with Russia, although many within the country argue that its sovereignty will only be fully secured by the withdrawal of Russian troops. Economic concerns have also provided an impetus to rapprochement. Russia remains its largest trading partner, while in 1996 the CIS still accounted for well over half of Georgia's overall trade. However, with the return of a degree of normality, economic reforms have got under way. Considerable progress has been made in the privatisation of state property and land, and Georgia's rate of inflation, which reached an annual average of more than 15,000 per cent at its height in 1994, has since slowed. Georgia has also begun to rethink its trade links. Turkey is almost as important a trading partner as Russia, and the majority of Georgia's imports now come from outside the CIS. Georgia has played a pivotal role in the formation of GUAM, which provides a basis for reducing its heavy dependence on Russia. Yet, given Moscow's interests in political stability in Transcaucasia and its role as mediator in the unresolved Abkhaz dispute, Georgia's geopolitical and economic security continues to remain vulnerable to Russian interests.

A Eurasian community: dead duck or phoenix?

Underpinning the continuation of the CIS are diverse bilateral and multilateral treaties that create a dense economic, geopolitical and cultural network of regional agreements. These include treaties on military co-operation, mutual recognition of borders, labour mobility, free trade, the co-ordination of new technologies and fighting the growing regionalisation of organised crime. Such treaties are as likely to reinforce as to weaken intra-bloc unity. Indeed, for integrationist-minded states like Kazakhstan and Kyrgyzstan, the main problem is one of creating more unions from within. Yet despite the tensions that have dogged the CIS from its inception, it has survived the difficult immediate transition from Soviet rule. Of significance both to the future of Eurasia and to the global economy more generally is whether the CIS can emerge not only as a successful regional trading bloc but also work towards the creation of a Eurasian community similar to the EU. In some respects, it is too early to envisage the CIS as a Eurasian community in the making. As one Russian economist put it, the CIS is not 'at a mature stage of development'.[34] For others, any comparison between the CIS and the EU is flawed. The CIS's purpose, Webber notes,

> is not akin to the international integration carried out by [the EU,] which involves the voluntary transfer of functions carried out by national governments to larger political units. The CIS has created institutional machinery among states, but there is no desire to erect decision-making machinery above states capable of making and enforcing obligatory decisions.[35]

In this sense, the CIS is an 'inter-governmental rather than a supranational body. It is, as its name makes clear, a commonwealth, not a confederation'.[36] Yet, when the Treaty of Rome was signed by the original six EU member states, few would have envisaged that 40 years later 15 member states (with a further five countries, including Estonia, scheduled for early admission) would be part of a federated superstate in which many of the limits to the mobility of capital and labour had been removed, and that the age of the European citizen would be a reality. Although they are at different stages of development, it is worth looking at some of the major similarities and differences in the evolution of these supraregional organisations (Table 7.4).

First, both regional trading blocs emerged out of a geopolitical crisis which was eased by a legacy of well-established interdependent trading systems and by large-scale Western economic intervention facilitating regionalisation following traumatic change. The original six EU member states probably faced the more gargantuan task – that of rebuilding their economies following the economic devastation caused by World War II. One of the most important economic building blocs for the EU was the US-sponsored Marshall Plan, launched in 1947 to reconstruct Europe's war-torn economies. Designed to ensure that western Europe was economically strong and sufficiently integrated to withstand pressure from the Soviet bloc, it was also intended to promote the formation of an economic partnership between western Europe and the USA, and led to the highly successful Trans-Atlantic Trading System. As Wallace notes, the presence of a supportive external hegemon, with surplus security and economic resources available, helped lessen the costs of EU integration.[37] For western Europeans, the existence of an external enemy – in the form of the Soviet bloc countries – also provided an important spur to integration. In contrast, the crisis facing the CIS countries, while also born out of geopolitical crisis, is due primarily to the failure of the Soviet model to provide an effective alternative to capitalism. The states to the east (at least of eastern Europe), prevented from becoming part of the Marshall Plan by the USSR in the late

Table 7.4 The CIS and EU compared

	CIS	EU
Membership	12	15
Fast-track members	Russian–Belarusian Union; Customs Union: Russia, Belarus, Kazakhstan, Kyrgyzstan, Tajikistan	11 countries in monetary union, 1999; 10 parties to Schengen Convention
Land area (km^2)	22.6 million	3.2 million
Population (1995)	286 million	372 million
Labour force	141 million (1995)	166 (civilian working population, 1994)
GDP ($ billion)	509 (1995)	8,588 (1996)
GDP ($ billion at PPP, 1996)	890 (estimate)	6,679
GDP per capita ($)	1,818 (1995)	23,051 (1996)
Real GDP growth (%, 1995)	−4.9	2.4
Crude oil production (million tonnes of oil equivalent, 1996)	352.6	145.6
Natural gas production (million tonnes of oil equivalent, 1996)	602.1	186.9
Consumer price inflation (%)	363 (year end change, 1995)	2.5 (1996, annual average)
Exports ($ billion, 1995)	129 (World Bank)	1,745 (EIU)
Imports ($ billion, 1995)	116 (World Bank)	1,648 (EIU)
Current account balance ($ billion, 1995)	6.9 (estimate)	59
Unemployment (% of labour force, 1995)	5.5[a]	10.7 (labour force surveys)

[a] Officially registered unemployed, except in Russia, where figures are calculated on the basis of labour force surveys.
Sources: *World Development Indicators 1997* (Washington DC, World Bank, 1997); Euromonitor, *European Marketing Data and Statistics 1998; International Marketing Data and Statistics* (London, Euromonitor, 1998); *Europe. Regional Overview*, EIU Country Forecast, 4th Quarter 1997; Eurostat (http://europa.eu); Economic Commission for Europe, *Economic Survey of Europe 1996–97* (New York and Geneva, UN, 1997); *Transition Report 1997* (EBRD, 1997).

1940s, are now able to tap into Western aid. But the conditions attached to the provision of aid today are far more rigorous and specific than those laid out in the Marshall Plan. The USA and major Western-dominated financial institutions such as the IMF, the World Bank and the European Bank for Reconstruction and Development (EBRD) make the disbursal of aid to CIS countries conditional upon the pursuit of stringent trade and price liberalisation policies (especially with regard to food and fuel), reform of the banking and financial-service sectors, a reduction in state subsidies to inefficient enterprises and cuts in state spending on and involvement in social welfare. While the countries of the east have benefited from this 'New Marshall

Plan', the scale of external support has been limited. It has been calculated that the sums involved in the post-war West European Marshall Aid programme would, at current prices, amount to around 300 billion ecu, a figure which still falls far short of current CIS needs. However, the West has given no serious consideration to providing that level of support.[38] Nevertheless, Western aid has helped to facilitate both regional trade and integration into the global economy.

Second, some similarities can be identified in the institutional development of the EU and the CIS. Both began as customs unions involving a group of core nation-states. The original EU Customs Union (Germany, France and the Benelux countries) has a parallel with the CIS Customs Union (Russia, Belarus, Kazakhstan, and later Kyrgyzstan and Tajikistan). The institutional development of the EU was gradually expanded and deepened less as a single enterprise than as a set of diverse but overlapping fields of activity on issues such as freedom of labour migration, the social chapter on workers' rights and a common currency. Within the CIS, integration is also proceeding through a series of overlapping bilateral and multilateral treaties among member states, some of which envisage the re-establishment of a common currency and monetary union, the integration of financial markets and investment flows, and the extension and deepening of freedom of labour migration. Moreover, as with the EU, the integration process has generated tension among member states. Russia, for example, wants to expand membership of the CIS Customs Union, while Belarus, whose economy is weak, fears expansion would undermine its present 'most favoured nation status' with Russia.

As a result of closer regional economic integration, the EU is now entering a phase of political integration. There are, of course, still considerable doubts about whether a post-Maastricht treaty will lead to the type of federal Europe that many of its founding members envisaged. But although the lack of a common European identity is often held up as the major obstacle to the realisation of an integrated Europe, there has been a certain diffusion of identities from the national to the supraregional among both national political elites and the general public. By contrast, the Eurasian idea remains very poorly developed, despite the fact that the Customs Union represents a balance of Asian and European member states. Also in contrast with the situation in the EU, which inherited firmly established inter-state political boundaries, the patchwork of contested post-Soviet borders continues to fuel division among nations which still aspire to the modernist idea that the national and political spaces of nation-states should be territorially congruent. The main threat to CIS integration is therefore the lack of a common post-Soviet identity capable of transcending the sovereign boundaries of the nation-state.

Finally, although much is often made of the leading role that Germany has played in shaping EU economic integration, a balance of influence exists within the EU which acts as a counterweight to the emergence of a regional hegemon. In contrast, not only does Russia dominate the CIS both economically and geopolitically, the borderland member states lack a coherent strategy to challenge Russia's pre-eminence. But while commentators have tended to latch on to the way in which Russia's dominance is likely to hinder voluntary integration, the role of Russia as regional hegemon may also provide stability. As Macfarlane notes in relation to the role of arbiter that Russia has been willing to play in internal security issues in a number of borderland states,

> hegemony by some accounts lays the basis for effective co-operation –
> in that the hegemon is both willing and able to provide the public
> good of order – but by its very nature is likely to turn the pursuit of
> order to the hegemon's own advantage.[39]

But the borderland states continue to treat such self-proclaimed leadership with suspicion. It fuels homeland nationalism and thus acts as an obstacle to further integration. If the CIS is to develop further from the ashes of the Soviet Union, its most powerful member state must recognise that the voices of the borderlands should be treated with equal respect.

The outsiders: the Baltic states

There is little doubt that it is the nature of their homeland nationalism which explains why the three Baltic states are the only post-Soviet borderland states to reject CIS regionalisation. Having regained the independent statehood they enjoyed between 1918 and their forcible incorporation into the Soviet Union in 1940, the Baltic states have remained vociferous opponents of membership in any Moscow-dominated regional trading bloc. For the Balts, reconnecting with the inter-war sovereign homeland – seen as a golden age based on *laissez-faire* economics – is inextricably bound up with again becoming part of a Western-oriented European common homeland. Thus, from the outset, the Baltic states possessed a clear vision of their place within the post-Soviet geoeconomic order: economic dependence on the Soviet market was to be severed and replaced by a westward orientation, while the Soviet economic model was to be replaced by a market economy based on private property.[40]

Despite, or rather in part because of, their small size, the Baltic states – with their combined population of only eight million – have managed to extricate themselves from dependence on the East and from central planning within a remarkably short period. Part of the reason for their success has been their capacity and willingness to transform their economies, a process which was already well under way by the late 1980s. During *perestroika*, not only did Moscow single out the Baltic republics as an experimental laboratory for many of its reform measures, but the Baltic states were the most enthusiastic of all the Soviet republics in their response to the centre's programme of economic decentralisation, market experimentation and opening up of trade with the West. This experience and association with flourishing, Western-style market economies, combined with the advantages accruing from a fully urbanised and highly educated and skilled labour force, explain much of the Baltic states' ability and willingness to adapt to socio-economic change. They have also been aided by geopolitics, notably by the presence of Western patrons in the form of their Scandinavian neighbours, particularly Finland and Sweden, who have played a key part in facilitating the integration of the Baltic economies into European trading systems. In short, the Baltic states, particularly Estonia, have emerged to play a pioneering role in the post-Soviet transition (Table 7.5).

The fact that the Baltic states twice won independent statehood in the twentieth century inevitably invites comparisons between the two periods.

Table 7.5　The Baltic states: socio-economic development in comparative perspective, 1991–96

	Estonia	Latvia	Lithuania
Population (millions, mid-1995)	1.5	2.5	3.7
GNP per capita ($, 1995)	2,860	2,270	1,900
Share of major sectors in GDP **(%, at current prices)**			
agriculture, 1991	21.8	23.2	20.2
agriculture, 1995	8.1	9.8	9.3
industry, 1991	35.3	38.2	45.3
industry, 1995	22.9	5.3	29.0
construction, 1991	7.9	5.8	5.0
construction, 1995	5.3	7.7	6.7
services, 1991	34.9	32.9	29.6
services, 1995	63.7	57.2	55.0
Consumer price inflation **(annual % change):**			
1993	89	109	410
1996	23	18	25
Unemployment (% of the workforce)			
1992	1.6[a]	2.3	3.6
1996	5.6[a]	7.2	6.2
Real net wages (% change over **same period of preceding year)**			
1993	3.9	5.0	–
1996	0.4 (Jan–Sept)	–7.2	1.2

[a] Registered jobseekers rather than the registered unemployed.
Sources: Economic Commission for Europe, *Economic Survey of Europe in 1996–97* (New York and Geneva, UN, 1997); *World Economic and Social Survey 1997* (Washington DC, World Bank, 1997).

Moreover, it is precisely because the Baltic states have the opportunity to revitalise their inter-war economic models to fit the conditions of the 1990s that commentators are more optimistic about their economic and political prospects than the other post-Soviet states. For some, the historic parallels should provide a source of solace. As Hiden and Salmon note, 'today's Baltic leaders, facing the problems of separation from the Soviet Union, can take comfort in the knowledge that their forebears faced no less daunting tasks in establishing the independent republics of Estonia, Latvia and Lithuania'.[41] But many would argue that today's transition is more difficult than the situation in the 1920s. What lessons, if any, may to be learnt from comparisons of the two periods?

In both 1918 and 1991, the Baltic states emerged as independent states from the chaos of revolutionary change at the heart of the empire. On both occasions, their economic and social situation compared favourably with the polities from which they had seceded. The republics created in November 1918 had been among the most urbanised and industrialised regions of the Tsarist Empire, with one in four of their total population living in cities. Similarly, in 1991, the Baltic republics were the most urbanised of the Soviet republics, with around 70 per cent of each republic's population living in cities. Finally, in 1918 as well as in 1991, a new beginning entailed a desire to turn away from Russia and the East, to create nation-states on the basis of West European political, economic and social models and to look to the West to provide the regional security architecture to ensure their continuing statehood.

The commitment to laissez-faire economics and to integrating their economic regimes into 'a new Europe' was as evident in the 1920s as it is now. In some respects it was easier for the Baltic states to extricate themselves from economic ties with the East in 1918 than it has been in the 1990s. The Baltic states had already established themselves as part of a European-based regional trading system before 1918. Earlier industrialisation than elsewhere in the Russian Empire, especially in Estonia and Latvia, had already propelled the Baltic region to the forefront of the Empire's trade with western and Scandinavian Europe. As part of capitalist Europe, the region already had in place native entrepreneurial classes well qualified and well equipped to facilitate the further transition to a market economy. By 1914, the region's largest port city, Riga, was already receiving 43 per cent of its imports from Britain, while Britain took 39 per cent of its exports. The region's development had been further stimulated by its gateway location at the interface between the West and Russia, and its position was consolidated by the establishment of an east–west railway network connecting the Baltic ports to both Western and Eastern markets. However, the then new states also had to cope with the mammoth task of rebuilding their war-torn industries and infrastructures. Instead of moving towards rapid industrialisation, they chose a path of de-industrialisation, reorienting their economies towards agriculture, which was to form the basis of their inter-war prosperity. Between 1918 and 1940, the Baltic states became successful agrarian-based economies finding markets for their products in Britain, Germany and Scandinavia. Estonia was typical in the scale and speed at which it reoriented its trade away from Russia. In 1922, 25 per cent of Estonia's trade was with that country, but by 1935 this figure had fallen dramatically to 3 per cent. Yet throughout, this Western-oriented project was motivated by fear of socialist Russia and the possibility that further industrialisation might give birth to a large urban-industrial proletariat sympathetic to the project of Bolshevism. As one 1920s Latvian politician put it,

> if we consider that the main priority of our country is to generate a healthy peasantry and to avoid the growth of a factory proletariat, we realise that it does not lie in the interests of Latvia to extend big industry but rather to promote such branches as are necessary for local requirements.[42]

Thus, as is the case today, the homeland nationalisms of the inter-war years were in part informed by a fear of the other – of a Russia again embarking upon the reconstruction of empire.

The current economic transition, after 5 decades of 'Sovietisation', has involved the wholesale restructuring of production. The Soviet legacy to the new state-makers of the 1990s included highly industrialised regional economies, dependent in particular on heavy industry. The two most industrialised republics, Estonia and Latvia, had become the most energy- and labour-dependent republics of the union. Latvia was importing 91 per cent of its total fuel and energy requirements from the rest of the Soviet Union. But despite the high degree of economic integration with Russia, the extent to which the Baltic states have managed to extricate themselves in terms of trade is notable, especially in the case of Estonia. The latter was more or less wholly dependent on Soviet trade before independent statehood, but by 1997 Russia accounted for only 18.8 per cent of Estonia's exports and 14.4 per cent of its imports. Finland is now Estonia's second-largest export partner, taking 15.7 per cent of total exports, while Sweden is third, with 13.5 per cent. The main source of Estonian imports is now Finland (23.4 per cent) while Germany (10.1 per cent) ranks third.[43] But trade with Russia and the other CIS countries continues, not least because Russia provides the cheapest energy. The Baltic states also have resources that Russia needs, most notably access to the Baltic ports, which means that Latvia and Lithuania in particular have a degree of leverage in negotiations over energy provision with their Eastern neighbour.

Despite the parallels mentioned above, it is a very different matter for the Baltic states to rejoin the West in the 1990s than it was 70 years ago. New states are now facing a global economy with faster rates of economic growth. Consequently, there is greater competition for markets than there was in the 1920s. Trade is also more regionalised as a result of the growth in regional trading blocs, and competition for European markets is stiffer. Geopolitically, the Baltic states are in a far weaker bargaining position than they were after World War I. In the 1920s, they were important buffer states between newly established Bolshevik Russia and the capitalist superpowers of Britain, France and a re-emerging Germany. As a result, they not only attracted Western capital to ensure that they were economically strong enough to stand up to pressure from their Eastern neighbour, but also benefited from increasing rivalry among the capitalist states for economic and political influence in the region, especially between Nazi Germany, on the one hand, and Britain and France, on the other. In the late 1990s, however, they are only three of a large number of newly emergent post-Cold-War states – including the Central European countries – that are seeking Western investment, new trading partners and global markets.

It is for these reasons that membership of the European Union forms the cornerstone of the Baltic states' foreign policies. In 1995, all three republics formally applied for EU membership, and at the EU's Luxembourg Summit in December 1997, Estonia, along with Slovenia, Hungary, Poland and the Czech Republic, was accepted for fast-track membership. Although NATO continues to treat the Baltic states as a regional unit, the EU's decision to single out Estonia, with its more successful economy, for privileged consideration marks a sea change in Western policy towards the Baltic states. Hitherto, as in the inter-war years, the West had continued to treat the Baltic states as a geopolitical unit, encouraging them throughout the 1990s to develop closer economic links with one another, not least because Baltic co-operation was seen as offering better prospects for a strong and stable region. To some extent, the Baltic governments continue to acknowledge that they have much in common, most notably a shared geopolitical space between Russia and the West. This recognition has led all three to promote the establishment of a Baltic Free Trade Zone, to co-ordinate their diplomatic positions on issues such as the withdrawal of Russian troops and to work towards joint membership of NATO.

Yet tensions are emerging among the Baltic states, particularly between Estonia and the other two republics. Before Estonia was singled out for special status by the EU, it demonstrated growing concern over Lithuania's slow transition to a market economy, fearing that this would act as a brake on the acceptance of Estonia for fast-track membership. For its part, Lithuania has accused Estonia of resorting to unfair practises in its efforts to 'sell itself' within European circles, even at the expense of its Baltic neighbours, and of attempting as part of its strategy to repackage itself as a Scandinavian rather than a Baltic state. Tension has also been exacerbated by what many businesses in Latvia and Lithuania see as unfair competition from more successful Estonian retail businesses and construction companies. While too small to tackle the large Russian market, many Estonian businesses have recognised the opportunities that accrue from economies of comparative advantage and are operating in Latvia and Lithuania.

While obstacles to EU membership still exist for all three, Estonia has made sufficient progress in most economic spheres to be recognised as a model applicant. Privatisation has progressed at breakneck speed, and Estonia has managed to keep both unemployment and inflation under control, despite the large-scale restructuring of its enterprises and labour force. By the late 1990s, 90 per cent of small and medium-sized firms in Estonia were in private hands, while two-thirds of the country's large firms have also been privatised. Although living standards fell dramatically in the first half of the 1990s, there has since been a slow but demonstrable recovery, adding to the growing gap between Estonia and the other post-Soviet states.[44] Nonetheless, living standards in Estonia remain far behind those of its western European counterparts. In terms of GDP per person as a percentage of the EU average in 1996 (where EU=100), Estonia stood at 22.0, far behind Greece (65.9), which has the lowest GDP of the EU countries, and the other four Central European countries seeking early admission: Slovenia (59.0), the Czech Republic (57.0), Hungary (37.0) and Poland (31.0).[45]

European institutions such as the EU, OSCE and Council of Europe also play an important role in influencing the nature of the political and economic transition in the 1990s, unlike equivalent inter-war global institutions such as the League of Nations. Although Baltic state-building in the 1920s began as a democratic project in which Scandinavia, Britain and Weimar Germany were used as models, by 1926 in Lithuania and by 1934 in both Estonia and Latvia, democracy had given way to authoritarian-nationalist regimes. Faced with economic devastation triggered by the global recession of the late 1920s, the newly established authoritarian dictatorships appealed to a form of homeland-nationalism in the hope of resecuring their economic and political stability. This included structuring their socio-political systems on the basis of strong leadership, appeals to national unity and the exclusion of their sizeable minorities – Germans, Jews, Russians and Poles – from participation in the socio-political and economic life of the country. As Latvia's dictator, Karlis Ulmanis, put it, 'only that class of the population which forms the heart and soul of the state is to govern and manage the economy of the country'.[46] In the late 1990s, however, European international political institutions have been able and willing to exert geopolitical leverage over the Baltic states to ensure a more successful and enduring path towards democratisation. For their part, the Baltic states have been keen to demonstrate their European credentials in order to attain the security, markets and distance from the East that membership of Europe offers. In order to secure inclusion, they have shown a willingness, when necessary, to abide by modern Western normative conceptions of what the European polity should be. In short, there is some truth in Norgaard's statement that 'the major factor preventing the Baltic states from slipping down the road towards authoritarian rule ... is the effort towards "Europeanisation"'.[47] A realization of the benefits of becoming a

full member of Europe and its political and economic institutions has therefore had a tempering effect on early 1990s hard-line attitudes, particularly
towards the republics' Russian minorities, making it less likely that the
states will repeat the mistakes of the 1930s.

Notes to Chapter 7

1 S. Novoprudskii, 'Dushanbe khochet ispravit' "chetverku" na "pyaterky" ',
   Russkii telegraf, 25 March 1998, p. 4.
2 M. Bradshaw, *The Economic Effects of Soviet Dissolution* (London, Royal
   Institute of International Affairs Report, 1993).
3 P. Goble, Testimony to the U.S. House of Representatives Foreign Affairs
   Committee, January 1992. Also in 'Misreading Russia. The costs to America',
   Washington Post, 19 January 1992.
4 R. Keohane and J. Nye, *Power and Interdependence. World Politics in
   Transition* (Boston, Little, Brown, 1977).
5 *Narodnoe khozyaistvo SSSR v 1989g* (Moscow, Goskomstat, 1990).
6 L. Orlowski, 'Indirect transfers in trade among the former Soviet Union
   republics', *Europe–Asia Studies*, 45(6), 1993, pp. 1001–24.
7 B. Islamov, 'Post-Soviet Central Asia and the Commonwealth of Independent
   States. The Economic Background of Independence', in B. Manz (ed.), *Central
   Asia in Historical Perspective* (Boulder, CO, Westview Press, 1994), pp. 202–31.
8 Islamov, 'Post-Soviet Central Asia and the Commonwealth of Independent
   States', p. 209.
9 G. Smith, 'Ethnic nationalism in the Soviet Union. Territory, cleavage and control', *Environment and Planning C. Government and Policy*, 3(1), 1985,
   pp. 49–74.
10 M. V. Belkindas and O. V. Ivanova (eds), 'Foreign Trade', in *Statistics in the
   USSR and Successor States*, World Bank Studies of Economies in Transition, no.
   18 (Washington DC, World Bank, November 1995); *Sodruzhestvo nezavisimykh gosudarstv v 1996 godu. Statisticheskii spravochnik* (Moscow, CIS
   Interstate Statistical Committee, 1997).
11 Belkindas and Ivanova (eds), 'Foreign Trade'; B. Kaminski, 'Factors Affecting
   Trade Reorientation of the Newly Independent States', in B. Kaminski (ed.),
   Economic Transition in Russia and the New States of Eurasia (Boulder, CO,
   Westview Press, 1997), pp. 386–416.
12 Data for 1991 are USSR official statistics, based on official and commercial
   exchange rates, cited in Belkindas and Ivanova (eds), 'Foreign Trade'. Data for
   1994 is from CIS Interstate Statistical Committee, *Official Statistics of the
   Countries of the CIS, 1997–2* [CD-ROM] (Moscow, CIS Interstate Statistical
   Committee, 1998).
13 Estimated from data in *Europe. Regional Overview*, EIU Country Forecast, 4th
   Quarter, 1997.
14 Only Estonia went straight to a national currency: Latvia, Lithuania, Moldova,
   Azerbaijan and Ukraine introduced transitional coupon currencies in 1992 initially on a par with the ruble before establishing their own national currencies or
   leaving the ruble zone in 1993.
15 M. Webber, *The International Politics of Russia and the Successor States*
   (Manchester, Manchester University Press, 1996), p. 15.
16 R. Whitlock, 'The CIS economies. Divergent and troubled paths', *RFE/RL
   Research Report*, 3(1), 1994.

17 *Nezavisimaya gazeta*, 23 May 1997.
18 International Monetary Fund, *Direction of Trade Statistics Yearbook* (Washington DC, 1997).
19 *Ukraine, EIU Country Report.*
20 G. Smith and A. Wilson, 'Rethinking Russia's post-Soviet diaspora. The potential for political mobilisation in eastern Ukraine and north-east Estonia', *Europe–Asia Studies*, 49(5), 1997, pp. 845–64.
21 ITAR-TASS, 17 October 1997.
22 J. Mroz and O. Pavliuk, 'Ukraine. Europe's linchpin', *Foreign Affairs*, 75(3), 1996, p. 57.
23 A. Wilson, *Ukraine. The Unexpected Nation* (Yale, Yale University Press, 1999).
24 O. Alexandrova and H. Timmermann, 'Integration und Desintegration in den Beziehungen Rußland-Belarus-GUS', *Osteuropa*, 47(10–11), 1997, pp. 1022–37.
25 *Moskovskie novosti*, 25 January–1 February 1998.
26 U. Markus, 'Imperial understretch. Belarus's union with Russia', *Current History*, 75(603), p. 335.
27 *Kommersant-Daily*, 23 March 1996, p. 3.
28 Alexandrova and Timmermann, 'Integration und Desintegration in den Beziehungen Rußland-Belarus-GUS'.
29 S. N. Macfarlane, 'On the front lines in the near abroad. The CIS and the OSCE in Georgia's civil wars', *Third World Quarterly*, 18(3), 1997, pp. 509–25.
30 E. Fuller, 'Transcaucasus. Doomed to strategic partnership', *Transition*, 15, 1996, pp. 29–31.
31 *Izvestiya*, 8 October 1993.
32 Y. Federov, 'Kaspiiskaya politika Rossii: k konsensusu', *Pro et Contra*, 2(3), 1997, pp. 72–89.
33 H. Gödeke, 'Transkaukasien nach dem Zusammenbruch der UdSSSR', *Osteuropa*, 47(12), 1997, pp. 1224–35.
34 V. Kirichenko, 'Sostoyanie i problemy ekonomicheskikh otnoshenii v SNG', *Voprosy ekonomiki*, 10, 1995, pp. 70–8.
35 Webber, *The International Politics of Russia and the Successor States*, p. 95.
36 Webber, *The International Politics of Russia and the Successor States*, p. 95.
37 W. Wallace, 'Rescue or Retreat? The Nation-state in Western Europe, 1945–93', in J. Dunn (ed.), *Contemporay Crisis of the Nation-State?* (London, Basil Blackwell, 1995).
38 I. Kearns, 'Eastern Europe in transition into the New Europe', in A. Gamble and A. Payne (eds), *Regionalism and World Order* (London, Macmillan Press, 1996), p. 71.
39 Macfarlane, 'On the front lines in the near abroad', p. 509.
40 O. Norgaard *et al.*, *The Baltic States after Independence* (Cheltenham, Edward Elgar, 1996).
41 J. Hiden and P. Salmon, *The Baltic Nations and Europe. Estonia, Latvia and Lithuania in the Twentieth Century* (London, Longman, 1991), p. 43.
42 *Rigasche Nachrichten*, 1923.
43 *Estonia, 1998* (Tallinn, State Statistics Department, 1998).
44 J. Grogaard (ed.), *Estonia in the Grip of Change* (Oslo, FAFO Report, 1996).
45 *The Economist*, 28 February–6 March, 1998, p. 47.
46 I. Krotoski, 'Nationalisation of the economic structure of Latvia', *Baltic and Scandinavian Countries*, 3(3), 1937, p. 461.
47 Norgaard *et al.*, *The Baltic States after Independence*, p. 214.

8

The state, economic liberalisation and the regions

While Russia has been among the most vociferous of the CIS countries in championing a reintegrated common economic space, paradoxically it has simultaneously faced a challenge to the coherence and legitimacy of its national economic space from its own regions. The challenge posed by the regions to the transition to an integrated national economic space is in part a product of the way in which Moscow has managed the country's introduction to capitalism. Abandoning 'the fig leaf capitalism' inaugurated during the *perestroika* era for a rapid transition to a market economy, Moscow began in 1991 to implement far-reaching neo-liberal economic policies, including large-scale industrial privatisation, the further opening up of trade and investment to the world economy, and extensive price liberalisation of basic goods and services. Faced with hyperinflation, the prospect of dramatic increases in both unemployment and poverty, and the likelihood of widespread social unrest, in 1993 Russia abandoned its fast-track transition to capitalism in favour of a more modest reform programme. At the same time, the regions began to adopt measures designed to protect their own individual economic interests, threatening to turn Russia into 'a collection of closed regional markets'.[1] Moreover, the centre has been relying ever more on its federated regions to take the lead in implementing capitalist reforms at the local level. The central state has increasingly taken a back seat to the regions in shaping the nature and tempo of economic transition and, as a consequence, the regions have emerged to play a powerful role in shaping the country's economic future.

This chapter explores the political interplay during the transition to a market economy between the central state and the regions. First, it examines why and in what ways the regions have become important in shaping the politics of Russia's economic transition. It then considers the nature of centre–regional economic relations and a geography of public finance shaped by the political interplay between the central state and the regional authorities. The remaining sections explore the nature of the developmental strategies being adopted by the regions by looking at regional privatisation, the growing internationalisation of regional economic relations and the extent to which strategies of inter-regional co-operation are empowering the regions *vis-à-vis* the central state.

The rise of the regional state

As noted in Chapter 6, one of the key political developments in Russia since the collapse of the Soviet empire has been the rise to prominence of the federated ethnorepublics and other regions. What has in effect occurred has been the emergence of what can be termed the 'regional state'. In other words, since the early 1990s, some of Russia's regions have increasingly been taking on many of the features usually ascribed to the modern nation-state, although they fall short of qualifying as nation-states, behaving rather as quasi-sovereign states. In some respects, such labelling might seem out of step with both regional demography and membership of such a powerful state as Russia. After all, the average population of Russia's federated regions is under two million. With the exception of the federated city regions of Moscow and St. Petersburg, only five regions have populations of more than four million (Bashkortostan, Krasnodar *krai* and Moscow, Rostov and Sverdlovsk *oblast's*). The central state, through the political, military and financial powers that it possesses, retains the capacity to exert considerable leverage over the regions to sanction local co-operation and punish dissent. Yet despite such constraints, three developments in particular would seem to justify such labelling.

First, political power has become more decentralised and thus regionalised, with federalism creating opportunities for regional political institutions to emerge. The regions have taken on a growing array of delegated responsibilities, including education, social services, housing and health as well as the right to exercise certain tax-raising powers. Responsibility for executing economic reforms – from the privatisation of industry and housing to reforming the rural economy – has also been devolved to the regions. In other cases, the regions have simply seized economic responsibilities in open contravention of federal laws. Such practices include imposing import duties on goods brought in from other regions, regulating labour markets and imposing certain local taxes on economic enterprises. Many regions also continue to violate their financial obligations to the centre by periodically refusing to contribute locally collected taxes to the federal budget. Consequently, the regional state is now in practice responsible for a whole range of socioeconomic activities which affect the well-being of the citizenry – a situation that would have been unimaginable only a decade earlier. However, some regions do exercise more say and control over their affairs than others, making such forms of diffused economic sovereignty highly uneven. In particular, the treaty-based power-sharing agreements concluded with Moscow have resulted in some regions – notably Sakha, Tatarstan, Bashkortostan and Chechnya – securing far-reaching economic and political powers. It is these regions in particular which can be most comfortably labelled regional states.

Second, the opportunities that have resulted from the opening up of the regions to economic globalisation have strengthened their powers *vis-à-vis* Moscow. As Castells observes more generally, 'once decentralisation of power occurs, local and regional governments may seize the initiative on behalf of their populations, and may engage in developmental strategies vis-a-vis the global system, eventually coming into competition with their own parent states'.[2] With the liberalisation of trade and the end of state control over flows of investment, the regions are now, autonomously from the dictates of the centre, able to negotiate their own niches within the global market place. For the first time in modern history, Russia's regions are therefore able to connect up directly with the global economy and its major economic institutions. And for their part, overseas capital, transnational corporations and some foreign countries are bypassing the central state, negotiating directly with regions keen to manage the rejuvenation of their own economies. As a consequence, the regions are in effect simultaneously going global and regional in terms of their strategies for local development. Citizens are therefore increasingly looking towards the region as a more relevant institutional instrument for providing the improved quality of life the central state has failed to deliver. In short, the regional state is seen by many as a more effective means of securing benefits from the opportunities opened up by the internationalisation of Russia's economy.

Finally, the rise of the regions has gone hand in hand with the emergence of a regional elite which increasingly puts the interests of the region before other political concerns. This does not imply that there has been a wholesale reshaping of the type of regional elite that administered the region and its economy during Soviet times. The *nomenklatura*, those members of the party-state apparatus who occupied key positions during the Soviet period, still wield considerable power. The *nomenklatura* are even more heavily represented in key regional positions than they are in central state institutions, constituting as much as four-fifths of regional political elites.[3] Moreover, analysis of elections to the regional assemblies in 1995–96 shows that the most significant outcome was the achievement of positions of dominance by previously established local administrative and economic elites. As Slider notes, 'overwhelmingly, the new [regional] assemblies consist of political and economic leaders who already dominated most institutions in a particular region . . .'.[4] So it is not so much who governs the regions that has changed but rather the changing nature of their political affiliations and loyalties that is important.

According to the political geographer Leonid Smirnyagin, and others, the prioritising of regional interests is also reflected in what he calls the de-ideologisation of electoral politics.[5] This thesis suggests that two phases are evident in the country's electoral geography. In the first phase, as reflected in the parliamentary and presidential elections of 1993, 1995 and 1996, a relatively clear pattern of regional voting began to emerge (Fig. 8.1). In these early years of transition, a north–south pattern of party political

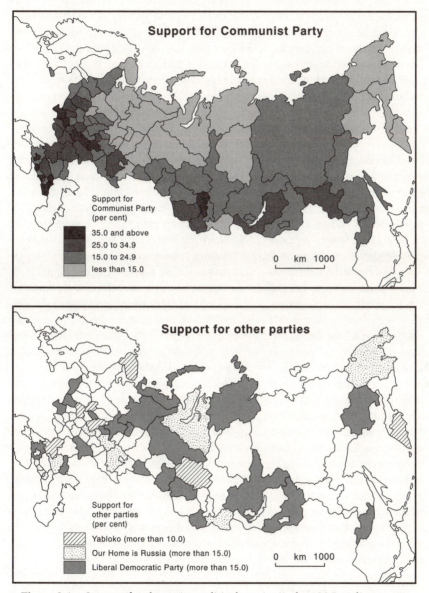

Figure 8.1　Support for the major political parties in the 1995 parliamentary elections in Russia. Source: *Vestnik Tsentral'noi izbiratel'noi komissii Rossiiskoi Federatsii*, 21, 1996; R. Orttung and S. Parrish, 'Russia after the elections', *Transition*, 23 February 1996, pp. 12–14.

voting could be detected. The democratic and centrist political parties tended to do well in the most heavily urbanised regions, especially in the larger and medium-sized cities in the north, which were also strongholds of market reform. In contrast, opposition political parties (notably communists and the ultra-nationalist LDPR) tended to do better in the least urbanised regions, especially in the small towns and rural areas, primarily in the south of the country. Thus, in the 1996 presidential election, it was possible to categorise regional leaders into those who supported the re-election of the Yeltsin administration (72 of the 89) and those who did not.[6] In short, regional political elites tended to affiliate along national party political lines by supporting either the incumbent central administration or opposition forces.

An important change is detectable in the 1996–97 regional (or gubernatorial) elections, when, for the first time, democratic elections were held for 'the heads of administration' or governors in the *oblast's* and *krais*. Previously, only republic presidents and the mayors of Moscow and St. Petersburg had been elected by popular vote. These elections heralded a new phase in regional political behaviour.[7] As Smirnyagin notes, the clear north–south voting pattern of previous parliamentary and presidential elections was no longer so evident. While the north–south and large city–countryside social cleavages in voting persisted, those candidates backed by the Kremlin tended to do better than expected in the rural areas than in the major cities. In turn, in some of the major cities the communists managed to do better than anticipated. This changing pattern suggests that political party labelling was now less relevant. Rather, the elections for regional governor were not so much fought along ideological lines (for example, privatisation versus state control, political party in power in the Kremlin versus communists), but rather by whether candidates made good practical regional managers. Those who could best convince their electorate of their regional credentials as managers – irrespective of ideology or political party affiliation – tended to do best. However, rather than staking their re-election by entering into a rhetoric of opposition to the federal centre, candidates tended to present their campaigns in terms of a willingness to work with the centre in order to ensure the maximisation of financial and economic benefits from the federal budget, widely interpreted in the regions as making good practical sense. Thus, Aleksandr Surikov, the newly elected Communist Party governor of Altai krai – a region long since a stronghold of support for the Communist Party and opposition to market reform – emphasised that he wanted to establish 'a non-partisan regional administration' which would prioritise regional interests by working with the central authorities in Moscow.[8] As Medvedev notes, 'the new regional agenda is not about political labels; it is day to day management of local affairs and the region's rights with respect to the centre'.[9] In short, the emergence of this new political geography represents what he calls 'a third force in Russia's politics', a new alternative to aligning with either the administration or with the main opposition political parties. According to one survey he draws upon, amongst the 45 regional governors elected by the end of 1996, 35 fell into the category of representing such 'a third force'.

It is of course important not to exaggerate the importance of the de-ideologisation thesis. Both candidates and voters are likely to behave differently in regional elections from the way they do in national elections, because there is invariably greater scope for prioritising regional interests when the election outcome will not directly affect national government. Nonetheless, a new regionalism has emerged in electoral politics. However, such a politics is not confined to the electoral map. A system of regional corporatist politics is also operating, whereby locally elected leaders and the regional administrations combine with the interests of local private capital to promote common regional goals – namely, maximising regional economic growth and extracting as much for their region from the federal budgetary system as possible, while at the same time striving to pursue economic policies compatible with maintaining local social stability.

Centre–regional relations: the politics of fiscal federalism

One of the central features shaping the political economy of transition is the role that federal politics plays in determining the allocation of financial resources to the regions. Who gets what, where and how in the allocation of public resources provides insight into the room for manoeuvre the regions have in influencing the geography of public finance. Such a politics of centre–regional financial transfers is often referred to as fiscal federalism.[10] On the one hand, it entails the transfer of public funds from the centre to the regions. This includes a wide range of flows of public funding: budget transfers – subventions, net mutual payments and budget loans, direct credit to support the agrarian economy, social welfare programmes; allocations through extra-budgetary funds, such as the pension fund or road fund; and other financial benefits, such as export privileges and hard currency allocations. On the other hand, as part of the federal budgetary equation, the regions have financial responsibilities to the centre for collecting and forwarding a proportion of taxes on businesses and individual citizens to the federal budget. This includes taxes from enterprise profits, value added tax and excise duty.

As a result of the increasing delegation of social budgetary responsibilities from the centre to the regions, local administrations have found it more and more difficult to balance their budgets. Besides having to meet their obligations to provide public services to their citizens, they have also faced the problem of meeting their tax obligations to the centre. For their part, the central authorities have found it increasingly difficult to satisfy the growing

demands of the regions for a greater share of scarce federal resources. As a
consequence, there has been a notable growth in regional budget deficits.
Compared with the early 1990s, when regional budget revenues exceeded
expenditures, deficits have now become the norm. Thus, in 1993, the consolidated regional budget deficit reached 10 per cent of expenditures,
increasing to 17.5 per cent in 1994.[11] While only 19 regions recorded a budget surplus in 1993, the following year a budget deficit was recorded for all
regions. Consequently, there is a considerable incentive for the regions to
extract as many subsidies from the federal budget as possible, while in turn
minimising or delaying their own payments to the centre. Thus, the number
of regional budgets being subsidised by the centre has grown by a third in
the 1994–97 period, from 65 to 81, and the number of regions which pay
more than they receive back in resource transfers has declined sharply.
Therefore, by 1997, only 8 of Russia's 89 regions were financially solvent
enough to qualify as net donor regions to the federal budget.[12]

There has, however, been some attempt by the federal authorities since
1994 to overcome this ongoing federal crisis by finding more efficient and
fairer means of redistributing resources. Previously, the budgetary system of
determining who paid and who got what was, in the absence of coherent
budgetary guidelines, characterised by an overly opaque, complex and arbitrary system. Ad hoc regional bargaining with the centre became the norm.
Invariably, who benefited depended upon the political influence and leverage that particular regions could exercise compared with others. Some
regions, notably Chechnya, Tatarstan, Sakha and Karelia, did not even contribute to the federal budget in some years, while more law-abiding regions
sought to extract preferential quotas, subsidies and aid money from the centre in return for promising to fulfil their tax obligations. The 1994 budgetary reforms attempted to resolve this fiscal anarchy, and two changes are
particularly notable.[13] First, the regions could independently establish a rate
for one of the basic federal taxes, the tax on enterprise profits. This provided
the regions with a degree of financial manoeuvrability and an additional
means of raising and legally retaining much needed additional local revenue.
Second, a fund for support of the poorer federated regions was created.
Designated for 'needy' and 'especially needy' regions, it represents the first
real attempt to try and use the federal budget as a means of reallocating
resources from the richer to the poorer regions.

While the reforms offer a greater opportunity to provide a more effective,
more efficient and fairer system of federal resource transfers, the new mechanism has run far from smoothly. In particular, the system of tax sharing
between the centre and the regions has been complicated by the introduction of the bilateral power-sharing agreements with the regions.
Consequently, certain regions, notably Tatarstan, Sakha and
Bashkortostan, have managed to extract special agreements from Moscow
under which the proportion of taxes forwarded to the federal authorities
has been reduced substantially, with payments open to annual renegotia-

tion. In exchange for a greater share of taxes collected being retained by the region, these more privileged regional administrations have, however, undertaken to finance a larger proportion of their own federal expenditures. Moreover, considerable shortcomings still persist with regard to the mechanism for determining budget allocations to the regions, with only a quarter of budget allocations by the mid-1990s being distributed according to the newly established formulas. Hence, despite the Komi republic's being the country's fourth richest oil-producing region, in 1994 it was allocated the largest subsidy from the centre, a decision Lavrov describes as 'purely political in nature'.[14] Informal procedures therefore continue to operate, encouraging 'behind the scenes' deals between the regions and the Federation's Ministry of Finance, and the flouting of established formulas continues to be widely regarded as the norm.

Given the complexity and range of types of fiscal flows and the extent to which a large proportion are allocated on a non-transparent and non-regionally determined basis, it is difficult to determine which regions are benefiting most from the present fiscal regime and which are contributing the greater share. From the official federal data that are made available, it is, however, possible to provide a picture of a fiscal geography of recipients and donors. The share of transfers received from the federal budget provides an indicator of those regions which are receiving the most subsidies (Fig. 8.2). In 1996, the regions which benefited the most were in the North Caucasus (Chechnya, Ingushetia, Dagestan, Kalmykia) and in the southern belt of Siberia (Agin-Buryatia, Tuva, Altai republic). Overall, this pattern reflects a general directional shift in the distribution of federal subsidies since the early 1990s from the north to the south and from west to east. The southern regions, notably the rural regions of the North Caucasus, some of the sparsely populated regions of the Northlands and the southern regions of Siberia appear to have benefited most since the mid-1990s, probably as a result of the new methods for distributing federal support according to the criterion of social need (Fig. 8.3). There is, however, also clear evidence that the ethnorepublics still tend to do better than the *oblast's*, and the urbanised-industrial *oblast's* better than the more rural-agricultural regions, although these differences are now less marked than previously.

Not surprisingly, the donor regions tend to be the richer republics and *oblast's*. As Fig. 8.2 shows, they are concentrated in the heart of the country, in western Siberia and in the south-east part of European Russia. In both 1996 and 1997, they included Moscow, Bashkortostan, Krasnoyarsk, Lipetsk, Samara, Sverdlovsk and the two sparsely populated national autonomous *okrugs* of Khanti-Mansi and Yamal-Nenets. Of the large number of oil-producing donor regions, these two autonomous okrugs, in particular, are of special importance to the federal authorities, not least because they account for 80 per cent of Russia's oil and gas production. A major problem is emerging. These okrugs want to become more fiscally autonomous, not least because, despite their enormous energy resources,

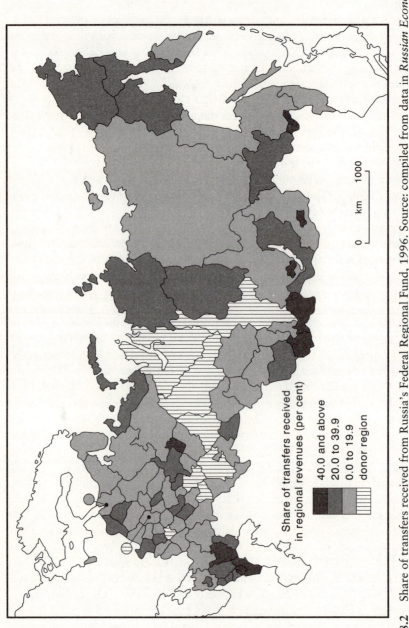

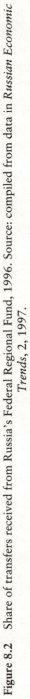

Figure 8.2   Share of transfers received from Russia's Federal Regional Fund, 1996. Source: compiled from data in *Russian Economic Trends*, 2, 1997.

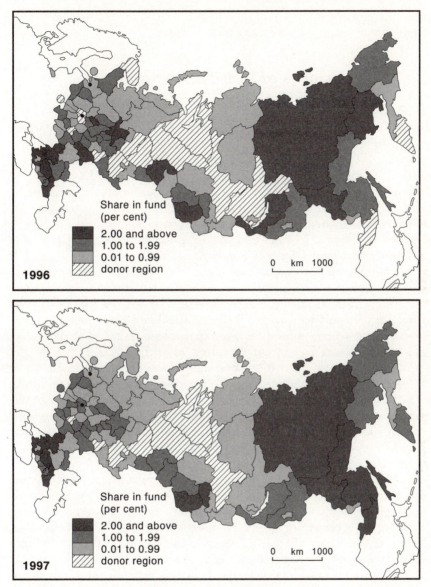

Figure 8.3   Share of the allocation of Russia's Regional Fund, 1996 and 1997.
Source: compiled from data in *Russian Economic Trends*, 2, 1997.

they are also underdeveloped and sparsely populated regions whose citizens'
living standards are amongst the lowest in the federation. Owing to the
large sources of revenue that local administrations can potentially acquire
from deals with Western oil companies, those regions have less incentive
than most to contribute to the federal budget. Moscow is well aware that

the reduction or withdrawal of their budget contributions could have disastrous consequences for the federation as a whole.

Theories of distributive (in)justice

Explaining what processes actually govern fiscal transfers to the regions is no easy task. Yet there is a general consensus that who gets what and where is not simply determined by objective allocation mechanisms or equitable accounting criteria. To shed light on the politics behind this fiscal and political geography, a number of theories of fiscal federal allocations that also draw upon the experiences of other federal regimes can be examined.

First, the federal authorities argue that intergovernmental transfers are based on its declared policy of working towards *mitigating the impact of regional economic disparities by ensuring a relative inter-regional equality in terms of a region's financial ability to meet the needs of its citizens*. It would be reasonable to expect that if this were the case the poorer regions would receive the lion's share of resource transfers, based on the premise that the centre uses such transfers to alleviate need and to work towards creating a more equitable society. There is little doubt that to meet such an objective, the federal authorities face a gargantuan task. Regional differentials are considerable whether measured by such indices as income per capita, social service provision, housing, education, infant mortality or access to medical care. While regional disparities did exist during the Soviet period, as Smirnyagin and others have noted, a degree of regional convergence was evident between 1965 and 1985.[15] With the advent of the market economy, however, regional differences and inequalities have grown apace. Thus, if regional gross domestic product (GDP) is taken as one indicator of socio-economic performance, data compiled for 1995 show that the unweighted average of the upper quintile of 89 regions was 4.6 times that of the lower quintile.[16] Such disparities are also evident from measures of per capita income, which show that Russia's richest *oblast'*, energy-rich Tyumen, has a per capita income 10 times greater than that of the poorest, Kalmykia.[17] In short, there is a general consensus that 'stratification into rich and poor regions has become more pronounced'.[18]

The centre's rhetoric that federalism is acting as an instrument for redistributing resources on the basis of need does not seem in practice always to be realised that effectively. During the early 1990s, federal resource allocations 'were random and were not justifiable at all from the standpoint of the objectives of federal regional policy'.[19] Overall, only 10 per cent of federal transfers in 1992–93 were being directed to the poorer regions, while the remaining 90 per cent were being allocated to the richer and more outspoken ethnorepublics. Tatarstan was receiving nearly one and a half times the national average, Bashkortostan double, and Sakha five times that figure.[20] Such findings are also borne out by a comprehensive study undertaken by

Bahl and Wallace.[21] They found that there was no evidence from federal revenue and expenditure data to suggest that the poorer regions were benefiting from fiscal allocations. In their examination of the relationship between fiscal capacity (using such indices as average monthly wages, the percentage of the population living in urban areas, and population size) and expenditure needs (for example, hospital beds per 10,000 population, the percentage of the population over 65 years old, infant mortality per 10,000 population), their findings showed that the per capita revenue retention of regions was positively related to their fiscal capacity. Thus, the differences between richer and poorer regions were simply reproducing themselves, and there was no evidence to suggest that reallocation was linked to the expenditure needs of regions. Thus, per capita retained revenues were greater for regions with higher average monthly wages, higher rates of wage growth and larger populations.

However, with the introduction of the Regional Support Fund, there has been a more concerted effort by the federal authorities to tackle more effectively the issue of regional inequality. Hanson argues that the federal redistribution of public money by means of the fund is already reducing the inequality of the regional budget revenues per head of population.[22] It does not, he contends, have the opposite effect of making this inequality greater, as some commentators have suggested. As Fig. 8.2 shows, there is evidence that some of Russia's poorest regions are receiving the largest subsidies. Thus, the largest net recipients tend to be the relatively rural, less developed regions of the North Caucasus and southern Siberia. In 1996, for instance, federal support (as a proportion of total regional budgets) was especially important for Russia's impoverished or war-torn southern regions, most notably Chechnya (80.7 per cent), Ingushetia (70.9 per cent), Agin-Buryat (65 per cent), Tuva (57.1 per cent) and Altai republic (54.8 per cent). Yet the amounts of such subsidies allocated to the regions remain small, making up less than 3 per cent of GDP. Given the small proportion of funds that are being made available, some commentators even go so far as to suggest that in the interests of achieving higher national economic growth, Moscow prefers to allocate a sizable proportion of its scarce federal resources and financial initiatives to the richer regions.[23]

The second thesis argues that if fiscal federal policies are not determined simply on the basis of objective criteria of need, it might be reasonable to suppose that the extent to which regional administrations fulfil their financial and economic obligations to the centre, and pursue policies that Moscow judges commensurate with national policy, might also have an impact on regional allocations. However, there is also little if any evidence to suggest that those republics and regions which are meeting their federal responsibilities by executing market reforms or paying their taxes on time are being rewarded in the next round of transfers, or that those which are not are being systematically penalised for non-compliance and non-payment. The president of Chuvashia, Nikolai Federov, whose republic has been among the most consistent in its support for the federation's economic and financial policies, notes that speedy payment of taxes to the centre does not result in higher transfer payments.[24] Rather, especially during the first half of the 1990s, the least reform-minded regions have tended to end up with the largest subsidies. According to one study, there is little incentive for the administrations of poorer regions to implement the centre's policy on privatisation, precisely because state-owned industries and rural collective farms within their territorial jurisdiction continue to be centrally subsidised.[25] Similarly, those regions that are contributing the lowest proportion of taxes to the centre (in particular, some energy or other resource-rich regions), seem to be doing well from net allocations from the federal budget.[26]

Third, it has been suggested that regions with access to key national leaders, central institutions and federal agencies like the Ministry of Finance tend to do better in securing federal resources. Here, political access and opportunity are key. One of the most cited practices is 'pork barrel politics'. Named after the experiences of other federations, notably the USA and Brazil, this refers to the practice whereby power in key congressional committees has assured federal benefits to members' home districts. It can therefore be hypothesised that regional elites who are influential at the centre can influence outcomes in favour of their own regions and local vested interests, thus ensuring greater material benefits for their locality. According to Medvedev, this practice is widespread, especially amongst representatives of the Federation Council, precisely because it is essentially a forum for

> personal meetings, lobbying and bureaucratic trading between the heads of the local executive and members of the federal government. The trading itself took place within committees and regional associations of the Federation Council, as well as within the federal ministries, most often in the Ministry of Finance. Regional governors and federal executives concluded package deals in which the central transfers, subsidies and subventions were traded for senators' votes in approval of government bills.[27]

Fourth, it has been suggested that resource transfers might be linked to the electoral process, whereby regions are rewarded not so much for their record of loyally voting for the central government or incumbent president but rather for changing sides, in the case of hitherto disloyal or electorally marginal regions. Thus, the centre may attempt to 'buy' key regional politicians or regional electorates in order to secure the re-election of the incumbent president or pro-government deputies by discriminating fiscally in favour of particular regions. There is widespread evidence to suggest that during the 1996–97 regional gubernatorial elections, the Yeltsin regime embarked upon a strategy of publicly promising certain regions additional subsidies and development aid in order to bolster its electoral prospects in

particular regions. It has been claimed that in the 1998 Krasnoyarsk gubernatorial election, Moscow announced extra federal funding before the second round of voting in an attempt to ensure the election of the pro-Yeltsin
candidate Valerii Zubov. This was not, however, enough to defeat the popular nationalist candidate Aleksandr Lebed.[28]

Finally, there is evidence to suggest that the more oppositional the region,
the more likely it is to be rewarded with subsidies. According to Lavrov's
findings,[29] the new methods for regulating inter-budgetary relations have
proven, on the whole, to be more beneficial to the oppositional regions than
to the politically loyal ones. Among the regions that supported the new federal constitution in the December 1993 referendum, 40 per cent gained from
the introduction of the 1994 procedures for distributing federal aid, while
26 per cent lost out. But among the regions that rejected the federal constitution, 55 per cent gained and only 18 per cent lost out. Thus, the centre
seems to recognise the need to create constituencies that will lend political
support to its continuing and perhaps expanding mandate. This is a well-
known phenomenon in centre–local politics.[30] Thus, it might be expected
that those regions that demonstrate the ability and resolve to threaten the
federal status quo are subsequently given larger net transfer payments.
Regions, in other words, are simply rewarded and bought off for their dis-
loyalty. As Berkowitz notes: 'threats of withholding taxes and secession
have become important ways for peripheral regions to influence centrally
controlled policies'.[31]

One of the most comprehensive studies to examine the relationship
between 'oppositional regions' and fiscal transfers is by Treisman. Using
1992 fiscal federal data for the regions, he examined the relationship
between fiscal transfers and a range of regional socio-economic and political variables. Multiple regression analysis showed that 'challenging
Moscow – whether by elite declaration, mass action or public voting – paid
off far better than complaisance'.[32] In particular, 'those regions that adroitly
manipulated the weapons of early sovereignty declarations, and where the
population was ready to back up demands with strikes, managed to extract
substantially more than those that were more docile'.[33] Moreover, those
regions that voted against Yeltsin in the 1991 Russian (RSFSR) presidential
election were also favoured. It would therefore seem that it is the geopolitical leverage and rhetoric of nationalist politics – the threat or perceived
threat of secession or withdrawal from the system of fiscal federalism – that
result in the greater likelihood of a region's securing economic benefits.
However, although it has been noted that in the mid-1990s the centre has
continued to favour regions in exchange for their commitment to the federation's territorial integrity, it may well be that use of the 'secessionist card' is
less effective than it was during the early years, when the prospect of federal
dissolution seemed greater.[34] There is some evidence to suggest that as a
geopolitical weapon secession is less effective for regional elites who engage
in such a form of oppositional politics. This has been the case with

Primorskii krai, the most recent region to engage in a politics of secession, which is designed less to establish a Far Eastern republic than to secure for the region certain economic and political demands from the centre, notably in relation to fiscal resource allocation, regional economic policy and the demarcation of the border with China. Despite the rhetoric of its leadership and a record of regional disobedience, there is no evidence that Primorskii krai has gained through resource allocations. In part, of course, this may be a product of the more limited economic or geopolitical leverage that it has at its disposal compared with such geopolitical heavyweights as Chechnya or Sakha.

The regional state and strategies for development, I: privatisation

Moscow has embarked upon the most ambitious scheme of privatisation ever conducted. In 1992, it began the process of denationalising state industrial enterprises and encouraging the decollectivisation of the rural economy, although the latter process has been slow, hampered by the lack of legislation on private land ownership. Many of Russia's public services have also been privatised. By 1997, about three-quarters of the country's smaller industrial enterprises had been denationalised through the so-called 'voucher system', whereby employees, managerial personnel and citizens could 'buy in' to these companies. Subsequently, a proportion of those shares were sold to private capital and have in turn been bought up by outside investors. However, while the centre has initiated the process of privatisation, it has been left to the regions to implement it. Despite the centre's wish to proceed apace, the regions have been generally slow to execute its wishes.

There is some evidence to suggest that, as might be expected, traditionalist local leaderships, especially where the Communist Party is still in power, have been more likely to resist privatisation, bent as they are on preserving as much of the state-controlled economic environment as possible. While there is a relationship between the type of regime in power locally and the extent to which market reform has been implemented, the response of regional elites is more complex than such ideological labelling might suggest. According to Hanson, the propensity of regional political elites to respond positively to centralised economic reforms has been conditioned largely by the incentive for regional elites to resist, steer or modify the process of privatisation, in order both to ensure that those within the region benefit (including local capital) and to maximise extraction of rents from local assets.[35] Selling off profitable state enterprises therefore may not be in the interests of financially hard-pressed regions concerned with raising the necessary public funds to sustain local employment or pay for public services. The regions thus pursue policies aimed at ensuring that they do not lose control over their more lucrative resources.

This preoccupation with maintaining local public control over highly valued state assets is illustrated by the case of Sakha's diamond industry. As the largest and most powerful region in Siberia, but with a population of only one million, Sakha is a resource-dependent republic, with diamonds by far the most important of its rich and varied natural resources. The republic produces over 99 per cent of Russia's diamonds and accounts for about a quarter of the world's supply. Thus, retaining control over the diamond industry is a high priority for the republican authorities because of the revenue and negotiating power it gives them *vis-à-vis* Moscow.[36] As a consequence, the Sakha authorities have created their own joint-stock company through which they retain a proportion of shares in the diamond industry. Moreover, rather than simply concerning themselves with the extraction of uncut diamonds for export – traditionally the mainstay of the region's diamond industry – the Sakha authorities have also provided capital to develop the processing of diamonds and other aspects of the industry, including purchasing, grading, marketing and selling. Bypassing Moscow, the Sakha authorities also subscribe directly to the International Diamond Cartel, De Beers, which is responsible for regulating the world market in diamonds. Thus, preventing outside capital from controlling the diamond industry and weakening Moscow's influence have been key to their local development strategy.

Regional political elites therefore appear to weigh up a series of factors in calculating the opportunities and costs presented by the process of privatisation. According to Slider's study of the regional response to the centre's privatisation programme, such opportunities include the possibility of the regional regime's using privatisation to retain a place for 'their people' in positions of power within reorganised industrial enterprises, as well as the prospects of raising income for the local budget from the proceeds of sales of enterprises.[37] In contrast, the main costs represented by privatisation identified by Slider were the prospects of loss of control by local administrators and economic managers over the running of the regional economy. This fear that privatisation could undermine the capacity of regional elites to manage their region was also bound up with a widespread concern that privatisation could eventually result in 'outsiders' exerting an inordinate influence over regional matters. In addition, the regional authorities also feared that newly privatised enterprises might risk bankruptcy, so raising the prospects of local mass unemployment, which could undermine the political legitimacy of those in power in the region.

The studies mentioned above signal two things in particular. First, the main disincentive to local privatisation is loss of control over the region's assets; second, regional elites are concerned about maintaining social stability. Understanding why some regions are likely to resist privatisation while others have embarked upon it can be analysed most fruitfully through comparative case studies. Two regions instructive in this regard are Ulyanovsk, one of the staunchest communist and anti-reformist regions, and Nizhnii Novgorod, widely regarded as 'the flagship of Russia's market reforms'. Both of these regions in central Russia are highly urbanised, with more than 70 per cent of their respective populations of 1.5 and 3.7 million living in cities. Although there are important differences in regional economic activities, both are dominated by a traditional manufacturing base, with a significant sector of their urban-industrial workforce dependent for their livelihood on the military–industrial sector.

Ulyanovsk is symbolically important to the Communist Party, not least because it is the birthplace of its twentieth-century icon, Lenin. Throughout the 1990s, it has remained staunchly communist, and in the 1996 presidential elections it voted for the Communist Party candidate Gennadii Zyuganov. Since 1991, it has been led by a populist governor, Yurii Goryachev, who was the head of the region's Communist Party in the 1970s. Although elected as governor in the regional elections of December 1996, he was not on this occasion backed by the Communist Party, which dominates the regional assembly. While there is little doubt that the longevity of Goryachev's career reflects his populist 'cult of personality' appeal, his position has also been reinforced by his opposition to local democracy. The local press has reportedly been subject to persecution and censorship, while local social movements have had little opportunity to challenge his authoritarian style of governance. Yet as Magomedev notes: 'Ulyanovsk's political system cannot simply be dismissed as nostalgia for the Soviet era or as desperate clinging to the past. Instead, it represents an attempt by existing local elites to adapt to the new epoch of mass politics'.[38]

Until the mid-1990s, the Ulyanovsk administration resisted both privatisation and liberalisation, preferring instead to keep tight administrative control over the local economy and public services. To do otherwise, it was argued, would lead to economic anarchy and to control over the region being ceded to the whims of venture capitalists.[39] In what can only be described as an appeal to populist politics, the regional government was one of only a handful of regions which continued to maintain local price controls and state subsidies. As a consequence, the population was shielded from the high food prices found in neighbouring regions as a result of the adoption of price liberalisation policies. By the mid-1990s, the citizens of Ulyanovsk enjoyed one of the lowest costs of living in Russia. Moreover, any incentive to privatise in order to raise additional public capital was offset by Ulyanovsk's continuing to receive large federal subsidies from the centre, although in an attempt to stimulate business activity the regional state did set up a network of local state-controlled commercial outlets.

Since 1996, however, Ulyanovsk has gradually been moving towards market exchange. Food and housing prices have been gradually rising to the Russian average as the region can no longer afford to subsidise its citizens. However, it has transpired that the populist policies pursued by the regional authorities were up until the mid-1990s largely financed by the region's huge automobile factory (UAZ): cars were sold at market prices and tax receipts were channelled into subsidising cheaper food and housing. By the late 1990s, however, the UAZ plant was finding difficulty in securing markets for its cars, and the system began to break down.[40] Thus, despite the official rhetoric, the regional state had been involved in a policy of selective economic liberalisation aimed at maintaining state-sector subsidies.

In contrast, Nizhnii Novgorod's regional elites seized upon the opportunities offered by democratisation and economic reform to establish a completely new type of regional economy in Russia. Led from 1991 to 1997 by a young technocrat, Boris Nemtsov, the region quickly embarked upon a radical set of economic policies. These included the mass sale of state industrial assets, the liberalisation of trade, house privatisation and the introduction of policies designed to encourage both local and outside private investment. By 1997, 95.5 per cent of the region's small enterprises were in private hands.[41] Three factors were key to Nizhnii's success. First, it had the support of market reformers at the centre, who were happy to see the region – containing Russia's third-largest city, Nizhnii Novgorod (formerly Gorkii) – serve as a laboratory where reforms that might later be applied elsewhere in Russia could be tested. As Buss and Yancer note, 'reformers [in Moscow] chose Nizhnii-Novgorod as a national demonstration site – it seemed a typical regional city and its political leadership were deeply committed to privatisation'.[42] Second, in contrast with most other regions, where attempts to introduce economic reform often ended up in deadlock owing to competing interests, the local authorities in Nizhnii displayed a remarkable degree of consensus in terms of both the adoption and the execution of economic policies. From the outset, the city and regional authorities were prepared to work together through a co-ordinating council, responsible for setting out the region's reform programme. Headed by Nemtsov, it quickly worked out a clear four-part development strategy that sought to promote privatisation from the bottom up, including the establishment of small businesses and the decollectivisation of farms; to privatise commercial and public transportation; to convert the defence industries to non-military production; and to reform social welfare. Finally, considerable financial and technical know-how was secured both from the federal budget and from overseas. This included support from the World Bank and its private sector affiliate, the International Finance Company. Massive capital investment from outside the region thus facilitated the process of privatisation in a region which benefited from a head start in economic reform. This helped to promote a massive expansion in local businesses, including privately owned local services, especially in the retail sector. In its social welfare reforms, Nizhnii has also managed to convince privatised firms to continue contributing to its citizens' social welfare, even though private firms are not obliged by law to do so. Private capital appears to see such a policy as a way of holding onto skilled labour that is at risk of being recruited by higher paying employers.

Nizhnii continues to be held up by the state's market reformers as a symbol of the new Russia, but, as with Ulyanovsk, its exceptional status can be overstated. Myths of regional exceptionalism persist, not least concerning Nizhnii's achievements since embarking upon the transition to local capitalism. While the region has been one of the country's few federal donor regions (with the exception of 1997), the region suffers from the near universal problem of wage, pension and other benefit arrears. Moreover, nearly one-third of the region's inhabitants live below the poverty line. The problem of the region's dependency on a large military–industrial sector has also not been resolved.[43]

The regional state and strategies for development, II: connecting up with the global economy

A notable feature of the politics of economic transition has been the way in which much of the responsibility and initiative for the globalisation of Russia's economy has passed from the centre to the regions. As a consequence of the limited effectiveness of the central state in wooing both outside investment and trading partners to Russia's provinces, the regions have accused Moscow of lacking a coherent and viable regional economic policy.[44] The provinces may have a point. By mid-1997, more than 60 per cent of all inward investment in Russia was going to Moscow, and 10 per cent to St. Petersburg, with the other 87 regions garnering less than 30 per cent between them. While the reasons why this has occurred are beyond the remit of this chapter, it does appear as though regions governed by the Communist Party are being shunned by overseas investors because their economies are perceived to be less open and less conducive to investment. Southern Russia's so-called 'red belt' has suffered as a consequence, as has the geopolitically unstable North Caucusus.[45]

Initially, however, it was the centre that was the key actor in opening up the regions to outside investment and overseas trade. The establishment of joint venture schemes in the late 1980s permitted the country's economic enterprises to form partnerships with foreign investors and overseas companies. Since the establishment of statehood, Russia's policies on trade and investment liberalisation have been extended greatly. Foreign enterprises have been granted similar investment opportunity rights as indigenous capital, including the right to purchase shares in Russian companies. The regional authorities, along with city and individual economic enterprises, can also become directly involved in investment opportunities abroad with overseas companies and transnational financial institutions, as well as trade internationally. In short, the liberalisation of investment and trade has become institutionally more regionalised.

Subsequently, however, the efficacy of measures taken by the central state to encourage trade and investment involving the regions has been limited. One of the few attempts to stimulate regional economy activity has entailed the creation of special (or free) economic zones (SEZs). Influenced initially by the success of the Chinese model of opening certain coastal cities to outside trade and investment, the central authorities earmarked certain 'beneficially located territorial enclaves' where foreign firms and joint ventures would enjoy special tax, customs and other incentives. In 1997, the state extended this scheme by permitting the creation of six types of SEZs: duty-free production and trading zones; special regional economic zones; zones for technological research and development; zones for the provision of international services; offshore banking centres; and tourist and recreational zones.[46] While some SEZs, like Kaliningrad *oblast'*, are exempt from import duties, others, like Nakhodka, benefit from tax breaks and simplified procedures for import and export operations. Although they are widely regarded as ineffective, the number of SEZs was increased from the initial 11 (seven of which were in Siberia) to 25 by 1998 (see Fig. 8.4).[47]

Such schemes have been widely criticised both in Moscow and the provinces on the grounds of underfunding, their unclear rubric, choice of localities and susceptibility to corruption. The fact that the regional authorities have had to find much of the resources to finance such schemes has on occasion had disastrous consequences. In October 1991, the Sakhalin SEZ, in an attempt to overcome a shortfall in the capital needed to encourage inward investment, wrecked its chances of attracting investment from leading Western oil companies by insisting that oil companies also invest in the region's physical and social infrastructure. There is also ambiguity surrounding the choice of localities. Some SEZs seem to have been chosen for geoeconomic reasons – to facilitate not only local regeneration but to stimulate growth in localities designated as hub or gateway regions, as in the case of Kaliningrad and St. Petersburg, with regard to Europe, and Chita and Sakhalin *oblast's* in relation to the Pacific Rim. Others seem to have been chosen for purely geopolitical reasons, as in the case of politically unstable Dagestan, Ingushetia and North Ossetia. Moreover, the central authorities have not been immune to using SEZs as political weapons in negotiating favourable terms in power-sharing agreements with the regions. This appears to have been the case with Ingushetia, whose 3-year privileges as an SEZ came abruptly to an end in 1997. While the Ingush authorities argued that abolishing the SEZ would create a severe economic and social crisis in a region where there were large numbers of refugees from conflict zones in neighbouring regions, Moscow's response was that it could no longer afford to exempt the region from federal taxes as part of its special status.[48] However, following the subsequent negotiation of a power-sharing treaty with Moscow, Ingushetia was reinstated as an SEZ. Finally, because of a lack of public accountability and transparency, federal funds to support the scheme have been susceptible to local corruption. In 1997, for example, the head of the Altai SEZ, created in 1995, was involved in siphoning off billions of rubles from federal subsidies that the region received as a result of its special status, in order to fund his campaign for election to the post of regional governor.[49]

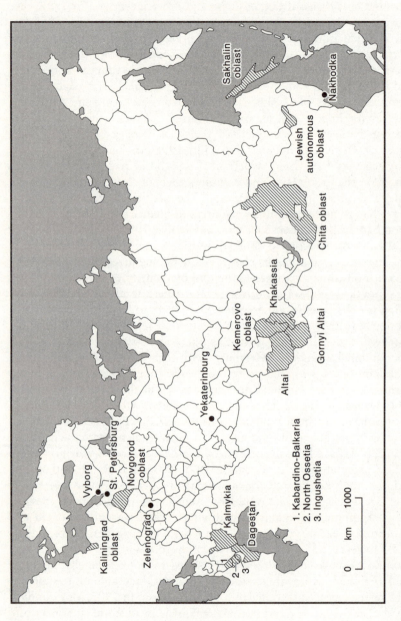

Figure 8.4 The main special economic zones in Russia, 1998. Source: S. Mitin and G. Charodeev, 'SEZ. Na svobodu s chestoi sovest'yu', *Izvestiya*, 10 July 1998, p. 2, and other sources.

In the absence of an effective regional policy, it is the increasingly proactive role being played by regional elites that has become crucial to shaping the geography of trade and inward investment. Some regions have seized the initiative by introducing their own schemes to attract local investment, including tax-free incentives for potential investors. Pioneered by Novgorod, the scheme entails offering short-term, local, tax-free incentives to foreign investors to put their money into local production facilities, by freeing would-be investors from local taxes until businesses become profitable. This has helped to create new jobs and improve the region's physical and social infrastructure. A further 15 regions have followed Novgorod's lead.[50]

How regions sell themselves within the global market place does, however, differ. Two of the most innovative are St. Petersburg and Novosibirsk which, like Moscow, Sverdlovsk, Nizhnii Novgorod and a handful of other regions, have foreign exchange bourses with a high turnover.[51] These regional states have either already managed to secure a niche as regions with global links or, through their strategies for regeneration, aspire to do so.

Both St. Petersburg and Novosibirsk have attempted to play on their status as cultural centres as a basis for selling themselves. In the case of St. Petersburg, this has entailed a strategy of 'civic boosterism' in which local budget funds have been used to promote the city's image as Russia's most European city and its 'window on the West' to attract outside venture and tourist capital, and to bolster local pride in the city's history and achievements. Thus, despite spending constraints throughout the 1990s, the city authority continued to earmark a significant proportion of public funds to city festivals, its sports teams and the local heritage industry. Mayor Anatolii Sobchak, in particular, saw the regeneration of local pride as central to the strategy of selling the city. As Mellor notes, 'his guiding vision was that of its restoration to its Petrine status as window to Western Europe, financial and cultural centre for Russia'.[52] Yet this attempt to make St. Petersburg a global city – which included an expensive but unsuccessful bid to stage the 2004 Olympic Games – exposed tension between those in the city leadership who espoused property-led regeneration strategies and those who favoured municipal social welfarism. Priority was given to attracting outside investment in modern communications, hotel complexes and a service industry geared towards foreign tourism at the expense of the social consumption needs of city inhabitants. Consequently, while the overtures to venture capital and access to Western technologies, as well as the resources released by privatisation, have helped to create a new wealthy class of young native entrepreneurs, the majority of city residents, particularly those dependent on the public sector for employment or social welfare, are suffering from deteriorating schools, health and other social services, and the problem of homelessness is growing.

Like St. Petersburg, Novosibirsk also aspires to a global role. Its strategy has been to repackage itself as the gateway region between Europe and Asia, and it hopes to make its major city and the country's fourth largest,

Novosibirsk, a rival to Moscow and St. Petersburg as a global financial centre. Indeed, 'internationalisation of the local economy appears to represent ... an attempt to argue for inclusion in "Asia" rather than (or as well as) Europe'.[53] Despite the comparative disadvantages of a largely uncompetitive economy and continuing dependency on the defence industry, the region's authorities – administrative, capital and labour – have displayed a marked degree of unity in opening up the local economy to global competition. This strategy has entailed drawing upon the city's Soviet heritage as an established scientific centre of research and development, and seeking to channel this expertise into a knowledge-based, high-value-added regional economy based on technical and organisational innovation. The promotion of research and development is a key component of this strategy. This policy is designed to make the region more competitive, so that it can adapt to the changing conditions of the global economy. Moreover, rather than being seen as a cost, local labour is presented as a resource whose contribution is vital to the region's success. However, Novosibirsk's political elites have had relatively little cash to play with. Indeed, the authorities complain that they receive ever more responsibilities for local public finance from Moscow but less and less federal funding.[54] Public sector wages and heating take up the bulk of the city's budget.

Some regions are also pursuing 'global strategies' more familiar to Europe's regions, with inter-regional civic links being used to bolster trade agreements and facilitate both inward investment and overseas markets. Thus, Nizhnii Novgorod has signed regional co-operation agreements with a number of European regions, including Nordrhein-Westfalen (Germany), Bouches-du-Rhône (France), Moravia (Czech Republic) and Rusenskii region (Bulgaria). And in October 1997, a special festival was held in Germany, attended by over 100 representatives from Nizhnii, in celebration of the success of the region's market reforms. While Nizhnii may be the most conspicuous regional state to use the market as a means of aspiring to 'global region' status, it is, as we have noted, not alone. For its part, the central state has tended to treat such regional activities with benign neglect if not active encouargement, since there is nothing at stake that threatens its territorial integrity.

Think globally, act regionally and lobby supraregionally

Rather than simply thinking globally and acting regionally, there is a third developmental strategy open to the regional state: the opportunity to use membership of inter-regional associations to press for concessions from Moscow through collective action. Since the formation of the Siberian Accord in 1991, the number of inter-regional associations has grown to eight, and now includes virtually all of Russia's regions (Table 8.1). While

Table 8.1 Russia's regional associations, 1999

Regional association	Members
Siberian Accord	*Republics*: Buryatia, Altai, Khakassia *Krais*: Altai, Krasnoyarsk *Oblasts*: Irkutsk, Novosibirsk, Omsk, Tomsk, Tyumen,[a] Kemerovo *Autonomous okrugs*: Agin-Buryat, Taimyr, Ust-Orda Buryat, Khanty-Mansi, Evenk, Yamal-Nenets
Far East and Baikal Association	*Republics*: Sakha, Buryatia *Krais*: Primorskii and Khabarovsk *Oblasts*: Amur, Kamchatka, Magadan, Chita, Sakhalin, Jewish autonomous oblast *Autonomous okrugs*: Koryak, Chukotka
Greater Volga Association	*Republics*: Tatarstan, Mordovia, Chuvashia, Mari-El[b] *Oblasts*: Astrakhan, Volgograd, Nizhnii Novgorod, Penza, Samara, Saratov, Ulyanovsk
Central Russian Association	*Oblasts*: Moscow, Bryansk, Vladimir, Ivanovo, Kaluga, Kostroma, Ryazan, Smolensk, Tver, Tula, Yaroslavl *City* of Moscow
Association of the North Caucasus	*Republics*: Adygeya, Dagestan, Ingushetia, Kabardino-Balkaria, Karachaevo-Cherkessia, North Ossetia, Kalmykia *Krais*: Krasnodar, Stavropol *Oblast*: Rostov
Black Earth Association	*Oblasts*: Orel, Voronezh, Belgorod, Kursk, Lipetsk, Tambov
Urals Association	*Republics*: Bashkortostan, Udmurtia *Autonomous okrug*: Komi-Permyak *Oblasts*: Sverdlovsk, Kurgan, Orenburg, Perm, Chelyabinsk
North-West Association	*Republics*: Karelia, Komi *Oblasts*: Kaliningrad, Kirov, Leningrad, Murmansk, Novgorod, Pskov, Arkhangelsk, Volgoda *Autonomous okrug*: Nenets *City* of St. Petersburg

[a] Tyumen oblast now belongs to the Urals Association (*Zaurale* [Kurgan], 10 July 1997).
[b] Mari-El has left the Greater Volga Association (*Jamestown Foundation Prism*, February 1998).
Sources: *Russian Regional Report*, 15 January 1997; *Moskovskie novosti*, 22–29 December 1996.

set up to facilitate the transition to the market economy through promoting inter-regional planning and trade between the regions, the associations quickly evolved to become an important means of strengthening the regions' individual lobbying efforts in their relations with Moscow. Hence, besides co-ordinating the region's economic restructuring, the Siberian Accord sought, through political co-operation, to give Siberia's regions a stronger voice to enable them to maximise their region's share of the federal budget and so reverse decades of dependence on European Russia.[55] Each association now possesses its own supraregional institutional structures: an executive (elected from the pool of regional governors) and various committees covering economic concerns such as energy, agriculture, the environment and industrial policy. Rather than opposing them, Moscow has generally welcomed the associations as a way of facilitating a more carefully co-ordinated transition to capitalism. In 1995, for example, as a result of its successful lobbying efforts, the Greater Volga Association managed to secure 15 per cent of the funds required to finance an economic modernisation programme for the Volga from the centre.[56] In periods of economic crisis in the regions, Moscow has also on occasion preferred to deal with the regional associations rather than with regions directly. This was the case during a miners' strike in Kemerovo *oblast'* in July 1998, in which the miners managed to disrupt the flow of essential goods to neighbouring Siberian regions by picketing the Trans-Siberian Railway.[57] By preferring to try to settle the strike by dealing with the chairman of the Siberian Accord (the governor of neighbouring Tomsk *oblast'*), Moscow used the association to exert pressure on Kemerovo to resolve the crisis. However, the central authorities are also well aware that, when necessary, the federal card of divide and rule can be used to weaken the power of the associations.

Not surprisingly, it is those regional associations with the most economic and political leverage that have emerged as the most effective regional lobbyists. Besides the Siberian lobby, these include the associations of the Urals, Volga and Central Russia. Thus, the Urals region, with its nine member regions, comprises a powerful lobby of eighteen representatives in the upper house of the Russian Parliament, the Federation Council. And the associations have not been slow to use their access to federal institutions to place regional initiatives on the national agenda. In one notable act of solidarity, members of the Volga region supported pioneering legislation passed in Saratov allowing citizens the right to buy and sell land.[58]

Nonetheless, doubts have been raised about the associations' accountability to their constituent regions, especially the way in which, despite a fixed term, regional governors elected to the presidency of an association tend to use the post as a way of promoting their particular region. During his presidency of the Greater Volga Association between 1994 and 1996, Samara's governor, Konstantin Titov, succeeded in turning Samara into the *de facto* capital of the Greater Volga Region. Samara managed to secure and subsequently retain a dominant role as the Volga's recognised regional

leader, and it became home of the regional association's executive direc-
torate and the major inter-regional committees. Holding the presidency of
inter-regional associations can also play an important role in launching
national careers for regional governors. As a consequence of holding the
presidency of a very powerful and successful regional lobby, that of the
Urals Region, Sverdlovsk Governor Eduard Rossel has been elevated to
national prominence. In short, presidency of the regional associations provides a stepping stone for regional politicians seeking to enter the national
political arena.

Yet the power of the associations to act as an effective force for regionalism has to compete with the self-interests of individual members. Progress
towards closer economic co-operation has thus often been undermined as
individual regions continue to carry out their own particular policies of
trade protection, cartelised capitalism and price subsidisation. Nor do members of the same regional association automatically give each other prefer-
ence over regions further afield. In 1997, for instance, Bashkortostan
bought 300 buses from a firm outside the Urals region, despite the fact that
neighbouring Kurgan could have supplied these vehicles more quickly and
cheaply.[59] Self-interest is also reinforced by the federal system, which tends
to pit one region against another. The Siberian Accord, which originally
included regions of the Far East and Baikal Association, fragmented in part
because the larger *oblast's* resented the way in which Sakha used its position
as Siberia's largest and most powerful ethnorepublic to secure considerable
economic and financial autonomy from Moscow. In other cases, unsettled
inter-regional territorial and ethnic claims have undermined solidarity,
which has even resulted in splits, as in the case of Kalmykia, which left the
Greater Volga Association following a territorial dispute with neighbouring
Astrakhan *oblast'*.

Conclusions

This chapter has offered an account of the rise to prominence of the regional
state in Russia and of the role that it is playing in remapping the country's
economic and political landscape. Increasingly, it would seem, the regions
are engaging in developmental strategies that maximise the benefits to their
own localities, although the extent to which such a process means engagement with democratic practices is not always apparent. It should also not be
assumed that opposition to central economic or fiscal policies is necessarily
tantamount to support for secession. Indeed, from a more global viewpoint,
there is nothing exceptional in some of the behavioural facets of Russia's
regions: pursuing strategies geared towards the regional interest, which also
includes the opportunity to connect directly with the global economy, has
become a characteristic feature of many regions elsewhere that enjoy federated or some form of autonomous status. The problem of regionalism, then,

may not be as intractable a political issue as has often been suggested. Not least, regionalism has now a greater opportunity to provide the space for localities to reconstitute a plurality of economic agendas which may or may not be a mirror image of the sort of agenda envisaged by the centre.

Notes to Chapter 8

1 *Kommersant-Daily*, 21 March 1997.
2 M. Castells, *The Power of Identity* (Oxford, Basil Blackwell, 1997), p. 272.
3 O. Kryshtanovskaya and S. White, 'From Soviet nomenklatura to Russian elite', *Europe–Asia Studies*, 48(5), 1996.
4 D. Slider, 'Elections to Russia's regional assembles', *Post-Soviet Affairs*, 12(3), 1996, p. 243.
5 *Rossiiskie vesti*, 3 December 1996.
6 R. Orttung and A. Paretskaya, 'Presidential election demonstrates rural–urban divide', *Transition*, 2(19), 1996, pp. 33–8.
7 S. Medvedev, 'Russia's regional elections. A step towards federalism', unpublished manuscript (Helsinki, 1997); S. Solnick, 'Gubernatorial elections in Russia', *Post-Soviet Affairs*, 14(1), 1998, pp. 48–80; L. Belin, 'All sides claim victory in 1996 gubernatorial elections', *Russian Regional Report*, 2(1), 8 January 1997 – L. Smirnyagin's observations on this appear in *Rossiiskie vesti*, 3 December 1996.
8 *Rossiiskie vesti*, 3 December 1996.
9 Medvedev, 'Russia's regional elections', p. 6.
10 C. Wallich, 'Reforming intergovernmental relations. Russia and the challenge of fiscal federalism', in B. Kaminski (ed.), *Economic Transition in Russia and the New States of Eurasia* (New York and London, M.E. Sharpe, 1997), pp. 252–76.
11 O. Bogacheva, 'Stanovlenie rossiiskoi modeli byudzhetnogo federalizma', *Voprosy ekonomiki*, 8, 1996, pp. 30–40.
12 L. Aidinova, 'Arifmetika lyubvi', *Vek*, 15, 10–16 April 1998, p. 4.
13 P. Kirkow, 'Distributional coalitons, budgetary problems and fiscal federalism in Russia', *Communist Economics and Economic Transformation*, 8(1), 1996, pp. 277–98.
14 A. Lavrov, 'Rossiiskii byudzhetnyi federalizm. Pervye shagi, pervye itogi', *Segodnya*, 7 June 1995, p. 5.
15 *Rossiiskie vesti*, 20 May 1997.
16 *Russian Economic Trends*, 2, 1997, p. 124.
17 Wallich, 'Reforming intergovernmental relations'.
18 Lavrov, 'Rossiiskii byudzhetnyi federalizm'.
19 Lavrov, 'Rossiiskii byudzhetnyi federalizm'.
20 *Moskovskie novosti*, 9 July 1993, p. 2.
21 R. Bahl and S. Wallace, 'Revenue sharing in Russia', *Environment and Planning C. Government and Policy*, 12(3), 1994, pp. 293–307.
22 P. Hanson, 'How many Russias? Russia's regions and their adjustment to economic change', *The International Spectator*, 32(1), 1997, pp. 39–52.
23 Wallich, 'Reforming intergovernmental relations'.
24 *Obshchaya gazeta*, 13 May 1998, p. 5.
25 D. Slider, 'Privatisation in Russia's regions', *Post-Soviet Affairs*, 10(4), 1994, pp. 367–96.
26 *Russian Economic Trends*, 2, 1997.
27 Medvedev, 'Russia's regional elections', p. 8.
28 *Segodnya*, 7 May 1998, p. 1.

29 Lavrov, 'Rossiiskii byudzhetnyi federalizm'.
30 S. Tarrow, *Power in Movement* (Cambridge, Cambridge University Press, 1998).
31 D. Berkowitz, 'Regional income and secession. Centre–periphery relations in emerging market economies', *Regional Science and Urban Economics*, 27(1), 1997, p. 19.
32 D. Treisman, 'The politics of intergovernmental transfers in post-Soviet Russia', *British Journal of Political Science*, 26(3), 1996, p. 322.
33 Treisman, 'The politics of intergovernmental transfers in post-Soviet Russia', p. 327.
34 Kirkow, 'Distributional coalitons, budgetary problems and fiscal federalism in Russia'.
35 Hanson, 'How many Russias?'.
36 P. Fryer and N. Lynn, 'National-territorial change in the republics of the Russian north', *Political Geography*, 17(5), 1998, pp. 567–88.
37 Slider, 'Privatisation in Russia's regions'.
38 A. Magomedev, 'The Ulyanovsk phenomeonon. From the Chinese path to the North Korean path', *Prism*, 4(4), 1997, p. 1.
39 F. Evers, 'Reformen und Soziales in der rußlandischen Provinz am Beispiel von Uljanowsk, *Osteuropa*, 3, 1997, pp. 256–66.
40 *Izvestiya*, 18 February 1996 and 5 March 1997.
41 *Russian Economic Trends*, 2, 1997.
42 T. Buss and L. Yancer, 'Privatising the Russian economy. The Nizhny Novgorod experience', *Environment and Planning C. Government and Policy*, 14(2), 1996, p. 213.
43 *Moskovskii komsomolets*, 4 June 1997.
44 *Izvestiya*, 13 November 1997.
45 *The Economist*, 3 January 1998, p. 32.
46 *Kommersant-Daily*, 6 February 1997.
47 *Izvestiya*, 10 July 1998, p. 2.
48 *Segodnya*, 9 July 1997.
49 *Trud*, 29 October 1997.
50 *Nezavisimaya gazeta*, 16 October 1997; *Izvestiya*, 13 November 1997.
51 Hanson, 'How many Russias?'.
52 R. Mellor, 'Through a glass darkly. Investigating the St. Petersburg administration', *International Journal of Urban and Regional Research*, 21(3), 1997, p. 489.
53 M. Bradshaw, A. Stenning and D. Sutherland, 'Economic Restructuring and Change in Russia', in J. Pickles and A. Smith (eds), *Theorising Transition. The Political Economy of Post-Communist Transformations* (London, Routledge, 1998), p. 163.
54 *Moskovskie novosti*, 12 May 1998, pp. 12–13.
55 J. Hughes, 'Regionalism in Russia. The rise and fall of the Siberian agreement', *Europe–Asia Studies*, 46(7), 1994, pp. 1133–61.
56 I. Malyakin, 'The Greater Volga Association', *Prism*, 4(3), 1998, pp. 1–2.
57 *Segodnya*, 10 July 1998, p. 5.
58 *Rossiiskaya gazeta*, 9 July 1998.
59 I. Stepanov, 'Urals Assocation strives to boost its cohesion and influence', *Russian Regional Review*, 3(15), 16 April 1998, p. 1.

Conclusions

|9|

Geopolitical futures

Chirot's observation that 'it is muddled transitional periods that dominate history, not the ideal types around which strong theories are built' is germane to framing any discussion of the post-Soviet transition.[1] While pessimists tend to latch on to the view that the post-Soviet states will be engulfed in further inter-communal violence, autocracy and economic crisis, more optimistic analysts argue that the dangers of transition associated with the initial breakdown of the Soviet Union have passed and that the prospects for democracy, greater economic security and regional stability are now brighter. What is indisputable is the existence of innumerable uncertainties, making any such predictions a daunting and often futile task. However, both comparative and geopolitical theory can help to put possible scenarios in context by facilitating an exploration of some of the main political, social and economic forces at work in mapping out possible outcomes. Such an approach uses both geopolitical theory and comparisons with other transitions as a way of interpreting, re-evaluating and clarifying events rather than engaging in pure prediction. This chapter takes a critical look at four of the most prominent theories of transition.

'Weimar Russia'

Russia's difficulties in coming to terms with the loss of the former homeland-empire and the challenges it faces in securing a stable democracy have generated interest in historical analogies with Weimar Germany. Various theories of regime breakdown that draw upon comparisons with the post-imperial and democratically fragile Weimar Republic (1918–33) have been formulated, based upon the assumption that unsuccessful attempts to secure democracy in Russia may, as in inter-war Germany, be superseded by the rise of a Far Right and the subsequent emergence of a totalitarian state. Others challenge the relevance of such comparisons by arguing that as history never repeats itself, analogies with Weimar Germany can do little to aid understanding of contemporary political events.[2] The main comparisons that have been made, either in part or in whole, are given below:[3]

1. Both Germany, after the internationally imposed Versailles Peace Settlement of 1919, and Russia, following the end of the Soviet Union, lost their homeland-empires. After World War I, large numbers of Germans residing in neighbouring countries were separated from what many regarded as their political homeland, just as a large Russian diaspora was stranded in the near abroad following the disintegration of the Soviet Union. In post-1991 Russia, as in inter-war Germany, the collapse of empire has greatly dented national pride, and generated mistrust of the West. A desire to reunite all members of the nation in one political homeland and to restore the country to its former national glory is envisaged as an important geopolitical project.

2. New and fragile democratic regimes were formed in both Germany in 1918 and Russia in 1991. Like the Weimar Republic, Russia has experienced a volatile political system which has had to cope with a series of ongoing and deep economic and financial crises. As with Weimar Germany, rampant inflation and dramatic falls in economic production threaten to undermine Russia's fledgling democratic institutions. Moreover, as in Weimar Germany, the dramatic fall in average living standards and mass impoverisation, combined with the loss in social status of particular social groups, have resulted in the alienation of key sections of society. Probably most significantly, this includes the military.

3. As in inter-war Germany, contemporary Russia has witnessed the emergence of a nationalist Far Right with the necessary organisational resources and means of social mobilisation to compete effectively for votes. Russia's Far Right also has a populist programme based upon centralised state control, national renewal and a radical set of policies which claim to be able to resolve the country's political and economic problems. In Germany, the nationalist Far Right, with a populist programme for imperial rejuvenation and economic renewal, became a credible electoral force by the late 1920s, and by 1932 the National Socialist (Nazi) Party had emerged as the single largest political party in the Reichstag. There is also a substantial base of electoral support for the Far Right in Russia. Although support for its largest political organisation, the Liberal Democratic Party of Russia, peaked in 1993, with 11.4 per cent of the party-list vote, the Russian electorate remains volatile and has proved capable of switching its affiliations from one end of the political spectrum to the other, as shown in the results of more recent parliamentary (1995) and presidential (1996) elections.

However, the process and consequences of imperial breakdown were very different in Weimar Germany compared with Russia. Not only was the German collapse born out of the experience of total war, but the Weimar

Republic was saddled with economic reparations imposed by the victorious Great Powers, and part of its territory was occupied by those very powers that had contributed to Germany's defeat in 1918. The sense of humiliation and grievance that such events imposed upon the vanquished left an indelible mark on virtually all sections of German society. In contrast, while Western triumphalism associated with the end of the Cold War and the Soviet Union's disintegration left many Russians resentful of the West, the death knell of the totalitarian state was an event welcomed by most of its citizens. Indeed, it is the collective memory of totalitarianism and in particular of the mass genocide associated with Stalinism which provides present-day Russians with a clearer benchmark for judging the value of democracy than inter-war Germans possessed. There the horrors of the totalitarian state and the Holocaust still lay in the distant future.

Rather than simply describe regime similarities and differences, a more instructive comparative approach is to focus on what has been called 'the Weimar syndrome'.[4] Here, the political and socio-economic factors behind inter-war Germany's transition from democratic to totalitarian rule are analysed and compared with developments in contemporary Russia. Thus, the suitability of the Weimar Russia label is assessed by identifying the conditions that facilitated Germany's political transition and looking at the extent to which they are present in today's Russia. Three factors in particular are considered here: the nature and extent of support for the ethnic patron's diaspora; the degree to which parallels can be drawn between the international economic and political situations facing inter-war Germany and post-1991 Russia; and the extent to which similarities exist in support for the Far Right amongst key strategic institutional and social actors.

The collapse of both empires, in Germany in 1918 and Russia in 1991, resulted in their successor regimes' being separated from large numbers of their ethnic brethren or diaspora. In the case of inter-war Germany, a substantial German diaspora came into existence in territories that had been ceded from Germany and the Austro-Hungarian Empire to neighbouring countries and in the newly created sovereign states such as Poland, Czechoslovakia (especially the Sudetenland) and Austria. Both Weimar Germany and post-1991 Russia also mapped out particular 'geographical spheres of influence', corresponding closely with the geographical settlement of their respective diasporas. Just as Russia has its 'near abroad', inter-war Germany talked about its 'new abroad', a zone of influence synonymous with the so-called *Grenzdeutsche* (borderland Germans). Calls among homeland nationalists to heed the plight of the diaspora in states which have been characterised as nationalising regimes were as evident in inter-war Germany as they have been in post-1991 Russia.[5] Although the German diaspora was numerically smaller than the post-1991 Russian diaspora, the diaspora issue was arguably more acute in inter-war Europe. While in the Russian state the definition of a Russian citizen is based on legal criteria and calls to support those dubbed 'compatriots abroad' remain ambiguous, in inter-war Germany there was from the outset a tendency to define Germanness in terms of blood ties rather than as a legal category. In Germany's 'new abroad', the sense of alienation amongst the diaspora and support from homeland nationalists were by the 1930s to lead to irredentist demands for the nation's reunification in one political homeland. The German diaspora was also highly organised and supported by Far Right nationalist organisations in Germany. In Russia's 'near abroad', however, as noted in Chapter 4, the position of the diaspora is quite different. After initially supporting re-unification with the metropole-homeland, the Russian diaspora, most significantly in Ukraine, where nearly half of their number are concentrated, now seem to be moving towards integrating into the polity in which they reside.[6]

The irredentist potential of the diaspora in the post-Soviet borderlands is therefore much weaker than it was in Weimar Germany's borderlands. Not only are diasporic identities less clear-cut and the relationship to the external homeland more ambiguous, but Russia's Far Right nationalist organisations do not possess the political resources or social networks that linked the diaspora with homeland nationalists in Germany. In particular, the analogies often drawn between the situation of the Sudetenland Germans and the Russians in Estonia and Latvia need to be treated with caution. Over three-fifths of Russians in 'the near abroad' who have taken out Russian citizenship are concentrated in Estonia and Latvia, providing Moscow with a precedent, if it wishes to exercise it, to come to the aid of its citizens in the same way as Hitler did in relation to the Sudeten Germans in 1938. However, in contrast with the three million German-speakers of the Sudetenland, there is no equivalent scale of political support in the Baltic states for the Russian nationalist Far Right. Nor is there the financial support in the external homeland from nationalist organisations for the equivalent of the *Sudetendeutsche Partei* to mobilise the diaspora into effective collective action.

Weimar Germany's and post-Soviet Russia's relationship with the international economic and political system also warrants consideration. As Hanson and Kopstein argue, the high level of international pressure for economic marketisation appears to be operating in post-Soviet Russia perhaps even more powerfully than in the case of the Weimar Republic.[7] Weimar Germany pursued a model of organised or monopoly capitalism. This included practising a high degree of state intervention in order to protect internal markets through policies of cartelisation and high tariffs. As a consequence, significant proportions of the national space economy were not subject to international competition. In addition, large state subsidies were provided to certain sectors of the economy, notably agriculture. Inter-war Germany also faced international pressures to manage and repay its huge external debt. The Allies had demanded huge reparations, especially severe for a country whose markets had shrunk considerably as a result of the loss of both large parts of its national space economy and its overseas colonies.

Faced with hyperinflation in 1922, Germany suspended its reparations payments. In order to ensure that it continued to fulfil its debt obligations, an international advisory group formulated the so-called Dawes Plan in 1924, which provided both a timetable to reorganise Germany's Western debt and provided for a large foreign loan. Despite receiving such support to finance its recovery, Germany was very badly hit by the 1929 global recession. With international pressure to remain tied to the gold standard, the Weimar Republic was severely affected by the economic crisis, which resulted in mass unemployment. Thus, 'the burden of reparations payments and the strains of maintaining currency parity after 1929 reinforced the credibility of the extreme right'.[8] Unable to counter recession effectively, the Weimar state entered a crisis of legitimacy from which it was unable to recover.

Russia faces similar pressures from the global market economy. In the early 1990s in particular, Western pressures to implement the prevailing Western neo-liberal economic model of rapid transition to the market helped fuel hyperinflation, wiping out the savings of many ordinary Russian citizens in ways not incomparable with Germany in the early 1920s. At the same time, political pressures within Russia ensure that state protection and subsidisation of certain key sectors of the economy, notably manufacturing industry, coalmining, transport and collectivised agriculture, are retained. And despite extensive borrowing from global financial institutions, Russia has been unable to make further progress with economic reform or balancing the state budget. So severe is Russia's economic crisis that in August 1998 Moscow announced that it was formally defaulting on its foreign debt repayments and devaluing the ruble, and the government was forced to resign for the second time in a year. As in inter-war Germany, economic crisis threatens to jeopardise Russia's political stability. Moreover, because of the inability of the Russian economy to function as an effective and integral part of a market economy, a significant proportion of both the public and private sector has fallen back on a system of barter as a strategy for economic survival, in what Shlapentokh labels the refeudalisation of Russia.[9]

However, compared with the situation in inter-war Europe, a dense political, legal and economic network of global institutions now exists which is capable of applying pressure on members of the international community embarking upon an imperial or a totalitarian agenda. Not only would such a regime now have to contend with more international political, economic and financial institutions, but present-day international organisations have proven more effective in influencing the form that regimes take. In contrast, the only major international body of the inter-war years, the League of Nations, was ineffective in countering the actions of recalcitrant member states. Its use of sanctions, when employed, proved ineffectual, and its claim to global status was weakened considerably by the USA's never becoming a member, the Soviet Union's joining only in 1934 and the only brief membership of Germany from 1926 to 1933. Its successor organisation, the United

Nations, is a truly global and more effective international player. Along with a number of other international bodies – NATO, the European Union and an unprecedented number of international human rights organisations – the global community has at its disposal a greater capacity to exert leverage and influence over states that are judged not to be conforming to acceptable forms of international conduct and norms of behaviour.

Finally, it is important to consider the part that strategic institutional and social actors can play in supporting the Far Right. As in Weimar Germany, in post-Soviet Russia there are key social actors who have been alienated as a consequence of regime change. Probably the most important is the military. As Pipes contends,

> most analogies between contemporary Russia and Weimar Germany fall wide of the mark, but parallels between the general officers of the two are striking: one sees the same sense of degradation and thirst for revenge. As in Weimar Germany, civilian authorities in Russia exert only nominal control over the military; the Ministry of Defence [in Russia] has a single civilian executive.[10]

In both Weimar Germany and post-Soviet Russia, the military have had to endure not only an economic crisis that has resulted in a dramatic fall in military expenditures but also changes in the country's world status that question their sense of purpose and mission. However, while Russia's remilitarisation is not out of the question, and its military potential, through its nuclear capability, is far greater than was Nazi Germany's, the poor state of Russia's economy significantly reduces the likelihood that it will act on any imperial ambitions.

Another key social group is the rich capitalist class. In inter-war Germany, this group showed little interest in supporting the Weimar regime. Not only was the state regarded as too accommodating to the interests of labour in its social and economic policies, it was also seen as too weak to counter the influence wielded by the Communist Party. In Russia, a small but highly influential class of rich capitalists has emerged more or less overnight and has established enormous business empires embracing the media, the energy industry, real estate and financial institutions. For the moment at least, it prefers to engage in a corporate relationship with government, thereby spawning the suggestion that Russia is ruled by an oligarchy of politicians and rich businessmen. This business elite played a significant part in financing President Yeltsin's 1996 re-election campaign. But as in Weimar Germany, Russia's rich capitalists fear a government of the Far Left, particularly the prospect of renationalisation and the disruption of further integration into the global market economy. Thus, while the business elite is unlikely to jeopardise its access to the world economy by supporting the election of a Far Right government that would cut ties with the West, the idea of a strong state able to provide economic and political stability has obvious appeal.

There are other important differences in the social base of support for the Far Right in Russia. During the Weimar period in Germany, that support was, as Peukert points out, notable 'particularly among the disorientated new and old middle classes, the unemployed, the *declassés* and a younger generation deprived of secure prospects for the future'.[11] This contrasts with the situation in Russia, where the much smaller middle class has shown little propensity to vote for the Far Right (Table 9.1). Instead, the new middle class holds more to Western-liberal and cosmopolitan values. Russia's new small-business class is thoroughly Westernised and supportive of the country's further economic liberalisation and democratic reforms. Similarly, the younger generation also tends to be Westernised in its cultural tastes, social values and political attitudes. Rather, in contrast with Weimar Germany, in Russia the most significant support for the Far Right comes primarily from certain sections of the urban-industrial working class. According to one of the most comprehensive studies of Russian voting behaviour, the profile of the typical Far Right voter at the time of the 1995 parliamentary elections was that of a male who 'was likely to be of working age, living in a rural or smaller town, an industrial or agricultural worker or in the police or armed services, poorer than average, and with fewer years of formal education'.[12] In short, the Far Right and its various political groupings appeal especially to the more marginal and socially excluded.

As in Weimar Germany, the Far Right in Russia has had to compete with the Far Left for workers' votes. Working-class communities, particularly those in the provincial and small towns of Russia's so-called 'industrial rust belt', have enjoyed few of the economic benefits of the new system. In fact, economic restructuring has often had disastrous consequences for such groups. Both market reform and the country's demilitarisation threaten the livelihood of those dependent on manufacturing industry and the military–industrial complex. In such urban-industrial communities, state-owned factories are finding it particularly difficult to secure the financial resources necessary for modernisation, and the workplace no longer carries the extensive housing, childcare and recreational supports that it did during the late Soviet period. Many of these provincial towns remain 'company towns', their inhabitants still dependent for employment, public services and even housing on one state enterprise. However, in contrast with Weimar Germany, where the nationalist Far Right was able electorally to outbid the Far Left, the trend in Russia since the mid-1990s has moved in the opposite direction, with most working-class voters supporting the Communist Party.[13] Gellner's conclusion therefore seems particularly apt: 'Russia resembles the Weimar republic – inflation, humiliation, criminalisation, illegitimate new wealth – except for one feature: in interwar Europe, the worst were full of passionate intensity; the best lacked all conviction. Now, fortunately, the worst also lack conviction'.[14]

Table 9.1 Social structure and party support in Russia, 1995 (in percentages)

	Neo-Soviet	Liberal		Statist		Neo-nationalist		Percentage of total voters
	CPRF	Yabloko	Russia's Choice (Gaidar)	Our Home Is Russia	Russia's Women	LDPR	Congress of Russian Communities	
Total % supporting each party	26	11	5	11	7	11	4	
Gender								
Male	26	10	4	10	4	16	5	45
Female	25	12	6	13	10	8	3	55
Age								
18–29	11	17	9	13	7	13	3	19
30–54	24	11	5	11	7	13	6	48
55 and over	37	8	3	10	7	9	2	33
Income								
lower	28	8	3	9	8	14	3	
Midddle	29	10	3	11	7	12	4	
High	18	15	10	14	6	9	5	
Settlement								
Big city	22	13	8	12	7	8	4	40
Small city	24	13	4	9	7	12	4	35
Rural	32	7	2	12	6	17	4	26

Occupation							
Independent entrepreneur	10	16	16	13	0	7	10	3
Manager, bureaucrat	19	18	8	18	5	11	5	5
Professional	14	16	11	12	9	4	6	15
Military, MVD, procuracy	20	9	0	6	0	20	14	3
Routine white-collar worker	13	17	1	15	6	8	5	7
Worker	29	9	2	10	5	21	5	26
Student, school student	5	23	12	12	7	5	0	4
Pensioner, housewife	38	7	4	11	8	8	2	32
Unemployed	22	10	2	8	13	13	2	6
Education							
Higher, incomplete higher	17	21	15	13	4	3	4	17
Secondary	21	11	4	13	8	11	5	45
Elementary	36	8	2	9	6	16	3	37
n =	299	130	58	131	80	135	48	

Sources: S. White, *et al.*, 'Parties and voters in the 1995 Russian Duma election', *Europe–Asia Studies*, 49(5), 1997, p. 786. Based on VTs10M survey data gathered after the December 1995 parliamentary elections.

The new Eurasia: the hegemonic challenge

In contrast to comparativists, geopolitical theorists of transition have tended to focus on the role that Russia and the other post-Soviet states are likely to play in shaping the post-Cold-War world political map. There seems to be a general consensus framing such discussions that, with the end of the Soviet Union, no state within the Eurasian continent is likely to emerge in the foreseeable future to challenge the primacy of the USA as the global hegemon.[15] However, it is also generally recognised that what happens in Eurasia will have a major bearing on whether and in what form the USA is able to continue to exert influence over that region's affairs. Various geopolitical theories have been put forward concerning the conditions in which a Eurasian challenger to the primacy of the USA may emerge. While many of these accounts have been rightly criticised for being ethnocentric and prescriptive,[16] they do provide certain insights, not least into Western geopolitical thinking.

One thesis is offered by one of the leading US theorists of the Soviet totalitarian model, Zbigniew Brzezinski.[17] In *The Grand Chessboard* (1997), the author frames his post-Cold-War anxieties concerning the prospects of an expansionist Russia and the need for the global system to maintain a balance of power. His thesis also takes its inspiration from the ideas of the early twentieth-century geopolitician Halford Mackinder, especially his concept of the geostrategic significance of the Heartland (roughly synonymous with the borders of the former Soviet Union) in mastery over Eurasia. Brzezinski argues that, as a result of the collapse of the Soviet Union, a power vacuum has been created in Central Eurasia which has the potential to destabilise the regional balance of power, potentially making the whole of Eurasia unstable. The geopolitical choices that Russia, as the most powerful state in Central Eurasia, makes are therefore critical. Those choices, he contends, are between becoming 'a European democracy' and prioritising its ties with Europe or becoming 'a Eurasian empire' through re-establishing Russian dominance over reluctant but weak post-Soviet neighbours. While the former will facilitate regional stability, the latter, the thesis contends, will lead to Russia's geopolitical isolation. Consequently, championing the interests of the USA means containing Russia by ensuring that the key borderland states are drawn into Western-dominated international organisations and security alliances. In holding to the classical geopolitical assumption that competition and control over territory still remain the primary driving forces conditioning relations between nation-states, Brzezinski draws a distinction between two types of Eurasian players. States designated as *geostrategic players* are defined as those capable of exercising power and influence over Eurasia. The only post-Soviet state identified as capable of playing such a role is Russia. In contrast, *geopolitical pivot states* are those players whose importance is not derived from their power and motivation but rather from their sensitive location and the consequences their potentially vulnerable economic or political condition have on the behaviour of geostrategic players. Two post-Soviet borderland states are singled out as geopolitical pivot states: Ukraine, because of its location between Russia and western Europe, and Azerbaijan, owing to its strategic position between Russia and two other geopolitical pivot states, Turkey and Iran. Primarily because of their location between Russia and China, Uzbekistan and Kazakhstan are also considered to have the potential to qualify for such status.

Crucial to countering what is assumed to be Russia's historic-spatial impulse to expand is integrating not only Central Europe and the Baltic states but also Ukraine into NATO and the European Union. Without becoming part of the West's main regional and economic security structures, it is claimed, Ukraine will not survive as a sovereign state. Moreover, without Ukraine, 'Russia ceases to be a Eurasian empire'.[18] Yet a variety of consequences for Eurasian security flow from bringing Ukraine closer to what is deemed the USA's 'democratic bridgehead', western Europe. As Colton and others note, having initially conceived European security as excluding Ukraine and the other post-Soviet states but subsequently envisaging NATO's membership extending eastwards, possibly to include Ukraine, the West has further fuelled Russia's fears of the intentions of European–Atlantic security interests.[19] For its part, Ukraine is conscious of itself becoming a pawn between the security interests of the West and Russia. Consequently, it has resisted any attempts to become locked into the hegemonic security structures of either.

It is, however, in the so-called 'Eurasian Balkans' where Brzezinski believes much of the fate of Eurasia's balance of power hangs. Besides including Azerbaijan and the other Transcaucasian states, this pivotal region is defined as encompassing all the post-Soviet South, including Central Asia. The emergence of new states here has undoubtedly brought to the fore regional tensions, which have the potential to draw Russia, Turkey and Iran into large-scale inter-state and civil wars (see Fig. 6.1). Halbach draws an analogy with the nineteenth-century European Balkans, noting that 'what was typical for the Balkans and what made it predestined as a landscape of conflict also seems to apply to the Caucasus'.[20] Just as the so-called Balkan 'Great Game' involved both local states and continental powers in a geopolitical rivalry that eventually became continental in scope, the mix of local political actors and neighbouring states with interests in the Caucasus, whose cultural heterogeneity and ethnic geography have already fuelled a series of territorial claims by states and ethnic groups, threatens to plunge the Eurasian region into further geopolitical instability. Yet any account of why this region should be singled out as pivotal to Eurasia's stability cannot be explained by recourse simply to its cultural heterogeneity geopolitical location. Rather, the region's current instability is primarily to do with two fundamental geopolitical developments: the emergence in the region of militant nationalism as a consequence of democratisation and global interest in the region's oil wealth.

Democratisation has fuelled rather than eased tensions by enabling a militant nationalism to emerge. Strictly contained and controlled by the Soviet regime until the mid-1980s, subsequent regional democratisation has somewhat paradoxically enabled nationalist regimes to emerge. As Macfarlane argues, the start of the late 1980s war between Armenia and Azerbaijan over the disputed territorial enclave of Nagorno-Karabakh can only be understood as a consequence of the Nagorno-Karabakh soviet's being able to take advantage of the Gorbachev regime's more permissive stance towards the region, which was voicing publicly its territorial demands for annexation to neighbouring Armenia, without the prospects of immediate retribution from the centre.[21] Throughout the 1988–94 Armenian–Azeri war, both states were able as a result of the region's democratisation to adopt a discourse of nationalism, which broadened the social base of support for the war and conferred popular legitimacy on such a large-scale military commitment. In particular, the liberalisation of education and the media enabled the two countries' cultural intelligentsias to play a crucial part in reinventing and publicising historical myths and events, which did much to justify the war and their respective claims to the disputed territory. Moreover, Russia's intervention in the debacle may also have been nurtured by its democratisation. Having been marginalised as a consequence of a more democratically accountable post-Cold-War government's cutting back on the country's defence budget, Russia's military lobby saw regional intervention as a way of achieving a more influential role in Kremlin politics and legitimising increased federal spending on the country's defence.

The elevation of the region's geopolitical importance is also bound up with the catapulting to global prominence of Caspian oil. Since the early 1990s, not only has Moscow lost a large degree of control over this vital resource but the region's oil wealth is seen by the region's new oil-producing states – Azerbaijan, Kazakhstan and Turkmenistan – as their passport to future economic prosperity. Moreover, Western corporations also have a major stake in developing the oil resources of a region whose oil reserves are estimated to be equivalent to those of Saudi Arabia or of the North Sea and Alaska combined. Who controls Caspian oil and how it is divided up remain a central and still unresolved issue within the region. While the countries bordering the Caspian have agreed that each has exclusive rights only to the sea floor up to 45 nautical miles from their shoreline, who controls access to the surface has still to be agreed.[22] Moreover, tensions also focus on transterritorial access to the oil wealth. Russia, with its control over the two major Caspian–Black Sea pipelines running through its territory, retains a monopoly over the east–west flow of the region's oil wealth, furnishing Moscow with considerable geopolitical leverage not only over the region's oil states but also over global oil prices. For their part, both US and Western oil companies would prefer to develop alternative pipelines through

Azerbaijan, Georgia and Turkey, especially as Washington refuses to consider the prospects of a route that runs through the territory of its *bête noire,* Iran.

Azerbaijan is therefore important not least because of its significance to Western geopolitical security and economic interests. The USA, keen to safeguard its interests in what it has designated 'a zone of vital interest', has signed defence-related agreements with Azerbaijan and Georgia. Moscow, for its part, is eager for Azerbaijan to remain a loyal member of the CIS. An oil-revenue-rich Azerbaijan might also have significant regional geopolitical implications. An Azerbaijani leadership, which has been reluctant to proceed further with democratisation may be willing, with more economic resources at its disposal, to reclaim Nagorno-Karabakh. Whether this would also bring in the region's other Muslim states in support of Azerbaijan is not clear. For its part, Iran is unlikely to welcome the prospects of a remilitarised and stronger Azerbaijan also capable of intervening in the secessionist claims of the Azeri diaspora in northern Iran.

Balkanisation and fragmentation

In his resignation speech as president of the Soviet Union in December 1991, Mikhail Gorbachev warned of the prospects of the post-Soviet states' following in the bloody wake of the disintegration of federal Yugoslavia. In the first half of the 1990s, in particular, many post-Sovietologists feared that ongoing inter-communal violence would become a central feature of the post-Soviet transition and raised the spectre of further Balkanisation, notably of Russia.[23]

While inter-ethnic and religious violence has been a feature of some regions in the early years of the post-Soviet transition, it has not occurred on the scale or with the intensity witnessed in Yugoslavia from 1990 to 1999. If the cases of inter-ethnic violence are mapped over the period of the post-Soviet transition (Fig. 9.1), it is clear that the occurrence of new violent ethnic conflicts has declined sharply since the early 1990s. Figure 9.1 charts the start date of occurrences of inter-communal violence throughout the post-Soviet states in the period from 1985 until 1998. Only acts of ethnic violence, rather than peaceful ethnic protest, have been included. As the post-Soviet transition unfolded, the incidence of inter-communal violence rose gradually in the late 1980s, reaching a peak in 1991–92. Since then the number of new occurrences has fallen dramatically, with no new incidents since June 1995. The number of conflicts that have been resolved or have run their course, compared with those which remain unresolved and ongoing, is also revealing. These, along with the total incidence of inter-ethnic violence, are listed in Table 9.2. According to my calculations, between 1985 and 1998 there were 28 new incidents of inter-ethnic communal violence, the majority of which have since been resolved. Many of those cases,

Table 9.2   Occurrences and present status of acts of inter-ethnic violence
initiated each year during the post-Soviet transition, 1985–98

Start date	Conflict	Status
1985		
January	Dushanbe, Tajikistan. Inter-ethnic riots	Riots reoccurred in February 1990. Since then, no reoccurrence
1986		
December	Alma-Ata, Kazakhstan. Inter-ethnic riots	Single incident. Resolved by Kazakhstan's becoming independent in 1991
1988		
January	Azerbaijan/Nagorno-Karabakh	Ongoing. Ceasefire, April 1994
February	Azerbaijan/Sumgait. Ethnic riots	Single incident
June	Georgians/Meskhetians clash in Georgia	Single incident
November	Armenian/Azerbaijani clashes in Nakhichevan Autonomous Republic	Single incident
December	Tashkent, Uzbekistan. Student ethnic riots	Single incident
1989		
April	Georgia/Soviet army	Single incident. Georgia became independent in 1991
April	Georgia/Abkhazia	Ongoing. Civil war 1992–93. An agreement in 1997 by the warring factions renouncing the use of force
May	Ashkhabad and Nebit-Dag, Turkmenistan. Ethnic riots in part directed against local Armenians	Single set of incidents
June	Uzbekistan/Ferghana Valley	Single incident
	Uzbeks/Meskhetians	Directed partly against Uzbekistan's Meskhetian minority
June	Novyi Uzen and other Kazakh cities. Inter-ethnic riots	Single set of incidents
July	Kyrgyzstan/Isfara district Intercommunal conflict between Kyrgyz and Tajiks concerning rights to land and water in the Isfara district	Ongoing
1990		
January	Azerbaijan/Baku riots	Single incident
June–July	Uzbeks and Kyrgyz in the Osh region, Kyrgyzstan	Single incident

Start date	Conflict	Status
1991		
January	Lithuania/Soviet army	Single incident. Lithuania became independent in 1991
January	Chechnya	Ongoing. Chechen war (1994–96). Ceasefire and settlement, October 1996
January	Georgia/South Ossetia	Ongoing; ceasefire, June 1992
April	Azerbaijan/Gestasen insurgency	Single incident
April	Georgia/Adzharia. Protests by Adzharians (Georgian Muslims) protesting against religious discrimination	Single incident
August	Moldova/Gagauz	Resolved. Autonomy agreement, July 1994
September	Moldova/Trans-Dniestria	Ongoing. Autonomy agreement, July 1996
1992		
Early 1992	Dagestan. Ethnic clashes between Chechens and Dargins, Laks and Avars in Aukh/Novolakskii districts	Ongoing. In April 1998, members of the self-styled Sword of Islam Organization were involved in acts of violence in the Novolakskii district. The group is demanding the return to Chechen jurisdiction of the Aukh and Novolakskii districts
May	Tajik civil war	Ongoing. Peace Agreement, June 1997
September	Kabardino-Balkaria	Single incident. Violent confrontation between demonstrators and the authorities
November	Ingushetia/North Ossetia	Ongoing
1993	Georgia/Mingrelians. Pro-Gamsakhurdia uprisings in Mingrelia (Western Georgia), motivated in part by tension between Georgians and Mingrelians	Single incident
1995		
June	Ukraine/Crimea. Crimean Tatars riot in several Crimean towns	Ongoing. In March 1998, Crimean Tatar demonstrators clash with the authorities in calling for accelerated citizenship

Sources: the above draws in part upon data assembled by Rubin (1998; see Note 24, p. 240). I have counted the Dushanbe riots as originating in 1985 and not in 1990. The additional 12 incidences that I have added to his original data set are recorded in the Soviet and Russian press.

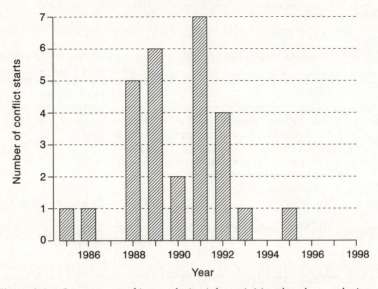

Figure 9.1   Occurrences of inter-ethnic violence initiated each year during the post-Soviet transition, 1985–98. Source: compiled from data in Table 9.2.

such as the inter-ethnic riots in Kazakhstan in 1986 or those involving the Soviet army in Georgia (1989) and Lithuania (1991) came to an end as a result of the Union republics' securing their independence from the Soviet Union.

However, as Rubin concludes from his observations regarding inter-communal tensions, 'while most of the conflicts of the post-Soviet transition are no longer violent, few have actually been resolved to the satisfaction of the parties, and tensions could reignite'.[24] By 1998, there were still 10 geopolitical flashpoints where inter-communal violence was ongoing, despite the fact that in some cases peace accords had been signed between the warring factions. As noted in Chapter 6, most of those conflicts involve secessionist or irredentist struggles. And they are concentrated exclusively in the post-Soviet South, in Transcaucasia (Nagorno-Karabakh, Abkhazia, South Ossetia), Central Asia (Kyrgyzstan, Tajikistan), southern Russia (Chechnya, Dagestan, North Ossetia) and in the south-western borderlands (Trans-Dniestria, Crimea).

What is also notable is that Russia has not undergone the Balkanisation which was widely predicted in the early 1990s. Since the formation of federal Russia, only one republic, Chechnya, has militarily fought for secession from the federation. According to one study, important differences in the scale of secessionist activism were detectable amongst the other ethno-republics in the 1990–94 period. The potentially most secessionist-minded was Tatarstan, closely followed by Bashkortostan and Sakha.[25] While to varying degrees all the ethnorepublics have continued to amass a variety of grievances against Moscow, clearly enmity alone has not been a sufficient condition for mobilising an ethnorepublic behind the cause of leaving the federation. Three possible explanations of why secessionism has not been as high on the political agenda of the ethnorepublics as was initially predicted merit consideration.[26]

First, in order to engage successfully in secessionist collective action, an ethnorepublic requires a regional political leadership willing and able to champion the secessionist cause. In most ethnorepublics there now exists a native-born political leadership which over recent years has become more titular in composition. It is a political leadership which has proven itself capable of commanding considerable respect and authority over its constituents. Yet members of this political elite have also had to limit their career ambitions largely to regional politics, in part because of a lack of opportunity to progress beyond the horizons of their own ethnorepublics. This may change if Russia takes on more of the features of Western-style federations, thus providing the channels necessary to ensure political elite mobility, which is important in pre-empting disillusionment with federation among ethnorepublic leaders. However, for the present, as Hanson notes, 'because there is still no effective structure of political parties linking the careers of local politicians to positions at the national level, most politicians . . . are not subject to any party discipline that would make them conform to Moscow's policies'.[27] Such political elites may therefore tend to look back to the ethnorepublic and engage in a rhetoric of federal politics that uses highly charged calls for sovereignty in order to maximise, fiscal benefits, in particular from the federation. Yet apart from Chechnya, such political elites have not called for outright statehood. In short, limited social mobility does not seem to be a sufficient reason for ethnorepublic political elites to engage in promoting a politics of secession.

Second, a sense of communal self-identity – of a strong ethnic, cultural or linguistic affinity among the local population – is an important condition for an ethnorepublic to engage in secessionist activism. The more clear-cut the local community's cultural-identity markers, the easier it will be for potentially secessionist-minded political and cultural elites to mobilise their constituents behind the cause of secession. The ethnorepublics possess their own native cultural intelligentsia who, given the occupational and status niches that they occupy within ethnorepublic institutions, have a vested interest in the promotion and survival of the titular language and culture.[28] The problem facing such cultural elites, however, is that as prospective supporters of secessionism, they need to appeal to a constituency whose sense of communal identity and solidarity is greatly weakened by multiple and cross-cutting markers – linguistic, religious, class and ethnic – that weaken mobilisation behind any titular-based secessionist movement. Thus, Russification has long since blurred clearly defined language boundaries, while any sense of a local ethnic division of labour – of the titular nation's occupying lower occupational niches within the ethnorepublic – is becoming far less evident because of their increasing promotion to positions of power and status. Moreover, Russia's ethnorepublics do not possess a pre-Soviet period of statehood to look back upon, which could provide a powerful national symbol to mobilise the nation behind the cause of secession in the way it did for the Baltic republics and Georgia in their struggles to secure independence from the Soviet Union.[29]

In some ethnorepublics, notably in Dagestan, the existence of a variety of indigenous ethnic groups with differing and often competing political interests also weakens the potential for secessionist mobilisation. Such ethnic groups focus on jockeying for control over their own republic rather than in mobilising behind the cause of Dagestani separatism. The position of local Russians in the ethnorepublics is also important, not least because they constitute a demographic majority in nearly half of them (see Table 6.2). For reasons of self-interest, Russians are more likely to continue to support the inviolability of what they unquestionably regard as their homeland, Russia, not least because independent statehood would be more likely to challenge their cultural rights, employment prospects and social status in a sovereign ethnorepublic dominated by the titular nation.

Finally, secession is unlikely to be supported irrespective of the probable economic costs to an ethnorepublic and its population. Although the ethnorepublics do not possess an information set regarding the likely economic implications of secession, constituents make judgements about its anticipated stream of costs and benefits. For the poorer republics, their economic dependency on the federation is likely to continue to outweigh the greater and uncertain economic costs of secession. Even for energy- or resource-rich ethnorepublics such as Sakha, Tatarstan and Bashkortostan, which are less dependent on economic subsidies from Moscow, a potential secessionist leadership would face an uphill task convincing its constituents that the relative security of a federal market should be jettisoned for dependency on a global trading regime, in which the likelihood of securing its own market niches as a sovereign state would be fraught with problems and uncertainties. If the ethnorepublics are not willing to bear the negative economic and social consequences that would undoubtedly follow from secession, the more acceptable and likely trade-off is to continue to pursue a strategy of securing what they can from the federal arrangement in tandem with working towards procuring a future for their ethnorepublic within the global market place.

For the present at least it would seem that the ethnorepublics are committed to obtaining as much as they can from the federation without losing completely those components of the federal arrangement that they value. However, the federation's inability to handle a series of ongoing political and fiscal crises could prompt the least economically dependent republics to re-evaluate their attitudes towards remaining part of Russia. Under such circumstances, Russia's transition from federation to confederation is not beyond the bounds of possibility.[30] The problems that an economically weak Russia faces in relation to economic globalisation may also play a role in such a transition, as different parts of Russia look increasingly for economic security towards the main regionalising growth centres of the world economy – Europe, East Asia and the Pacific Rim – while at the same time remaining part of a loose political confederation of states. While Fig. 9.2 captures the economic spirit of such globalising pressures, any confederal arrangement is unlikely to take the particular political form that the map suggests.

Competing on the margins: the Latin-Americanisation of the post-Soviet states

At first glance Latin America's political transition from military-authoritarian rule in the so-called Southern Cone countries (Brazil, Argentina, Uruguay and Chile) from the late 1980s onwards appears to have little in common with the transition experienced by the post-Soviet states – not least because in Latin America the establishment of capitalism preceded the transition to democracy, while in the post-Soviet states the transition to democracy instituted the transition to capitalism. Consequently, the post-Soviet states do not possess the scale of market institutions or the well-developed middle class that Latin America did to facilitate transition. The latter also possessed a large private sector and history of private enterprise, whereas, with the exception of the Baltic republics, there is no such recent legacy for the post-Soviet states to draw upon. Thus, for the post-Soviet states, transition involves both economic reform and democratisation, while for the Latin American states it has been primarily a matter of establishing democratic institutions and forms of more open and participatory governance. Moreover, for the countries of Latin America the process of democratisation has not had the added dimension of establishing new territorial states or having to cope, as in the case of Russia, Georgia and Moldova, with a series of crises generated by the possibility of their fragmentation.

Yet, as comparativists have noted, not only are there striking similarities between the post-communist states and Latin America, but as the 1990s have unfolded the former are taking on many of the features of the latter. The major similarities identified either in part or in whole by comparativists are as follows:[31]

1. Both the Latin American and post-Soviet states compete on the margins of the world economy and are heavily dependent on core-dominated global financial and economic institutions, notably the World Bank and the International Monetary Fund (IMF), to facilitate economic restructuring. States in both transitional regions comprise a mix of private and state-owned sectors, which have been undergoing changes owing to market reforms and extensive privatisation. Although the state is less

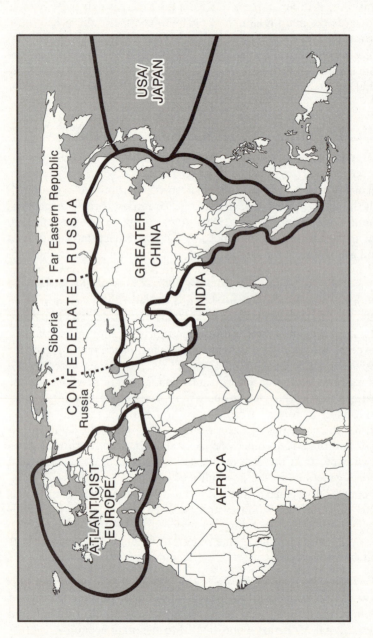

Figure 9.2 The geoeconomic fragmentation of Eurasia. Source: redrawn from Z. Brzezinski, 'A geostrategy for Eurasia', *Foreign Affairs*, 75(5), 1997, p. 60.

involved in the national economy than in the 1980s, the public sector is still very significant, and accounts for a large proportion of economic production. As in Latin America, most of the post-Soviet states have borrowed heavily from both the World Bank and the IMF, especially Russia, but such loans have also played a vital role in Ukraine, Kazakhstan and Uzbekistan. Many of the economic and fiscal requirements and much of the economic advice given by the IMF have drawn upon the Latin American experience, with prospective debtor countries expected to redress budget deficits, cut public expenditures and successfully demonstrate tight fiscal control before trade credits and loans are granted. Consequently, both Latin America and the post-Soviet states have experienced a strained relationship with global financial institutions.

2. Latin American countries, like the post-Soviet states, differ in the extent to which they have developed effective democratic institutions. Some countries have succeeded in managing the tensions and contradictions that have arisen as a result of the abandonment of the previous authoritarian/totalitarian model, leading to regime stability (e.g. Chile, Argentina, Brazil, Estonia, Latvia, Lithuania, Ukraine). Others have succumbed to those tensions and authoritarian rule has either been re-established or is threatening to make a comeback (e.g. Columbia, Mexico, Russia, Belarus, Uzbekistan). Symptoms of the inability of the system of political representation to manage relations between conflicting interests include wide-scale social violence, corruption and organised crime. Freedom of speech and of the mass media exists, but even in the most democratised states it is limited in such a way that it does not interfere with the exercise of political power.

Probably the major challenge facing both Latin America and the post-Soviet states is that their economies are competing on the margins of the global economy. Consequently, both regions suffer from the handicap of re-entering the world economy from semi-peripheral or peripheral positions. Semi-peripheral economies – which would include Russia, the Baltic states and Ukraine – are characterised by features that combine elements found in core states (relatively high wages, advanced technology and a diversified production mix) with periphery processes (low wages, more rudimentary technology and a simple production mix), which are characteristic of the Central Asian states. As with Latin America, the post-Soviet states aspire to core status within the world economy. Indeed, since the late 1980s, states in both regions have been prepared to jettison their previous developmental models for 'modernisation via internationalisation'.[32] However, while both regions previously embraced developmental strategies that envisaged economic growth in terms of national development, there were also important differences. The Latin American model was based on private property, an active role for the state and protectionism reflected largely in a policy of import-substitution industrialisation. In contrast, the Soviet model was based on state ownership of productive resources, allocation through centralised command and an autarkic development strategy led by producer goods industries. In replacing their differing strategies with 'modernisation via internationalisation', both Latin America and the post-Soviet states have reframed their normative understandings of transition by embracing those features characteristic of core states: democracy, markets and an individualistic consumption-oriented culture. According to Przeworski, 'in this strategy, modernisation therefore becomes synonymous with the international system: integration into the world economy, combined with an imitation of economic, political and cultural patterns prevalent in advanced capitalist economies'.[33] In turn, the core states have been keen to see these countries buy into their neo-liberal economic visions of globalisation and democracy.

In the drive for modernisation via internationalisation, the task facing the post-Soviet states is by far the more daunting. The scale of privatisation and the Western-imposed austerity programmes that the post-Soviet states must implement as a requisite to full membership of the world economy is far greater. Moreover, unlike the Latin American states, Russia and most of the other post-Soviet states have to tackle the legacy of converting their former military–industrial complex into forms of economic activity acceptable to Western financial and political institutions. For Russia, this is an especially formidable task. In many of its regions, the military–industrial complex is still responsible for the economic livelihoods of the majority of inhabitants. Conversion of these plants means draconian cuts in employment. In all, owing to the nature of its previous developmental model, the finance and scale of reorganisation required to facilitate the wholesale restructuring of the post-Soviet space-economies are of a far greater magnitude.

To facilitate marketisation, the post-Soviet states have secured large-scale economic assistance from the West. And for its part, through the World Bank, the IMF and other global financial institutions, the West has been ready and willing to lend Russia and the other post-Soviet states large sums of capital in order to secure greater global economic and political security. Geared towards liberalising trade and investment as well as favouring wholesale privatisation, the structural adjustment programmes which both the World Bank and the IMF have prescribed bear a striking similarity to those employed in Latin America. As Allan Smith notes,

> It can be argued that the problems of indebtedness and hyper-inflationary pressures in Russia are very similar to those experienced in Latin America and that economic recovery will be impossible without stringent monetary and fiscal policies, which are also necessary to prevent the misuse of funds.

But, as he goes on to say,

> The principle counter-argument is that economic reform will be impossible without major Western assistance and that the scale of the

international problems which could result from the failure of Russia's reforms is of an altogether different magnitude from projects that the IMF has overseen on an economic basis in the past.[34]

Russia, in particular, has amassed a formidable foreign debt, and in August 1998 it defaulted on its repayments. However, its debt crisis was not only a product of debts it had accumulated during the 1990s. Following the Soviet Union's collapse, the successor states agreed that Russia should accept responsibility for the entire Soviet debt along with all foreign assets accrued during Soviet rule. Russia has continued to borrow heavily from the IMF and other global financial institutions ever since. Its total debt to the West, primarily due to borrowing from global financial institutions, has been rising steadily throughout the 1990s. In 1990, it stood at US$50.8 billion, increasing to $83.7 billion in 1993 and to $102.4 billion by 1995.[35] In 1998 alone, the IMF and World Bank, along with the Japanese government, approved a further loan of US$22.6 billion on condition that it be spent on further privatisation and on introducing a more effective tax-collecting system in order to boost the state's revenue base.

Despite global assistance, Russia has lacked the political means to execute the radical neo-liberal policies envisaged by the IMF and World Bank. To this end, the observations of Linz and Stepan are especially sobering:

> the best studies of the [post-communist states] region are confirming a pattern about state power already documented in Latin America, that effective privatisation (often mistakenly equated with 'state shrinking') is best done by relatively strong states that are able to implement a coherent policy. . . In a context of post-communist, post-command economy, a state with rapidly eroding capacity simply cannot manage a process of effective privatisation.[36]

Thus, they note, the most successful Latin American country to bring about wholesale privatisation reasonably effectively was Chile, precisely because privatisation began in the late 1980s before the transition from military to democratic rule was under way. If these conclusions hold sway, then it would indicate that democracy is not necessarily a precondition for economic liberalisation as the standard story would suggest. Indeed, a number of commentators go even further by noting that democratisation does not necessarily have a beneficial impact on economic liberalisation.[37] As Offe argues, 'democratic politics may block or distort the road to privatisation and hence marketisation'.[38] This can be a consequence of tensions concerning the equitable distribution of the costs of economic liberalisation, especially for poorer citizens, which can lead to the prospects of economic crisis, social unrest and political instability that neither a democratising elite nor its citizenry are prepared to endure. Similarly, the optimism of Western triumphalists that accelerated economic reform can reduce the likelihood of authoritarianism has also only limited foundation. Although the rapid privatisation of the post-Soviet space-economies may be interpreted as the solution to democratic transition by the West and its global financial institutions, as Feigenbaum and Henig warn with regard to post-communist countries like Hungary, Poland and the Czech Republic, 'privatisation policies do not necessarily lead to such propitious outcomes . . . the wrong policies may place the fragile democracies in eastern Europe in jeopardy'.[39] Indeed, large-scale and rapid privatisation may occur most effectively under a dirigiste political system, where pressures to cut public expenditures and the consequences of social dislocation can be effectively controlled by the coercive state. This would seem to be borne out by the experiences of the post-1978 market reforms in China, where the success of Beijing's economic restructuring policies appears to be due in part to the absence from its political agenda of democratisation.

As was the case regarding Latin America, the policies of the West and global financial institutions towards the post-Soviet states have been criticised as being insensitive to local conditions. Sachs argues that the West and global financial institutions should rethink their policies towards the former Soviet Union.[40] He advocates democratising the G8 to include a form of democratic geo-governance whereby key decisions affecting the post-communist world would not be limited to a handful of Western states which have an inordinate say in the policies of global financial institutions. IMF–World Bank programmes would be far more sensitive to local conditions in the way they condition foreign aid, and the West would no longer channel foreign aid exclusively through individual states but through regional organisations that could put peer pressure rather than Western pressure on their members. While such a programme might succeed in the case of MERCOSUR, (the common market of Brazil, Argentina, Uruguay and Paraguay), despite the declaration by Russia and the other four members of the CIS Economic Union of their commitment towards closer economic integration, as noted in Chapter 7, the realisation of a regional economic bloc with which the West and global financial institutions could deal is fraught with problems because of internal rivalry and dissent. For the moment, the West and its global financial institutions seem reluctant to see a strong CIS emerge, no doubt fearing that it could act as a catalyst in strengthening Russia's geopolitical influence over northern Eurasia. Other valuable lessons could also have been drawn from the success of what Strange calls 'the missing Marshall Plan' of the 1990s. As she notes, for post-communist Europe, the 'problems were not so much that they had debts that they could not repay as that they had not been given the right sort of credit in sufficient amounts for their needs'.[41] Besides helping the post-Soviet states, a Marshall Plan would also have benefited prospective Western donor states by providing them with new consumer markets in the East in a similar way that the USA benefited from the original Marshall Plan for western Europe.

What both the Latin American and post-Soviet experiences therefore demonstrate is that neither economic liberalisation nor democracy necessarily facilitates one another, and nor do they automatically progress in a linear fashion. As Yergin and Gustafson suggest, like some Latin American countries, 'Russia may not necessarily progress down a smooth path to the market, but instead could swing between extremes of acceptance and rejection – of the West, of the market, and of democracy'.[42] Thus, if there is a lesson to be learnt from the Latin American experience, it is that Russia and most of the other post-Soviet states are likely to be caught up in a continual process of oscillating between periods of reforms and counter-reforms, stagnation and growth, authoritarianism and democracy, and social stability and crisis.

Notes to Chapter 9

1 D. Chirot, 'The rise of the West', *American Sociological Review*, 50, 1985, p. 193.
2 W. Laqueur, *Black Hundred. The Rise of the Extreme Right in Russia* (New York, Harper Perennial, 1994).
3 See, in particular, R. Brubaker, *Nationalism Reframed. Nationhood and the National Question in the New Europe* (Cambridge, Cambridge University Press, 1996); K. Dawisha and B. Parrot, *Russia and the New States of Eurasia. The Politics of Upheaval* (Cambridge, Cambridge University Press, 1994); E. Gellner, 'Return of a native', *The Political Quarterly*, 67(1), 1996, pp. 4–13; S. Hanson and J. Kopstein, 'The Weimar/Russia comparison', *Post-Soviet Affairs*, 13(3), July–September 1997, pp. 252–83; A. Motyl, 'After Empire. Competing Discourses and Inter-state Conflict in Post-imperial Eastern Europe', in B. Rubin and J. Snyder (eds), *Post-Soviet Political Order. Conflict and State-Building* (London, Routledge, 1998), pp. 14–33.
4 Hanson and Kopstein, 'The Weimar/Russia comparison'.
5 Brubaker, *Nationalism Reframed*.
6 G. Smith and A. Wilson, 'Rethinking Russia's post-Soviet diaspora. The potential for political mobilisation in eastern Ukraine and north-east Estonia', *Europe–Asia Studies*, 49(5), 1997, pp. 845–64.
7 Hanson and Kopstein, 'The Weimar/Russia comparison', p. 264.
8 Hanson and Kopstein, 'The Weimar/Russia comparison', p. 260.
9 V. Shlapentokh, 'Early feudalism. The best parallels for contemporary Russia?', *Europe–Asia Studies*, 48(3), 1996.
10 R. Pipes, 'Is Russia still an enemy?', *Foreign Affairs*, 76(5), 1997, p. 72.
11 D. Peukert, *Inside Nazi Germany. Conformity, Opposition and Racism in Everyday Life* (London, Penguin, 1989), p. 245.
12 S. White, M. Wyman and S. Oates, 'Parties and voters in the 1995 Russian Duma election', *Europe–Asia Studies*, 49(5), 1997, p. 785.
13 White, Wyman and Oates, 'Parties and voters in the 1995 Russian Duma election', p. 786.
14 Gellner, 'Return of a native', p. 12.
15 See, in particular, J. Agnew and S. Corbridge, *Mastering Space. Hegemony, Territory and International Political Economy* (London, Routledge, 1995).

16 A. Lieven, 'The paranoid Pole', *Prospect*, May 1998, pp. 64–7.

17 Z. Brzezinski, *The Grand Chessboard. American Primacy and its Geostrategic Imperatives* (New York, Harper Collins, 1997).

18 Brzezinski, *The Grand Chessboard*, p. 46.

19 T. Colton *et al.*, 'Five years after the collapse of the USSR', *Post-Soviet Affairs*, 13(1), 1997, pp. 1–18.

20 E. Halbach, 'The Caucasus as a region of conflict', *German Foreign Affairs Review*, 48(4), 1997, p. 358.

21 S. N. Macfarlane, 'Democratisation, nationalism and regional security in the North Caucasus', *Government and Opposition*, 10, 1998, 399–420.

22 *Moskovskie novosti*, 19–26 April 1998.

23 For one of the more informative comparisons between the end of the Soviet Union and Yugoslavia, see V. Vujacic and V. Zaslavsky, 'The causes of disintegration in the USSR and Yugoslavia', *Telos,* Summer, 1991, pp. 120–40.

24 B. Rubin, 'Managing normal stability', in B. Rubin and J. Snyder (eds), *Post-Soviet Political Order. Conflict and State-Building* (London, Routledge, 1998), p. 171.

25 D. Treisman, 'Russia's "ethnic revival". The separatist activism of regional leaders in a postcommunist order', *World Politics,* 49(1), 1997, pp. 212–49.

26 G. Smith, 'Russia, ethnoregionalism and the politics of federation', *Ethnic and Racial Studies*, 19(2), 1996, pp. 391–410.

27 P. Hanson, 'The centre versus the periphery in Russian economic policy', *RFE/RL Research Report*, 3(17), 1994, p. 23.

28 L. Drobizheva, 'Processes of Disintegration in the Russian Federation and the Problems of Russians', in V. Shlapentokh, M. Sendich and E. Payin (eds), *The New Russian Diaspora. Russian Minorities in the Former Soviet Republics* (London, M.E. Sharpe, 1994), pp. 45–58.

29 As noted in Chapter 6, the only ethnorepublic in the Russian Federation to experience a previous period of independent statehood was the southern Siberian republic of Tuva. Because it is one of Russia's poorest republics, the main reason why secession has not been on its agenda is probably bound up with its high degree of economic dependency on Russia and therefore the economic costs that would result from becoming a sovereign state.

30 *Kommersant-Daily,* 3 September 1998.

31 J. Linz and A. Stepan, *Problems of Democratic Transition and Consolidation. Southern Europe, South America, and Post-Communist Europe* (Baltimore, The Johns Hopkins University Press, 1996); A. Przeworski, *Sustainable Democracy* (Cambridge, Cambridge University Press, 1995); A. Smith, *Russia and the World Economy. Problems of Integration* (London, Routledge, 1993); D. Yergin and T. Gustafson, *Russia 2010 and What it Means for the World* (London, Nicholas Brealey Publishers, 1994).

32 Przeworski, *Sustainable Democracy.*

33 Przeworski, *Sustainable Democracy*, p. 3.

34 Smith, *Russia and the World Economy,* p. 236.

35 Economic Commission for Europe, *Economic Survey of Europe in 1996–1997* (New York and Geneva, United Nations, 1997), p. 156.

36 Linz and Stepan, *Problems of Democratic Transition and Consolidation,* p. 436.

37 See, in particular, A. Leftwich (ed.), *Democracy and Development* (Oxford, Polity Press, 1996).

38 C. Offe, *Varieties of Transition. The East European and German Experience* (Oxford, Polity Press, 1996), p. 45.

39 H. Feigenbaum and J. Henig, 'Privatisation and democracy.' *Governance,*

an *International Journal of Policy and Administration,* 6(3), July 1993, p. 438.
40 J. Sachs, 'Global capitalism', *The Economist,* 12–18 September 1998, pp. 23–5.
41 S. Strange, 'The new world of debt', *New Left Review,* 230, July/August 1998, p. 113.
42 Yergin and Gustafson, *Russia 2010 and What it Means for the World,* p. 206.

Appendix

Appendix

Post-Soviet-state membership of major global and regional organisations, 1999

	UN	WTO	NATO	Partnership for Peace, North Atlantic Co-operation Council	Western European Union	OSCE/CSCE	Council of Europe	European Union	CIS	EFTA	CEFTA (Czech Republic, Hungary, Poland, Romania, Slovakia, Slovenia)	Baltic Assembly/Council of Ministers	CIS Customs Union	GUAM	Central Asian Economic Space
Russian Federation	Yes	Observer status; applied to join		Yes		Joined 1992	Yes		Yes				Yes		
South-western borderlands															
Ukraine	Yes	Observer status; applied to join		Yes		Joined 1992	Yes		Yes					Yes	
Belarus	Yes	Observer status; applied to join		Yes		Joined 1992	Applied		Yes				Yes		
Moldova	Yes	Observer status; applied to join		Yes		Joined 1992	Yes		Yes					Yes	
Baltic states															
Estonia	Yes	Observer status; applied to join	Seeks membership	Yes	Associate partner since 9 May 94	Joined 1991	Yes	Applied 24 Nov 95; accession negotiations began in 1998 following July 97 EU recommendation		Free trade agreement signed Dec 95	Bilateral free trade agreements with 3 CEFTA members, in negotiations with 3 others	Yes			

Latvia	Yes	Observer status; applied to join	Seeks membership	Yes	Associate partner since 9 May 94	Joined 1991	Yes	Applied 13 Oct 95; accession question to be re-examined annually	Free trade agreement signed Dec 95	Bilateral free trade agreements signed with 4 CEFTA members	Yes			
Lithuania	Yes	Observer status; applied to join	Seeks membership	Yes	Associate partner since 9 May 94	Joined 1991	Yes	Applied 8 Dec 95; accession question to be re-examined annually	Free trade agreement signed Dec 95	Bilateral free trade agreements signed with 4 CEFTA members	Yes			
Transcaucasia														
Armenia	Yes	Observer status; applied to join		Yes		Joined 1992	Applied	Yes						
Azerbaijan	Yes	Observer status; applied to join		Yes		Joined 1992	Applied	Yes					Yes	
Georgia	Yes	Observer status; applied to join		Yes		Joined 1992	Applied	Yes					Yes	
Central Asia														
Kazakhstan	Yes	Observer status; applied to join		Yes		Joined 1992		Yes				Yes		Yes
Uzbekistan	Yes	Observer status; applied to join		Yes		Joined 1992		Yes						Yes
Kyrgyzstan	Yes	Observer status; applied to join		Yes		Joined 1992		Yes				Yes		Yes
Tajikistan	Yes			Yes		Joined 1992		Yes				Yes		
Turkmenistan	Yes			Yes		Joined 1992		Yes						

Glossary

apparatchik	middle or low level bureaucrat
CIS	Commonwealth of Independent States. Set up in December 1991, it includes all the post-Soviet states with the exception of the three Baltic republics
COMECON	Council for Mutual Economic Assistance. Established in 1949, it constituted the main form of economic alliance between the Soviet Union and its east European satellite states
CPRF	Communist Party of the Russian Federation
CPSU	Communist Party of the Soviet Union
Duma	the lower house of the Federal Assembly
EBRD	European Bank for Reconstruction and Development
ethnorepublic	a constituent unit of the Russian Federation. There are 21 such ethnorepublics (see Fig. 6.2)
Federal Assembly	the Russian Parliament, which came into existence in 1993; the lower house is called the Duma and the upper house the Federal Assembly
G8	the Group of Seven, an association made up of seven of the world's most powerful states – the USA, Canada, France, Germany, the UK, Italy and Japan – with the addition of Russia
glasnost'	Gorbachev's policy of greater openness
GUAM	a regional bloc, formed in 1997, which includes Georgia, Ukraine, Azerbaijan and Moldova
KGB	*Komitet gosudarstvennoi bezopasnosti*, the Soviet state security police
krai	a territory which forms part of the Russian Federation
LDPR	Liberal Democracy Party of Russia
near abroad	*blizhnee zarubezhe* – the term in official Russian foreign policy circles that refers collectively to the states of the post-Soviet borderlands

NEP	New Economic Policy, referring to the mixed economy of the 1921–28 Soviet period
nomenklatura	a list of high-ranking officials within the CPSU
oblast'	a region which forms part of the Russian Federation
okrug	a district which forms part of the Russian Federation
OSCE	Organisation for Security and Co-operation in Europe
Partnership for Peace	a NATO programme which is designed to offer affiliation but not membership to NATO for certain countries of eastern Europe
perestroika	Gorbachev's programme for restructuring the Soviet economy (1986–90)
RSFSR	Russian Soviet Federative Socialist Republic (or 'Russia proper'). The RSFSR formed the largest of the 15 Union republics of the Soviet Union
Union republic	the major nationality-based administrative unit of the Soviet Union: there were 15 of them. It is these Union republics which now constitute the post-Soviet states

Select bibliography

Primary sources

CIS Interstate Statistical Committee, *Demograficheskie yezhegodnik 1994* (Moscow, CIS Interstate Statistical Committee, 1995).

CIS Interstate Statistical Committee, *Official Statistics of the Countries of the CIS, 1997–2* [CD-ROM] (Moscow, CIS Interstate Statistical Committee, 1998).

CIS Interstate Statistical Committee *Sodruzhestvo Nezavisimykh Gosudarstv v 1997 godu* (Moscow, CIS Interstate Statistical Committee, 1998).

Economic Commission for Europe, *Economic Survey of Europe in 1996–1997* (New York and Geneva, United Nations, 1997).

Euromonitor, *European Marketing Data and Statistics 1998; International Marketing Data and Statistics* (London, Euromonitor, 1998).

European Commission, DGIA, NIS/Tacis Services, *Belarussian Economic Trends,* 1997–98 issues; *Kazakstan Economic Trends,* 1997–98 issues; *Russian Economic Trends,* 1996–98 issues; *Uzbekistan Economic Trends,* 1997–98 issues.

Goskomstat Rossii, *Demograficheskii yezhegodnik Rossiiskoi Federatsii 1997* (Moscow, Goskomstat, 1997).

Goskomstat Rossii, *Regiony Rossii 1997,* 2 vols. (Moscow, Goskomstat, 1997).

Goskomstat Rossii, *Sotsialno-ekonomicheskoe polozhenie Rossii, 1997 g* (Moscow, Goskomstat, 1997).

Natsional'nyi sostav naseleniya SSSR (Moscow, 1990).

Russian Federation Ministry of Internal Affairs, Russian Federation Justice Ministry, CIS Statistical Committee, *Prestupnost' i pravonarusheniya (1991–1995). Statisticheskii sbornik* (Moscow, 1996).

Secretariat of the UN, *Economic Survey of Europe in 1996–1997* (New York and Geneva, UN, 1997).

Vybory presidenta Rossiiskoi Federatsii 1996. Elektoral'naya statistika (Moscow, Ves'mir, 1996).
World Bank, *World Development Report 1997* (New York, Oxford University Press, 1997).

Newspapers consulted

The following were used extensively for 1990–98:
Argumenty i fakty (Moscow); *Atmoda* (Riga); *Baltic Independent* (Tallinn); *Delovoi mir* (Moscow); *Diena* (Riga); *Izvestiya* (Moscow); *Kazakhstanskaya pravda* (Almaty); *Kommersant-Daily* (Moscow); *Komsomol'skaya pravda* (Moscow); *Literaturnaya gazeta* (Moscow); *Molodezh Estonii* (Tallinn); *Moskovskie novosti* (Moscow); *Nezavisimaya gazeta* (Moscow); *Panorama Latvii* (Riga); *Rossiiskaya gazeta* (Moscow); *Rossiiskie vesti* (Moscow); *Rossiya* (Moscow); *Russkii telegraf* (Moscow); *Segodnya* (Moscow); *Vek* (Moscow).

Main bibliography

Abdulatipov, R (1995) *O federativnoi i natsional'noi politike Rossiiskogo gosudarstva* (Moscow, Slavyanskii dialog).

Adams, W and Brock, J (1993) *Adam Smith Goes to Moscow. A Dialogue on Radical Reform* (Princeton, Princeton University Press).

Afanas'ev, Y (1992) *God posle avgusta, gorech i vybor* (Moscow, Literatura i politika).

Agnew, J and Corbridge, S (1995) *Mastering Space. Hegemony, Territory and International Political Economy* (London, Routledge).

Akiner, S (1997) 'Melting pot, salad bowl or caldron? Manipulation and mobilisation of ethnic and religious identities in Central Asia', *Ethnic and Racial Studies,* 20(2), pp. 362–98.

Alexandrova, O and Timmermann, H (1997) 'Integration und Desintegration in den Beziehungen Rußland-Belarus-GUS', *Osteuropa,* 47(10–11), pp. 1022–37.

Andersen, E (1997) 'The legal status of Russians in Estonia's privatisation', *Europe–Asia Studies,* 49(2), pp. 303–16.

Andreev, A (1996) 'Etnicheskaya revolyutsiya i rekonstruktsiya postsovetskogo prostranstva', *Obshchestvennye nauki i sovremennost',* 1, pp. 105–14.

Arnason, J (1993) *The Future that Failed. Origins and Destinies of the Soviet Model* (London, Routledge).

Arutynian, Yu V, *et al.* (1992) *Russkie. Etnosotsiologicheskie ocherki* (Moscow, Nauka).

Avineri, S (1992) 'The End of the Soviet Union and the Return to History', in M. Keren and G. Ofer (eds), *Trials of Transition. Economic Reform in the Former Communist Bloc* (Boulder, CO, Westview Press) pp. 11–18.

Bahl, R and Wallace, S (1994) 'Revenue sharing in Russia', *Environment and Planning C. Government and Policy,* 12(3), pp. 293–307.

Bahry, D and Way, L (1994) 'Citizen activism in the Russian transition', *Post-Soviet Affairs,* 10(4), pp. 330–66.

Bassin, M (1991) 'Russia between Europe and Asia. The ideological construction of geographical space', *Slavic Review,* 50(1), pp. 1–17.

Beissinger, M (1995) 'Persistent ambiguities of empire', *Post-Soviet Affairs,* 11(2), pp. 149–84.

Berkowitz, D (1997) 'Regional income and secession. Centre–periphery relations in emerging market economies', *Regional Science and Urban Economics,* (27), pp. 17–45.

Bogacheva, O (1996) 'Stanovlenie rossiiskoi modeli byudzhetnogo federalizma', *Voprosy ekonomiki,* 8, pp. 30–40.

Borodaj, R and Nikiforov, A (1993) 'Between east and west. Russian renewal and the future', *Studies in Eastern European Thought,* 47 (1 and 2), pp. 61–116.

Bradshaw, M (1993) *The Economic Effects of Soviet Dissolution* (London, Royal Institute of International Affairs Report).

Bradshaw, M, Stenning, A and Sutherland, D (1998) 'Economic Restructuring and Change in Russia', in J. Pickles and A. Smith (eds), *Theorising Transition. The Political Economy of Post-Communist Transformations* (London, Routledge), pp. 147–71.

Brubaker, R (1996) *Nationalism Reframed. Nationhood and the National Question in the New Europe* (Cambridge, Cambridge University Press).

Brunetti, A, *et al.* (1997) 'Institutional obstacles to doing business. Region-by-region results from a worldwide survey of the private sector', *World Bank Policy Research Paper,* no. 1759.

Brzezinski, Z (1997) *The Grand Chessboard. American Primacy and its Geostrategic Imperatives* (New York, HarperCollins).

Buchanan, A (1991) *Secession. The Morality of Political Divorce from Port Sumter to Lithuania and Quebec* (Boulder, CO, Westview Press).

Bunce, V (1995) 'Should transitologists be grounded?', *Slavic Review,* 54(1), pp. 111–26.

Burawoy, M (1996) 'The state and economic involution. Russia through a China lens', *World Development,* 24(6), pp. 1105–17.

Buss, T and Yancer, L (1996) 'Privatising the Russian economy. The Nizhny Novgorod experience', *Environment and Planning C. Government and Policy,* 14(2), pp. 211–25.

Castells, M (1997) *The Power of Identity* (Oxford, Basil Blackwell).

Chinn, J and Kaiser, R (1996) *Russians as the New Minority. Ethnicity and Nationalism in the Soviet Successor States* (Boulder, CO, Westview Press).

Clarke, S, *et al.* (1993) *What about the Workers? Workers and the Transition to Capitalism in Russia* (London, Verso).

Clarke, S, Fairbrother, P and Borisov, V (1995) *The Workers' Movement in Russia* (Aldershot, Edward Elgar).

Cohen, R (1997) *Global Diasporas. An Introduction* (London, Routledge).

Colton, T, *et al.* (1997) 'Five years after the collapse of the USSR', *Post-Soviet Affairs,* 13(1), pp. 1–18.

Cook, L J (1993) *The Soviet Social Contract and Why it Failed. Welfare Policy and Workers' Politics from Brezhnev to Yeltsin* (Cambridge, MA, Harvard University Press).

Dale, N (1996) 'The globalisation of the Latvian economy since 1991', *International Politics,* 33(1), pp. 97–108.

Davies, R, Harrison, M and Wheatcroft, S eds (1994) *The Economic Transformation of the Soviet Union, 1913–1945* (Cambridge, Cambridge University Press).

Dawisha, K and Parrot, B (1994) *Russia and the New States of Eurasia. The Politics of Upheaval* (Cambridge, Cambridge University Press).

Dawisha, K and Parrot, B (1997) *Conflict, Cleavage and Change in Central Asia and the Caucasus* (Cambridge, Cambridge University Press).

Diligenskii, G (1997) 'Chto my znaem o demokratii i grazhdanskom obshchestve?', *Pro et Contra,* 2(4), pp. 5–21.

Drobizheva, L (1994) 'Processes of Disintegration in the Russian Federation and the Problems of Russians', in V. Shlapentokh, M. Sendich and E. Payin (eds), *The New Russian Diaspora. Russian Minorities in the Former Soviet Republics* (London, M. E. Sharpe), pp. 45–58.

Drobizheva, L ed. (1994) *Natsional'noe samosoznanie i natsionalizm v Rossiiskoi Federatsii nachala 1990-kh godov* (Moscow, IEA).

Dugin, A (1996) *Misterii Yevrazii* (Moscow, Arktoreya).

Dugin, A (1997) *Osnovy geopolitiki. Geopoliticheskoe budushchee Rossii* (Moscow, Arktoreya).

Duka, A (1997) 'Transformation of local power elites. Institutionalisation of social movements in St. Petersburg', *International Journal of Urban Regional Research,* 21(3), pp. 430–44.

Dunlop, J (1997) 'Russia. In Search of an Identity?', in I. Bremmer and R. Taras (eds), *New States. New Politics. Building the Post-Soviet Nations* (Cambridge, Cambridge University Press), pp. 29–95.

Dunlop, J (1998) *Russia Confronts Chechnya* (Cambridge, Cambridge University Press).

Elster, J, Offe, C and Preuss, U (1998) *Institutional Design in Post-Communist Societies. Rebuilding the Ship at Sea* (Cambridge, Cambridge University Press).

Evers, F (1997) 'Reformen und Soziales in der rußlandischen Provinz am Beispiel von Uljanowsk', *Osteuropa,* 3, pp. 256–66.

Federov, B (1994) *Chto: kak budem delat'* (Moscow).

Federov, Y (1997) 'Kaspiiskaya politika Rossii. K konsensusu', *Pro et Contra,* 2(3), pp. 72–89.

Feigenbaum, H and Henig, J (1993) 'Privatisation and democracy', *Governance, an International Journal of Policy and Administration,* 6(3), July, pp. 438–53.

Foweraker, J (1995) *Theorising Social Movements* (London, Pluto Press).

Fraser, N (1997) *Justice Interruptus. Critical Reflections on the 'Post-socialist' Condition* (London, Routledge).

Friedrich, C, *et al.* (1969) *Totalitarianism in Perspective. Three Views* (New York, Praeger).

Fryer, P and Lynn, N (1998) 'National-territorial change in the republics of the Russian north', *Political Geography,* 17(5), pp. 567–88.

Fukuyama, F (1992) *The End of History and the Last Man* (London, Hamish Hamilton).

Gall, C and De Waal, T (1997) *Chechnya. A Small Victorious War* (London, Pan).

Gamble, A and Payne, A eds (1996) *Regionalism and World Order* (London, Macmillan Press).

Gellner, E (1996) 'Return of a native', *The Political Quarterly,* 67(1), pp. 4–13.

Gellner, E (1997) *Nationalism* (London, Weidenfeld and Nicholson).

Gödeke, H (1997) 'Transkaukasien nach dem Zusammenbruch der UdSSSR', *Osteuropa,* 47(12), pp. 1224–35.

Goldman, M (1996) 'Why is the Mafia so dominant in Russia?', *Challenge,* January–February, pp. 39–47.

Gorbachev, M (1986) *Politicheskii doklad tsentral'nogo komiteta KPSS XXVII S"ezdu Kommunisticheskoi Partii Sovetskogo Soyuza* (Moscow).

Gorbachev, M (1987) *Perestroika. New Thinking for our Country and the World* (London, Collins).

Greenfeld, L (1992) *Nationalism. Five Roads to Modernity* (Cambridge, MA, Harvard University Press).

Grigorievs, A (1996) 'The Baltic Predicament', in R. Caplan and J. Feffer (eds), *Europe's New Minorities. States and Minorities in Conflict* (Oxford, Oxford University Press), pp. 120–37.

Grogaard, J ed. (1996) *Estonia in the Grip of Change* (Oslo, FAFO Report).

Gurr, T (1993) *Minorities at Risk. A Global View of Ethnopolitical Conflicts* (Washington, DC, United States Institute of Peace Studies).

Halbach, E (1997) 'The Caucasus as a region of conflict', *German Foreign Affairs Review,* 48(4), 358–67.

Hanauer, L (1996) 'Tatarstan and the prospects for federalism in Russia. A commentary', *Security Dialogue,* 27(1), pp. 81–6.

Hanneman, A (1995) 'Independence and group rights in the Baltic States. A double minority problem', *Virginia Journal of International Law,* 32(2).

Hanson, P (1997) 'How many Russias? Russia's regions and their adjustment to economic change', *The International Spectator,* 32(1), pp. 39–52.

Hanson, S and Kopstein, J (1997) 'The Weimar/Russia comparison', *Post-Soviet Affairs,* 13(3), July–September, pp. 252–83.

Hauner, M (1992) *What is Asia to Us? Russia's Asian Heartland Yesterday and Today* (London, Routledge).

Hiden, J and Salmon, P (1991) *The Baltic Nations and Europe. Estonia, Latvia and Lithuania in the Twentieth Century* (London, Longman).

Hinton, H (1995) 'Urban administration in post-Soviet Russia. Continuity and change in St. Petersburg', *Environment and Planning C. Government and Policy*, 13, pp. 379–93.

Holmes, L (1993) *The End of Communist Power. Anti-Corruption Campaigns and Legitimation Crisis* (Oxford, Polity Press).

Hughes, J (1994) 'Regionalism in Russia. The rise and fall of the Siberian agreement', *Europe–Asia Studies*, 46(7), pp. 1133–61.

Huntington, S (1993) 'The clash of civilisations', *Foreign Affairs*, 72(3), pp. 22–49.

Islamov, B (1994) 'Post-Soviet Central Asia and the Commonwealth of Independent States. The economic background of independence', in B. Manz (ed.), *Central Asia in Historical Perspective* (Boulder, CO, Westview Press).

Ivanov, V, Ladodo, I and Naraov, M (1996) 'Sostoyanie mezhnatsional'nykh otnoshenii v Rossiiskoi Federatsii (po rezul'tatam issledovanii v regionakh RF)', *Sotsial'no-politicheskii zhurnal*, 3, pp. 33–49.

Jenkins, J and Klandermans, B eds (1995) *The Politics of Social Protest. Comparative Perspectives on States and Social Movements* (London, University of London Press).

Kagarlitsky, B (1995) *The Mirage of Modernisation* (New York, Monthly Review Press).

Kagarlitsky, B (1995) *Restoration in Russia. Why Capitalism Failed* (London, Verso).

Kaminski, B ed. (1997) *Economic Transition in Russia and the New States of Eurasia* (New York and London, M.E. Sharpe).

Kennedy, P (1989) *The Rise and Fall of the Great Powers* (London, Fontana).

Keohane, R (1990) 'The institutionalisation of the new world order', *Relazioni Internazionali*, pp. 3–17.

Keohane, R and Nye, J (1977) *Power and Interdependence. World Politics in Transition* (Boston, Little, Brown).

Kerr, D (1995) 'The new Eurasianism. The rise of geopolitics in Russia's foreign policy', *Europe–Asia Studies*, 47(6), pp. 977–88.

Khakimov, R (1996) 'Prospects of federalism in Russia. A view from Tatarstan', *Security Dialogue*, 27(1), pp. 69–80.

Kirichenko, V (1995) 'Sostoyanie i problemy ekonomicheskikh otnoshenii v SNG', *Voprosy ekonomiki*, 10, pp. 70–8.

Kirkow, P (1996) 'Distributional coalitons, budgetary problems and fiscal federalism in Russia', *Communist Economics and Economic Transformation*, 8(1), pp. 277–98.

Kolosov, V and Treivish, B (1996) 'Etnicheskie arealy sovremennoi Rossii.

Sravnitel'nyi analiz riska natsional'nykh konfliktov', *Polis*, 2(32), pp. 47–55.

Kolstoe, P ed (1998) *Nationbuilding and Ethnic Integration in Bipolar Societies. The Cases of Latvia and Kazakstan* (Oslo, University of Oslo).

Kozyrev, A (1994) *Preobrazhenie* (Moscow, Mezhdunarodnye otnosheniya).

Kristof, L (1969) 'The Russian Image of Russia. An Applied Study in Geopolitical Methodology', in C. Fisher (ed.), *Essays in Political Geography* (London, Methuen), pp. 345–87.

Laitin, D (1996) 'Language and nationalism in the post-Soviet republics', *Post-Soviet Affairs*, 12(1), pp. 4–24.

Lane, D (1990) *Soviet Society under Perestroika* (London, Unwin Hyman).

Lane, J and Ersson, S (1997) *Comparative Politics* (Cambridge, Polity Press).

Laqueur, W (1994) *Black Hundred. The Rise of the Extreme Right in Russia* (New York, Harper Perennial).

Leftwich, A ed. (1996) *Democracy and Development* (Oxford, Polity Press).

Lewin, M (1991) *The Gorbachev Phenomenon. A Historical Interpretation*, 2nd edition (Berkeley, University of California Press).

Lieven, A (1993) *The Baltic Revolution. Estonia, Latvia, Lithuania and the Path to Independence* (Yale, Yale University Press).

Lieven, D (1995) 'The Russian empire and the Soviet Union as imperial polities', *Journal of Contemporary History*, 30, pp. 605–36.

Linz, J and Stepan, A (1996) *Problems of Democratic Transition and Consolidation. Southern Europe, South America, and Post-Communist Europe* (Baltimore, The Johns Hopkins University Press).

Liuhto, K (1996) 'Entrepreneurial transition in the post-Soviet republics. The Estonian path', *Europe–Asia Studies*, 48(1), pp. 121–40.

Lysenko, V (1996) 'Naskol'ko prochna dogovarnaya osnova federativnykh otnoshenii', *Federalizm. Teoriya, praktika, istoriya*, 3, pp. 11–34.

Macfarlane, S N (1997) 'On the front lines in the near abroad. The CIS and the OSCE in Georgia's civil wars', *Third World Quarterly*, 18(3), pp. 509–25.

Macfarlane, S N (1998) 'Democratisation, nationalism and regional security in the North Caucasus', *Government and Opposition*, 10, 399–420.

Malcolm, N and Pravda, A (1996) 'Democratisation and Russian foreign policy', *International Affairs*, 72(3), pp. 537–52.

Markus, U (1996) 'Imperial understretch. Belarus's union with Russia', *Current History*, 75(603), pp. 335–9.

Matveeva, S Ya (1997) 'Natsional'nye problemy Rossii. Sovremennye diskussii', *Obshchestvennye nauki i sovremennost'*, 1, pp. 52–62.

McAuley, M (1997) *Russia's Politics of Uncertainty* (Cambridge, Cambridge University Press).

McGarry, J and O'Leary, B eds (1993) *The Politics of Ethnic Conflict Regulation* (London, Routledge).

Mellor, R (1997) 'Through a glass darkly. Investigating the St. Petersburg administration', *International Journal of Urban and Regional Research*, 21(3), pp. 481–503.

Melvin, N (1995) *Russians Beyond Russia. The Politics of National Identity* (London, Royal Institute of International Affairs).

Mikhaleva, N A (1995) 'Konstitutsionnye reformy v respublikakh-sub"ektakh Rossiiskoi Federatsii', *Gosudarstvo i pravo*, 4, pp. 3–10.

Morvant, P and Rutland, P (1996) 'Russian workers face the market', *Transition*, 2(13), pp. 6–11.

Mostov, J (1994) 'Democracy and the politics of national identity', *Studies in East European Thought*, 46, pp. 9–31.

Mroz, J and Pavliuk, O (1996) 'Ukraine. Europe's linchpin', *Foreign Affairs*, 75(3), pp. 52–62.

Neumann, I (1996) *Russia and the Idea of Europe* (London, Routledge).

Norgaard, O, *et al.* (1996) *The Baltic States after Independence* (Cheltenham, Edward Elgar).

Offe, C (1996) *Varieties of Transition. The East European and German Experience* (Oxford, Polity Press).

Orlovsky, D ed. (1995) *Beyond Soviet Studies* (Washington, DC, Woodrow Wilson Center Press).

Orlowski, L (1993) 'Indirect transfers in trade among the former Soviet Union republics', *Europe–Asia Studies*, 45(6), pp. 1001–24.

Orttung, R (1995) *From Leningrad to St. Petersburg. Democratisation in a Russian City* (London, Macmillan Press).

Penter, T (1997) 'Die Republik Tywa (Tiuwa). Nationale und Kulturelle Wiedergeburt einer ehemaligen Sowjetkolonie', *Osteuropa*, 47(7), pp. 666–83.

Pickvance, K (1997) 'Social movements in Hungary and Russia. The case of environmental movements', *European Sociological Review*, 13(1), pp. 35–54.

Pilkington, H (1998) *Migration, Displacement and Identity in Post-Soviet Russia* (London, Routledge).

Pipes, R (1997) 'Is Russia still an enemy?', *Foreign Affairs*, 76(5), pp. 65–78.

Pridham, G and Vanhenen, T eds (1994) *Democratisation in Eastern Europe. Domestic and International Perspectives* (London, Routledge).

Przeworski, A (1995) *Sustainable Democracy* (Cambridge, Cambridge University Press).

Resler, T (1997) 'Dilemmas of democratisation. Safeguarding minorities in Russia, Ukraine and Lithuania', *Europe–Asia Studies*, 49(1), pp. 89–106.

Roeder, P (1994) 'Varieties of post-Soviet authoritarian regimes', *Post-Soviet Affairs*, 10(1), pp. 61–101.

Rubin, B and Snyder, J eds (1998) *Post-Soviet Political Order. Conflict and State-Building* (London, Routledge).

Ruble, B (1995) *Money Sings. The Changing Politics of Urban Space in Post-Soviet Yaroslavl* (Cambridge, Cambridge University Press).

Rutland, P (1990) 'Labour unrest and movement in 1989 and 1990', *Soviet Economy*, 6(4), pp. 345–84.

Sakwa, R (1997) *Russian Politics and Society*, 2nd edn (London, Routledge).

Schelter, K (1997) 'Bedrohung durch die russische Mafia', *Internationale Politik*, 52(1), pp. 31–6.

Schmitter, P and Karl, T (1994) 'The conceptual travels of transitologists and consolidologists. How far to the East should they attempt to go?', *Slavic Review*, 53(1), pp. 173–85.

Shenfield, S (1994) 'Post-Soviet Russia in Search of Identity', in D. Blum (ed.), *Russia's Future. Consolidation or Fragmentation?* (Boulder, CO, Westview Press), pp. 5–16.

Shmelev, N and Popov, V (1990) *The Turning Point. Revitalising the Soviet Economy* (London, I.B. Tauris).

Slider, D (1994) 'Privatisation in Russia's regions', *Post-Soviet Affairs*, 10(4), pp. 367–96.

Slider, D (1996) 'Elections to Russia's regional assemblies', *Post-Soviet Affairs*, 12(3), pp. 243–64.

Smith, A (1993) *Russia and the World Economy. Problems of Integration* (London, Routledge).

Smith, G ed. (1994) *The Baltic States. The National Self-determination of Estonia, Latvia and Lithuania* (London, Macmillan, and New York, St. Martin's Press).

Smith, G ed. (1995) *Federalism. The Multiethnic Challenge* (London, Longman).

Smith, G (1996) 'The ethnic democracy thesis and the citizenship question in Estonia and Latvia', *Nationalities Papers*, 24(2), pp. 199–216.

Smith, G (1996) 'Russia, ethnoregionalism and the politics of federation', *Ethnic and Racial Studies*, 19(2), pp. 391–410.

Smith, G ed. (1996) *The Nationalities Question in the Post-Soviet States*, 2nd edn (London, Longman).

Smith, G (1998) 'Russia, multiculturalism and federal justice', *Europe–Asia Studies*, 50(8), pp. 1393–411.

Smith, G (1998) 'Russia's politics of multicultural recognition', *Peace Review. An International Quarterly*, 10(2), pp. 165–71.

Smith, G (1999) 'Transnational politics and the politics of the Russian diaspora', *Ethnic and Racial Studies*, 22(3), pp. 502–25.

Smith, G and Wilson, A (1997) 'Rethinking Russia's post-Soviet diaspora. The potential for political mobilisation in eastern Ukraine and north-east Estonia', *Europe–Asia Studies*, 49(5), pp. 845–64.

Smith, G, Law, V, Wilson, A, Bohr A and Allworth, E (1998) *Nation-Building in the Post-Soviet Borderlands. The Politics of National Identities* (Cambridge, Cambridge University Press).

Solnick, S (1998) 'Gubernatorial elections in Russia', *Post-Soviet Affairs*, 14(1), pp. 48–80.

Solnick, S (1998) 'Will Russia Survive? Centre and Periphery in the Russian Federation', in B. Rubin and J. Snyder (eds), *Post-Soviet Political Order. Conflict and State-Building* (London, Routledge), pp. 58–80.

Solzhenitsyn, A (1991) *Rebuilding Russia. Reflections and Tentative Proposals* (London, Harvill Press).

Solzhenitsyn, A (1998) *Rossiya v obvale* (Moscow, Russkii put').

Sorensen, G (1993) *Democracy and Democratisation* (Boulder, CO, Westview Press).

Steen, A (1996) *Elites, Democracy amd Policy Development in Post-Communist States. A Comparative Study of Estonia, Latvia and Lithuania* (Oslo, Forskningsrapport 02, University of Oslo).

Stroev, E (1996) 'Rossiiskii federalizm. Nuzhno idti dal'she obshchikh formul', *Federalizm. Teoriya, praktika, istoriya*, 3, pp. 3–10.

Szablowski, G and Derlien, H-D (1993) 'East European transitions, elites, bureaucracies, and the European Community', *Governance*, 6(3), pp. 304–24.

Szporluk, R ed. (1994) *National Identity and Ethnicity in the New States of Eurasia* (London, M.E. Sharpe).

Tarrow, S (1998) *Power in Movement. Social Movements and Contentious Politics* (Cambridge, Cambridge University Press).

Tavadov, G T (1997) 'Sovremennye federatsii i ikh sub"ekty', *Sotsial'no-politicheskii zhurnal*, 1, pp. 38–45.

Tishkov, V (1997) *Ethnicity, Nationalism and Conflict in and after the Soviet Union. The Mind Aflame* (Oslo, Prio, and London, Sage).

Trautmann, L (1996) 'Fuhrungswechsel an der Newa. Burgermeister- und Prasidentenwahlen in St. Petersburg', *Osteuropa*, 46(11), pp. 1124–405.

Treisman, D (1996) 'The politics of intergovernmental transfers in post-Soviet Russia', *British Journal of Political Science*, 26(3), pp. 299–335.

Treisman, D (1997) 'Russia's "ethnic revival". The separatist activism of regional leaders in a postcommunist order', *World Politics*, 49(1), pp. 212–49.

Trenin, D (1997) *Baltiiskii shans. Strany Baltii, Rossiya i zapad v skladyvayushcheisya bolshoi Evrope* (Moscow, Carnegie Endowment for International Peace).

Tsepkalo, V (1998) 'The remaking of Eurasia', *Foreign Affairs*, 77(2), pp. 107–26.

Tsygankov, A (1997), 'From international institutionalism to revolutionary expansionism. The foreign policy discourse of contemporary Russia', *Mershon International Studies Review*, 41, pp. 247–68.

Tunador, O, *et al.*, eds (1997) *Geopolitics in Post-Wall Europe. Security, Territory and Identity* (London, Sage).

Vaksburg, A (1991) *The Soviet Mafia* (London, Weidenfeld and Nicolson).

Valentei, S (1996) 'Rossiiskie reformy i rossiiskii federalizm', *Federalizm. Teoriya, praktika, istoriya*, 2, pp. 23–36.

Varese, F (1994) 'Is Sicily the future of Russia? Private protection and the rise of the Russian mafia', *Archives Européennes de Sociologie*, 35(2), pp. 224–58.

Vishnevskii, A ed. (1997) *Naselenie Rossii 1996* (Moscow, Center of Demography and Human Ecology).

Walter, R (1996) 'Rußland und die NATO-Osterweiterung', *Osteuropa*, 46(8), pp. 741–57.

Walzer, M (1992) 'The new tribalism. Notes on a difficult problem', *Dissent*, Spring, pp. 164–71.

Webber, M (1996) *The International Politics of Russia and the Successor States* (Manchester, Manchester University Press).

White, S, Wyman, M and Oates, S (1997) 'Parties and voters in the 1995 Russian Duma election', *Europe–Asia Studies*, 49(5), pp. 767–98.

Wilson, A (1999) *The Ukraine. The Unexpected Nation* (Yale, Yale University Press).

Yanitsky, O N (1996) 'The ecological movement in post-totalitarian Russia. Some conceptual issues', *Society and Natural Resources*, 9(1), pp. 65–76.

Yergin, D and Gustafson, T (1994) *Russia 2010 and What it Means for the World* (London, Nicholas Brealey Publishers).

Z (pseudonym for Malia, M) (1991) 'To the Stalin Mausoleum', in W. Brinton and A. Rinzler (eds), *Without Force or Lies. Voices from the Revolution of Central Europe in 1989–90* (San Francisco, Mercury House Books), pp. 380–434.

Zakaria, F (1997) 'The rise of illiberal democracy', *Foreign Affairs*, 76(6), pp. 22–43.

Zaslavsky, V (1992) *The Neo-Stalinist State. Class, Ethnicity and Consensus in Soviet Society*, 2nd edition (London, M.E. Sharpe).

Zevelev, I (1996) 'Russia and the Russian diaspora', *Post-Soviet Affairs*, 12(3), pp. 265–84.

Zhirinovsky, V (1993) *Poslednii brosok na yug* (Moscow, TOO Pisatel).

Zubov, R (1997) 'Sovremennoe russkoe obshchestvo i "civil society". Granitsy nalozheniya', *Pro et Contra*, 2(4), pp. 22–37.

Zyuganov, G (1995) *Rossiya i sovremennyi mir* (Moscow, Obozrevatel').

Zyuganov, G ed. (1995) *Sovremennaya russkaya ideya i gosudarstvo* (Moscow, RAN).

Index